D0152659

# Swing Dancing

# Swing Dancing

Tamara Stevens

*With editorial contributions by Erin Stevens*

The American Dance Floor
*Ralph G. Giordano, Series Editor*

**GREENWOOD**

AN IMPRINT OF ABC-CLIO, LLC
Santa Barbara, California • Denver, Colorado • Oxford, England

WILLARD LIBRARY, BATTLE CREEK, MI

Copyright 2011 by Tamara Stevens and Erin Stevens

All rights reserved. No part of this publication may be reproduced, stored in a retrieval system, or transmitted, in any form or by any means, electronic, mechanical, photocopying, recording, or otherwise, except for the inclusion of brief quotations in a review, without prior permission in writing from the publisher.

**Library of Congress Cataloging-in-Publication Data**

Stevens, Tamara.
  Swing dancing / Tamara Stevens ; with editorial contributions by Erin Stevens.
    p. cm. — (The American dance floor)
  Includes bibliographical references and index.
  ISBN 978–0–313–37517–0 (hard copy : alk. paper) — ISBN 978–0–313–37518–7 (e-book)
1. Swing (Dance) I. Title.
GV1796.S85S74   2011
793.3'3—dc22         2010053906

ISBN: 978–0–313–37517–0
EISBN: 978–0–313–37518–7

15 14 13 12 11    1 2 3 4 5

This book is also available on the World Wide Web as an eBook.
Visit www.abc-clio.com for details.

Greenwood
An Imprint of ABC-CLIO, LLC

ABC-CLIO, LLC
130 Cremona Drive, P.O. Box 1911
Santa Barbara, California 93116-1911

This book is printed on acid-free paper ∞

Manufactured in the United States of America

# Contents

# Series Foreword

From the Lindy hop to hip hop, dance has helped define American life and culture. In good times and bad, people have turned to dance to escape their troubles, get out, and have a good time. From high school proms to weddings and other occasions, dance creates some of our most memorable personal moments. It is also big business, with schools, competitions, and dance halls bringing in people and their dollars each year. And as America has changed, so, too, has dance. The story of dance is very much the story of America. Dance routines are featured in movies, television, and videos; dance styles and techniques reflect shifting values and attitudes toward relationships; and dance performers and their costumes reveal changing thoughts about race, class, gender, and other topics. Written for students and general readers, The American Dance Floor series covers the history of social dancing in America.

Each volume in the series looks at a particular type of dance such as swing, disco, Latin, folk dancing, hip hop, ballroom, and country & western. Written in an engaging manner, each book tells the story of a particular dance form and places it in its historical, social, and cultural context. Thus each title helps the reader learn not only about a particular dance form, but also about social change. The volumes are fully documented, and each contains a bibliography of print and electronic resources for further reading.

# Preface

My sister Erin and I have written this book from the perspective of being avid Swing dancers ourselves. We live and breathe it most nights of our lives through our business, the Pasadena Ballroom Dance Association (PBDA), which we founded in Pasadena, California, in 1983. We have always referred to our business as "a school of social dance," offering classes and dances in all styles of American social dance, and the concept of Swing as a "social dance" is important here. In 1924, when the Imperial Society of Teachers of Dancing mapped out a structure and a set of rules governing ballroom dances, two distinct styles of dance emerged: International Ballroom, and American Social dance. Dance historian and author Ralph G. Giordano gives this excellent explanation of the International style: "Ballroom dancing is marked by a pursuit of perfection on set routines danced with the same partner" (2007, Vol. II, 45). Social dancing, however, is an entirely different art form. Based not upon choreography but on a dancer's ability to lead or follow, Social dance entails spontaneity and constant interplay between the music and the partner. The pursuit of perfection for a Social Swing dancer means being able to dance gracefully and skillfully with a variety of partners; leading or following with a flair of individual expression in a tandem duet of synchronized energy. It doesn't matter if it's a fast song or a slow song, one you've never heard before, or a tune you've danced to over and over again. You don't feel exactly the same way twice, so you dance it differently each time. And when it all comes together—when you've clicked with the music and your partner, you're in sync with the rhythm and your entire body's moving with effortless ease—everything feels exactly right. There is elation and joy, as satisfying as any perfectly executed choreographed performance routine. Those are what great social dancing moments are made of.

In the 1990s, at the height of the second era of swing, a number of styles of Swing were popular, but the Lindy Hop became a global phenomenon. This was due, in large part, to one of the original Savoy Ballroom Lindy Hoppers, Frankie Manning, who shared his expertise in the dance worldwide. His 2007 autobiography, *Frankie Manning: Ambassador of Lindy Hop*, co-authored by Cynthia Millman, is a wonderful record of his life and will ensure that his legacy, and the dance that he so loved, will be preserved for future generations. Manning passed away at the age of 94, as we were writing this book. Like so many people around the world, we feel lucky to have known him. We will always treasure the time we spent with him over the years: dancing with him, talking to him, and calling him our friend. Along with the Lindy Hop, this book also delves into West Coast Swing, a vital offshoot of the Lindy Hop, as well as many other styles including Jitterbug, East Coast Swing, Shag and Balboa, to only name a few.

This is not an instructional guide to learning Swing dancing, but is instead a look back at the remarkable history of Swing and its evolution over the years in the multiethnic melting pot of America. It may seem odd that we start with the subject of slavery in the United States, but that's where the story begins. It progresses through the years of minstrelsy, the jazz age, the big band era of swing music, bebop, and the decline of partnered dance in the 1960s, then traces Swing's development and resurgence in the late 1990s, continuing through more contemporary trends of the twenty-first century. We have chosen to focus mainly on the East and West Coasts of America— New York and Los Angeles—the two areas where Swing, in general, has had the most notoriety. However, many other regions contributed to the development of the dance, and by the second era of Swing, many of the smallest cities in the most remote areas of the country were playing significant roles in keeping it vital.

The evolution of music parallels this story, as the connection between swing music and the dance known as Swing is undeniable. Besides its many talented musicians, American history is filled with innovative dancers who created new steps and new styles, often testing the limits of social acceptability in the process, but advancing the cause of Swing. But it clearly took the right combination of elements—the music, the social climate of the time, and previous dance trends to springboard from—to produce the Lindy Hop, the original style of Social-partnered Swing dancing in America. It was a similar combination of elements that produced the second era of Swing, along with one extra important element: some of the original first era dancers being on hand to help guide its course.

In writing this book, we've walked a tricky tightrope in regards to our own contribution in "bringing Swing back" from its original heyday of the 1930s and 40s. Erin and her dance partner in the 1980s, Steven Mitchell, are credited with bringing Frankie Manning out of "dance retirement," and our PBDA has been unique in its large numbers of students and its longevity as a vibrant part of the international social dance community. While we recognize that we have played an integral role in the Swing story, there are clearly people who are more important to the overall history of Swing dancing, and we personally know a number of people equally qualified to have written this book. They would have each chosen different stories to tell, and had their own focuses based on their areas of expertise; their finished products would all be interesting and equally valuable. For the subject of Swing dancing is multilayered, multidimensional, and vast, and its history is not one story, but many. We hope this book gives the honor due to all original and subsequent Swing dancers, event organizers, instructors, historians . . . all the people who throughout the years have pushed for the preservation of Swing dancing (and social dancing in general), as well as those with new interest in the subject.

The story of Swing is still unfolding in the twenty-first century, with contemporary trends driving social dance in new directions. However, as of this writing, Swing dancing has become clearly defined as a long-lasting cultural tradition steeped in history, an American folk dance, an American treasure.

# Acknowledgments

My sister Erin leads one of the busiest lives of anyone I have ever known, and although I took the lead in writing this book, it would not have happened without her enormous contribution of good ideas and sound editorial input for which I am very grateful. We have always worked closely together in running the Pasadena Ballroom Dance Association; it has always been a true family business. While Erin and I taught the classes, our parents were fully involved behind the scenes—and although they were both excellent dancers in their own right, they had the "business sense" which helped us make our dance dreams real. In all our endeavors in life, our parents remain our biggest fans, and we appreciate them more than we can ever say. Erin and I both met our husbands as a result of our dance business. They both have careers of their own, but they have always been wonderfully supportive of ours and have often worked (and danced) right along with us. Erin's husband, Jim Key, a general contractor, has devoted many hours to our dance hall and our various events. My husband, Scott Price (a piping-design engineer who is also an amazing dancer), took time to read each chapter as I completed it, and I have appreciated his critical eye and thoughtful comments. His entire family has been extremely supportive and helpful, too. We also want to thank our editor George Butler, Erin Ryan, and our friend Rhonda Hicks for helping me with preproduction details. Jessica Cheatwood, Kevin and Richard Price, Larry Schulz, Mary Collins, Alycia Keys, Jean Veloz, and Paul Armstrong are just a few of the people who made photographic contributions.

Ralph G. Giordano's remarkable 2007 two volume set *Social Dancing in America*, inspired us tremendously. We're grateful for the opportunity he gave us to write this book, along with his confidence in us and his continuous support along the way. We also want to thank the staff and all the students of PBDA (as well as all the attendees of Swing Camp Catalina over the years) for their enthusiasm and for continuing to inspire us. We appreciate all the talented musicians who have ever inspired us to move, and all the wonderful partners who have shared happy moments with us on the dance floor.

On a more personal note, I want to thank my sister Erin for bringing Frankie Manning into our world as our lives have been enriched many times over by knowing him. (I know I'm not alone in this sentiment.) A special thank-you as well to Frankie's son Chazz Young and Frankie's longtime companion Judy Pritchett for their friendship and encouragement. A big thank-you to Norma Miller for her continued efforts in keeping the Swing flame burning brightly. Jean Veloz, Skippy Blair, Jack Carey, and Annie Hirsch, are only a few of the dancers who took the time, either in person or by telephone or e-mail, to give me their thoughts and historical insights. Cynthia Millman contributed some wonderfully written words to this book's conclusion (and both she and Chazz Young contributed wonderful photographs of Frankie Manning, which added immensely to the final product). But it is truly my sister Erin who set me "dancing" on my life's course, and I have always been inspired by her love of dance, her continued enthusiasm for teaching dance, and her dedication to preserving the important American art form known as "Swing."

Finally, for all Swing dancers everywhere, this history belongs to you, as you are a part of it. I hope that our sincere love of dance shines through, as it should, throughout all the pages of this book. And I hope it is an interesting and inspiring read, which encourages Swing dancing's continued preservation.

# 1

# Swing Dance: Born in the USA

Ballroom dance styles differ greatly one from another. Cha-Cha, for instance, paints an entirely different picture and creates a different mood than a Tango or a Foxtrot. And an onlooker, even one with no prior dance knowledge or experience can immediately recognize that a Viennese Waltz doesn't look anything like a Samba or a Rumba. Some styles of social dance are best described as sultry or sensuous, while others are graceful and refined, performed with an epitome of elegance and high-class style. Swing aficionados generally use words like "happy" and "fun," when describing their dance, and Lindy Hop, the original style of Swing, is often referred to as "an outward expression of an inner joy." Sometimes silly, sometimes cool, it's a dance that lifts the spirits. And to those who catch the bug (the "Jitter"-bug, that is), it's an addictive thrill. Instead of shouting out loud with joy, a Swing dancer jumps up in the air and kicks or spins around in some such display of happy exuberance.

The word "Swing" when used today, in reference to social dancing, is generally an umbrella term covering Lindy Hop, Jitterbug, Jive, West Coast and East Coast styles, plus Balboa, Shag, and many regional variations of all of these (such as Carolina Shag and Hollywood-style Swing, etc.). While there are distinct differences between the various styles of Swing, they all share similar rhythmic components and character traits and are clearly branches from the same family tree. But where did this dance called "Swing" come from? What are the origins of its birth?

It is impossible, of course, to pinpoint the exact moment a seed for any future dance style is planted. It may take years for that seed to develop its own set of characteristics and, finally, acquire a name of its own. But in the case of Swing dancing, historians have determined at least the geographical region where the dance started, and that it is consummately American in its beginnings and its evolutions. It is an American vernacular dance, a true American folk dance. More precisely, it's categorized as an "Afro-American" dance, whose roots extend across the continent deep into the heart of Africa. And this joyous, jubilant style of dance began its historical evolution, remarkably, in one of the most sorrowful and tragic chapters in American history: the African slave trade to North America.

Between the settlement of the first British colony at Jamestown in Virginia in 1607 and the end of the seventeenth century, slave trade had developed into a well-established practice in the United States. Southern plantation owners ensured a profitable return on their sugar and tobacco crops and rice harvests by maintaining an organized system of slave labor. By the eighteenth century, increasing numbers of African men, women, and children were rounded up, forced onto slave ships, and shipped off to mainland America. The slave trade was big business (Peter Kolchin, 1993, 3).

In 1793, when Eli Whitney (1765–1825) invented the cotton gin, dramatically increasing production and revolutionizing the industry, cotton became "king." The international market price for cotton was set at the Cotton Exchange in Savannah, Georgia, and as white gold brought hard currency to the region, it also brought more enslaved Africans into the flourishing Southern colonies. In 1803 alone, over 20,000 slaves were brought from Africa into Georgia and South Carolina to work in the cotton fields. The institution of slavery became so deeply entrenched in the agricultural South that it affected the legal, political, and economic workings of all the colonies (*Africans in America*, "Brotherly Love," pbs.org; Kolchin, 26–27).

Most contemporary scholars put the total number of African slaves who sailed to the Americas at somewhere between 9 and 12 million. It is difficult to even approach the subject of slavery without shuddering at the horrors and sufferings endured by so many during that time in American history. But there can be no denying that the traditions of those African slaves had a profound influence on many aspects of culture in the New World, perhaps most notably in the American art forms of music and dance. The journey that connected the tribal dances of Africa to the vernacular American dance called Swing may have begun with the slaves' literal journey from Africa across the Atlantic Ocean on human cargo transports—the various sailing vessels best referred to as the "slave ships."

The wretched conditions for slaves onboard the sailing vessels have been well documented. There are many eyewitness accounts of the lack of food, the cargo holds overstuffed with human cargo, the chains, the stench, and the horrific cruelties of the slave traders. An eighteenth-century slave ship surgeon, Alexander Falconbridge, describes how slaves were generally chained together, two by two, in handcuffs and leg irons, and were often forced to lay down, one on top of another, in cramped spaces too low to stand up in. He comments, however, that some captains treated their captives more humanely than others (he sailed under one captain whom he described as "one of the very best men in the trade," and another whom he described as "brutal"), and he notes that, although it varied from vessel to vessel, there was at least some social contact between crewmembers and slaves. According to Falconbridge, slaves were often made to dance as a form of exercise, to keep them stronger and healthier on their transatlantic journey, a practice that became known as "dancing the slaves." The onboard dancing was also thought to combat scurvy; the true cause of the disease, unbeknownst to anyone at the time, was a deficiency of vitamin C (Alexander Falconbridge, 1788, 209; Kolchin, 1993, 21).

Historian Marcus Rediker asserts in *The Slave Ship: A Human History*:

> Captains and doctors alike believed that exercise was essential to the health of the enslaved aboard the ship, so they organized dancing on deck every day, for men and women prisoners, assisted sometimes by music but more commonly by whips . . . (Rediker, 2008, image caption, np)

Dance historians Marshall and Jean Stearns agree that during the slave ships' voyages from Africa, captors forced slaves to dance to keep them fit and healthy. But the Stearns also suggest that the slaves were exposed to European dance forms. The dancing of the slaves may have provided entertainment for crewmembers; it isn't hard to imagine European crewmembers occasionally adding their own dance steps and showing off their own dance styles on board. So those slaves who survived the journey to the United States may have already absorbed something of British-European dance (Stearns and Stearns, 1994, 16).

Traversée: *Danse de Nègres* (Dancing the Slaves). This engraving of a slaving vessel from *La France Maritime*, Amédée Gréhan, ed., 1837, shows how slaves were often forced to dance on deck. This kept them healthy for their journey to the New World. (Jerome Robbins Dance Division, New York Public Library for the Performing Arts, Astor, Lenox, and Tilden Foundations.)

The African slaves who made it to the New World brought with them their religious beliefs and their cultural traditions. They arrived with their own tribal subcultures and their own tribal languages, of course, all distinct one from another. But they were all intrinsically African. Dancing is an important African tradition, a tradition that transcends language. And for slaves in America, dancing became a communal link, connecting them to each other, and reconnecting them to their shared heritage. It gave them back a tiny bit of all they had lost, a bit of their homeland, a bit of themselves.

As the traditions of slaves from various tribes and different villages of origins meshed—including traditions of music and dance—they became "Afro-American" in nature. This fusion of cultures was actually twofold: African slaves with other African slaves, and Africans with the varied European citizenry of North America. The blending of styles created something—not totally African, not wholly European, but a completely new style of American dancing.

## The Ring Shout

Their hands clapped the percussive rhythms. Their chants and moans, repeated words and vocal melodies, became their music. They danced in circle formations after-hours on their Southern plantations. They were slaves, captured in Africa and shipped overseas for lives of forced labor in North America. During work hours they tilled the soil, picked the cotton, cleared the rice fields, and spent their days in indentured servitude. But at night, in the hours belonging just to them, they formed a Ring Shout circle, and they shuffled and they stomped, with every movement resonating as a deep part of their heritage, tying them to their homeland a vast ocean away. Dance historians and scholars are in agreement that the Ring Shout, with its shouting, clapping, and counterclockwise movements, is a clear example of an African dance that survived in the United States.

In the late 1930s, as part of President Roosevelt's Works Progress Administration, the U.S. government hired unemployed writers to compile a folk history of slavery in the United States. The writers conducted interviews with former slaves in a massive effort to document the stories of their lives. Seventeen volumes of typewritten records prepared by the project are housed today in the archives of the Library of Congress under the title *Federal Writers' Project: Slave Narratives, 1936–1938*, providing tremendous historic insight into the times and daily lives of former slaves. There are numerous references to the Ring Shouts in these narratives. Silvia King was born in Africa, stolen from her husband and three children, brought to the United States, and sold into slavery in Texas. King recalls dancing with other slaves in the Texas backwoods, and gives a good description of a Ring Shout (which she calls a "Ring Dance") in this following narrative:

> De black folks gits off down in de bottom and shouts and sings and prays. Dey gits in de ring dance. It am jes' a kind of shuffle, den it git faster an' faster and dey gits warmed up and moans and shouts ... Sometimes dey sings and shouts all night.... (*Slave Narratives*, Vol. 16, part 2, 294)

With one dancer following directly behind another in the basic geometric pattern of a circle, the plantation slaves could incorporate the nuances of their various tribal dance traditions. They could also add their own individual movements and improvisational steps within the framework of the group dance. In Africa, however, the circle dances of the tribes were not only social, they were also spiritual; they were expressions directly linked to African religion. According to historian P. Sterling Stuckey, the Ring Shout enabled the African slaves to connect with each other not only at a social level, but also spiritually (2002, 44).

Early paintings, illustrations, and firsthand descriptions of the Ring Shouts certainly bring to mind church gatherings and revival meetings. The participants' body positions, such as outstretched arms reaching skywards, create scenarios resembling church service assemblies and revival meetings. Dance historian and author Ralph G. Giordano notes that "in later years, the Ring Shout was actually an integral part of Sunday religious church worship among African Americans" (2007, Vol. I, 150).

Music was another primary element in African sacred rituals. Over the centuries, tribal drumming in African religious ceremonies had produced percussive music with sophisticated rhythms. Staggered time and offset beats were often blended together in a choir of rhythmic patterns. But music incites emotions, and the power of the drum to connect the slaves to each other and to the cultural heritage of their African tribal villages intimidated plantation owners. They often banned drumming, fearing that the rhythms would rally the slaves and produce large-scale revolts. Slave Codes enacted in the Southern states restricted the lifestyles of the slaves and expressly prohibited the use of drums for dancing, or any other purpose. Giordano explains that violators of the Slave Codes were subject to severe punishments "including whippings or even death" (Vol. I, 149). So, without drums, the plantation slaves used their own bodies to re-create the polyrhythmic complexities of their African tribal music. Brushing two hands together in combination with claps and snaps can produce various shades of sounds. Adding vocal tones, from sharp and shrill to guttural and soulful creates layers of rhythms. Then, striking an arm to the chest or the upper thigh (like a drumstick pounding on a drum) creates more percussion and, finally, using the feet to tap and stomp adds pulses between the beats and within the multi-layers of sound.

The term for this type of musical accompaniment, the clapping and slapping routines, became known as "patting juba," and there are many references to it in the literature of the Old South.

Mark Twain writes of rafts men on the Mississippi River in the 1840s:

> Next they got out an old fiddle, and one played and another patted juba, and the rest turned themselves loose on a regular old-fashioned keelboat breakdown. (Quoted in Stearns and Stearns, 1994, 29)

A "breakdown" was a general term used, in early literature and historic accounts, to describe any type of percussive solo dancing. But at some point the word "juba" was definitely applied to a specific shuffling dance. For example, in *The Speakers Garland Literary Bouquet*, published in 1892, a poem by Frances E. Wadleigh titled *Pattin' Juba* is prefaced with the following explanation:

> "Pattin' Juba" is the darky expression for a shuffling dance in which the hands accompany the motion with a rhythmic patting. (Vol. VIII, xxx, 85)

In her studies of West Indian dancing, in the late 1930s, scholar Katherine Dunham notes that the Juba (or "Jumba" dance) was "primarily a competitive dance of skill" (1941, 997). And the *New York Public Library's African American Desk Reference* states that:

> The Juba (based on the African *Giouba*) was a competitive dance, in which participants would demonstrate all their skills moving in a counterclockwise circle and rhythmically shuffling their feet. (1999, 407)

Typical to African dance in general, the Ring Shout focused on individual soloists against the background of the group. Similar to the "jam circles" known to Swing dancers (where one dancing couple at a time "swings out" into the middle of a formed circle to be highlighted briefly with their fanciest footwork and aerials), soloists moved into the middle of the ring one by one, improvised their footwork (their Juba dancing), and then merged back into the circle's perimeter again. Some of the best improvised moves of the Ring Shouts were mimicked, remembered, and rehearsed, and took on lives of their own.

It would be a mistake to assume that the white slaveholders never witnessed the Ring Shouts. In fact, in some cases they even encouraged their slaves to dance. It wasn't that unusual for North American plantation owners to bring their slaves up to the "Big House" for talent exhibitions. Eventually the slaveholders hosted competitions and gave

prizes to their most "dance-talented" slaves (Richard Nevell, 1977, 49).
Besides the Juba, some of the other improvised steps that were eventually given names were: The Hornpipe, the Buck, and the Jig.

## Precursors to Swing: The Hornpipe, the Buck Dance, and the Jig

There are many factors that led to the creation of Swing dancing and
many prior dances, and former dancers, who contributed to its birth.
(Many more, it should be added, than there is room to mention in the
pages of this book.) But several early dance styles can be viewed as
rungs on the evolutionary ladder leading to the creation of both Tap
dancing and to the Lindy Hop, the original style of Swing. While the
Hornpipe, the Buck dance, and the Jig differ in point of origin, they
are all percussive styles, adapted and danced by African American
slaves in the United States. And while each is a "solo" dance, with its
own set of rhythmic subtleties, the variations in the footwork patterns
were blended with African dance traditions. Subsequent variations
gave rise to vernacular jazz steps, which eventually set the stage for
the emergence of Swing dancing.

The Hornpipe, a Country-dance of English origin, is generally
described as a lively solo Jig with intricate footwork that could be performed in a very small space. It became a favorite dance of sailors onboard ship and is historically linked to British sailors, who danced to
entertain themselves and each other on long sea voyages. In the early
eighteenth century, the Hornpipe was danced in bare feet on the wet
slippery decks of ships. (Even into the nineteenth century, sailors only
wore shoes for formal occasions and worked onboard ships in bare
feet.) Eventually, however, the dance became associated with
the rhythms and sounds of the sailors' heavy sea boots, stamping on
the floorboards of the open decks (e-mail interview with Margaret
Newman, Royal Naval Museum).

T. P. Cooke, a Victorian stage actor who specialized in nautical roles,
is credited with bringing a "sailor's version" of the Hornpipe to the
stage. Eventually, the Hornpipe's association with the British sailor
became so strong that the dance became part of standard naval training
in Britain. But it was American actor and stage dancer John Durang
(1768–1822) who catapulted the Sailor's Hornpipe into nationwide
popularity. Durang created his own stylized version of the Sailor dance

and documented his choreography on paper, so it has been well preserved for posterity. (Durang's son Charles published the choreography
in the 1855 *Ball-room Bijou*.) Durang's notes are subject to interpretation,
of course, but he uses a number of terms which seem less nautically
inspired and more in keeping with the Afro-American jazz vernacular,
such as "Cut the buckle down," and "Grasshopper step down," and
"Jockey crotch down" (Durang's choreography is reprinted in Stearns
and Stearns, 1994, 38). Whatever Durang actually meant by the word
"jockey," it's interesting to note that the closed position of the Lindy
Hop is sometimes referred to as the jockey position. And to hang-time
in closed position (as in waiting to swing-out on count one of a
phrase, or in waiting to swing-out into a jam circle) is sometimes called
"jockeying." Legendary Lindy Hopper Frankie Manning described
how his original dance troupe used the term. He hunched down low,
imitating an eager horse ready to break out of the starting gate, and
explained:

> You know when you go the racetrack and you see the horses all ready to
> start a race? They're all ready to go, right? We'd all be standing there,
> looking down the line, like the horses do at the starting point. When do
> we start? When do we start? (PBDA video archives, 1988)

There is also a specific step in the Lindy Hop called the "Sailor Step,"
in which a couple rolls back to back while maintaining a hand-to-
hand hold. Locked in position with their backs against each other, both
partners lean to the right, hopping on one foot while kicking back with
the other, propelling themselves around in a clockwise circle. The
move replicates the look and feel of a hornpipe.

Dance author/historian Mark Knowles writes in *Tap Roots: The Early
History of Tap Dancing* that Durang's Hornpipe "later fused with
African American rhythms to create American Tap" (2002, 75). The
same historical link that connects Durang's Hornpipe to Tap dance
also connects it to Swing.

In the Appalachian Mountains, European folk dances blended together to create a toe-heel, stepping, shuffling dance style called
"Clogging." While a traditional American style of Clogging originated
in the Appalachian communities, with standardized specific footwork
developing later on, Afro-American slaves across the southeastern
states also danced versions of Clogging, and it is mentioned throughout
the Federal Writers' Project, *Slave Narratives*. One of the original versions

of the Clog, with definite Afro-American ties, was the Buck dance, which is one of the most difficult dances to define. As dancer/historian Ruth Pershing of the Cane Creek Cloggers of North Carolina points out,

> The phrase "Buck dance" means different things to different people, and greatly depends on geography, race, age, tradition, communities, as well as the quirks of language and individual experience. (E-mail interview)

The word "buck" has long been used in reference to a young man: the Buck dance may have originally been created as a catchall title, covering all male solo styles of dance. Into the twenty-first century, what some dancers call Buck dancing might also be called "Flatfoot Dancing," "Big Circle Clogging" (with looser, larger leg movements) or just plain "Clogging" by others. Tap dancers may also describe what they do with their feet as "Buck dancing." For example, in the 1933 Hollywood musical motion picture *42nd Street*, actress dancer Ruby Keeler Tap danced her way throughout the film with a notably different style than her Tap dancing contemporaries, Fred Astaire and Ginger Rogers. Keeler herself described what she was dancing as "Buck dancing." Tap dance historian/swing preservationist Rusty E. Frank interviewed Keeler for the 1995 book *Tap: The Greatest Tap Dance Stars and Their Stories*, and quotes Keeler as saying:

> I never wore taps. Never. I wore wooden soles like Bill Robinson. . . . I used to call them "My Buck Shoes." (1995, 36)

In the nineteenth century, the Buck dance was certainly well known to Southern plantation slaves. It is mentioned throughout the *Slave Narratives* in much the same manner as it is here in this narrative by former slave Agatha Babino:

> We have dance outdoors sometime. Somebody play fiddle and banjo. We dance de reel and quadrille and buck dance. (*Slave Narratives*, Texas, XVI, part 1, 38)

James Wiggins, a former slave born in Maryland circa 1850, reported: "As a child I was very fond of dancing the jig and buck" (*Slave Narratives* Maryland, Vol. 8, 67, 68).

It is generally agreed that the Buck dance performed by African American slaves on Southern plantations was a forerunner of Rhythm Tap, although Tap dancing didn't evolve until the early twentieth

George Primrose and William West owned one of the largest minstrel companies of the late nineteenth century, employing both white and black (always segregated) performers. This 1895 poster image advertises some of their African American cast members as "Buck Dancers." During this period, Buck dances could also be referred to as, "Breakdowns" or "Jigs"; the footwork was generally a low-to-the-ground, flat-footed, solo percussive style of stomping and shuffling. (Library of Congress.)

century. But there is still much speculation on where and how the dance originated. Knowles suggests that the Buck dance "is a reference to the boisterous movements of buccaneers and later was connected to the bucking of a male deer" (2002, 208). Some of the dance variations of the buck were imitations of the kicking and bucking movement of horses, mules, and deer, and may have given the dance its name. Lawrence McKiver, born in 1915, remembers:

> I used to cut the buck . . . when I was young, and more supple, I could cut just as much buck as any mister man, make like the mule bucking, like the mule trying to throw you off, and every such stuff as that . . . (McKiver quoted in Art Rosenbaum and Johann S. Buis, 1998, 93)

There are also increasing suggestions that Native American traditions inspired the Buck dance. Throughout North American Indian tribes there are ritualistic dances celebrating the deer. Some are performed to bring luck in the hunt, while others pay tribute to the deer as an important food source. Native Americans often wear buckskins while dancing, and the term "cut the buck" may refer to the actual cutting of the animal skin to wear as a dance costume. Amongst the Cherokee Indian tribe, for example, it was common practice to wear buckskins while dancing. Cherokee dancing is generally described as "low to the ground, with shuffling and stamping steps" (Richard Alan Straw, 2004, 142). Such descriptions match those of the early style of Buck dancing as, for example, when dance historian Marshall Stearns uses the words "close to the floor," "shuffle," "flatfoot," and "stamping" when referring to it (Stearns and Stearns, 1994, 65, 176).

Ruth Pershing comments that in North Carolina's western mountain regions there were many Cherokee dancers who were members of Clogging teams from the late 1920s through the 1950s. And it is often suggested that the Cherokee may have been the original creators of Appalachian team Clogging (E-mail interview; Straw, 2004, 142). But there may be another possible connection between Native Americans (specifically the Cherokee) and the Buck dance. Many North American

THE GHOST DANCE OF THE SIOUX INDIANS IN NORTH AMERICA

This wood engraving from 1891 ("Ghost Dance of the Sioux Indians") depicts the typical dancing style of North American Indians: low to the ground, with flat-footed shuffles and steps, similar to Buck dancing. (Library of Congress.)

This 1923 photograph is titled "White Deerskin Dance Costume—Hupa." It is a good example of how some Native Americans "cut the buck" and wore the deerskin for ceremonial dancing. (Edward S. Curtis/Library of Congress.)

Indian tribes held harvest dances in celebration of corn, and Phil Towns, in the Georgia *Narratives*, is one of many early observers who noted the "similarity" between the Cherokee "Green Corn Dance" and "Buck dancing." And, interestingly, the Green Corn Dance was also often called a "busk." The words: "busk" and "green corn dance" have long been used interchangeably by authors and historians, which brings up the question, might the word "busk" have metamorphosed, at some point, into the word "buck"? (Towns, Vol. IV, part 4, 40; Livingston Farrand, 1906, 170–171).

There is no denying that there were ethnic mixings between African Americans and Native Americans, particularly in the Southern mountain states. In fact, a large percentage of runaway slaves in the early nineteenth century in Tennessee, Georgia, and the Carolinas were suspected of "making for the Cherokee Nation" (Wilma A. Dunaway, 2003, 225). And in the Federal Writers' Project *Slave Narratives*, many former slaves give insight into the fusion of the two cultures and traditions. Jerry Sims, a former slave, born in Mississippi in 1859, asserts:

> I'm more Indian than anything else . . . Chief Sims was my Grandpa. He
> was Indian, full blood. His wife was a Choctaw Indian. (*Slave Narratives*, Arkansas, Vol. II, part 6, 160)

Betty Robertson, a former slave from Oklahoma, states:

> My Mammy was a Cherokee slave, and talked it good. My husband was a
> Cherokee born Negro. . . . (*Slave Narratives*, Oklahoma, Vol. XIII, 266)

Another example is ex-slave Tom Windham, [who] was stolen from a
Southern plantation by a Creek Indian (who became his master), and
was raised in a tepee on a large plantation owned by the Indians (*Slave Narratives*, Arkansas, Vol. II, part 7, 213).

Considering this ethnic mixing, it seems reasonable that Native
American dances could certainly have influenced African American
dance traditions, and may have had a direct connection to Buck dancing.

While the Hornpipe, Clog, and Buck dance were all popular concurrently in the nineteenth century, there was another important solo
dance being danced at the same time: the Jig. With its characteristic
hop steps and taps, the Jig was especially popular as a competitive
dance (Lilly Grove, 1907, 203). Today, the word "jig" conjures up visions
of the *Lord of the Dance* Irish Step-dancers and St. Patrick's Day
celebrations. In the eighteenth and nineteenth centuries in America,
however, the word could be used to describe any solo variation of
European Country-dancing. Whatever distinguishing characteristics
the different varieties of Jigs had, they all involved a fast and fiery
stamping of the feet, with very little other body movement employed.
Hands hung limp and open, while arms dangled without tension.
When an easy balance was set, the dancer's feet could accelerate in time
with the music in a dazzling display of toe-and-heel-taps, stomps, hops,
and whirls.

Between the years of 1846 and 1860, the Irish potato famine brought
an estimated two million Irish immigrants into the United States. They
were mostly farmers with no means of buying land or property,
who tended to cluster in neighborhoods in the larger cities. These
immigrants helped create the first American ghettos (Robert V. Rimini,
2008, 131). Dance halls were prevalent in the ghetto neighborhoods
and, as African Americans and Irish Americans co-mingled in these
communities, dancing was a popular pastime. Historian Henry Kmen

asserts that in New Orleans, mixed-race social dances, with both blacks and whites in attendance, became "a recreational institution." The African American slaves, the free blacks, and the poorer-class Country-dancing whites (mostly Irish Americans) were all mixing it up together and borrowing elements from each other's dances and step variations. The dances of the separate cultures were definitely merging (Kmen in Stearns and Stearns, 1994, 20).

Some of the slaves made names for themselves as accomplished dancers. In the pre-Civil war years, a "Negro" known only as "Tom" is documented as being "the jigginest fellow ever was." Apparently Tom could move his feet at lightening quick speed while balancing a glass of water on his head. He'd jab at the floor with hammer-like strikes, even spin around, all the while keeping his head and neck perfectly still. And he wouldn't spill a drop of water from the glass (Stearns and Stearns, 37).

Besides the traditional European dances, formal plantation parties eventually featured popular Country-dances like the Clog, the Buck, and the Jig. As dance historian Richard Nevell points out, using slaves as musicians at the "Big House" formal balls was a common practice. The slaves were trained to play the Quadrilles, Contredanses and Minuets, and also the popular Jigs (1977, 45).

Southern slaves became renowned for their musical skills and dancing prowess. The tribal dance steps of the Ring Shouts, having blended with European courtly dances, the Hornpipes, Clogs, various plantation Buck dances, and Jigs, plus Native American traditions, were producing new dance forms that audiences across America and Europe clamored to see. But instead of audiences getting to view touring representatives of the dance (the Southern slaves themselves), their curiosity gave rise to a strange social phenomenon, an entirely new form of entertainment in the American theater known as "blackface minstrelsy."

# 2

# Bred in Minstrelsy, Raised in Rhythm

For much of the nineteenth century, minstrelsy was the most important form of entertainment in the United States. Minstrels were touring song-and-dance professionals, typically white males (women were banned from the stage until the 1870s), from northern urban communities. They were most often small-time actors who set out on the minstrel circuit as a way to break into big city theater. Constantly in search of new and exciting material for their shows, minstrels began to borrow heavily from the dance talents of slaves they observed in the Southern colonies. They blended their own straight up, buoyant styles of the Hornpipes, Clogs and Jigs with the looser, lower-to–the-ground shuffling steps of the Southern slaves, and added these new dance techniques to their onstage performances. They blackened their faces with greasepaint or burnt cork residue, in caricature of Southern slaves, and the genre became defined by their "blackface" performances. The blackface minstrel show is generally considered to be the first truly American form of musical theater.

As Alexander Saxton reminds us, the Southern slaves, in general, received no credit for being the source of the minstrel's material. But it was through that material, through the influences of the Afro-American dance traditions, that the entire minstrelsy profession was molded and shaped (Saxton, "Blackface Minstrelsy" in: Bean, Hatch, and McNamara, 1996, 70–71).

Dancing was an important part of minstrelsy entertainment, and as the two separate traditions of European and African dance styles began to fuse, cross-cultural trends developed and new dance forms emerged. Yet each retained certain characteristics at the heart of those original, separate traditions. The European stylistic trends included straighter legs, pointed toes, a "lilt" or "airy spring" in the steps, which produced nimble buoyancy. African dancing (like Native American dancing) was based on a bend, or a crouch, through the body and knees. The dancing stayed closer to the earth, with flatter feet and looser, more relaxed movements in the hips and legs. The fusing of the traditions was most certainly a two-way street, with white dancers borrowing from the Afro-American styles and black dancers "Africanizing" the European dances. This term "Africanizing" has been used before in reference to both dance and to music. For example, the first chapter of Ted Gioia's *The History of Jazz* is subtitled, "The Africanization of American Music." And Mark Knowles writes in *Tap Roots*: "European dances were Africanized and therefore transformed." But it was through minstrelsy that the two dance traditions merged into something uniquely American (Gioia, 1997, 3; Knowles, 2002, 41).

Deeply rooted in European folk culture, blackface can be traced to the fifteenth century, although most historians agree that its origins pre-date that time. The black-faced Moor was a common theatrical character in Europe. Shakespeare's *Othello*, for instance, regularly featured actors in blackface in the title role. And costuming for masquerade balls, rural festivals and parades, often used blackface as a theatrical device.

In Europe, in general, early stage representations of slaves were handled gently, with a degree of sympathy and pathos toward the enslaved. In fact, it is often suggested that the eighteenth-century English blackface singers helped rid Europe of slavery, as their songs rallied public sentiment against it. In early America, however, those theatrical trends took on a different tone. Colonial Americans loved comedy, farces, and burlesque. While there was a small elite audience who preferred thespian orations and classical productions, the general masses wanted nothing more from their entertainers than to be entertained. American blackface productions, always brash and satirical in nature, became increasingly popular. But they also became increasingly derogatory, conveying a general prejudice against the slaves. The minstrels' songs and dances began to caricature slave culture to the point of depicting the African American person as a dimwitted and comical character (*American Experience*, "Daniel Decatur Emmett, 1815–1904," pbs.org.). However, as the minstrels toured the country, Americans were further exposed to this new cross-cultural dance blend.

Early African American dancing possessed a number of distinctive characteristics that made it unique unto itself. Three key elements shaped the minstrel performers' shows and helped pave the way toward Swing: The first was the use of percussive rhythms to "fool around with" the strict tempos of the Jigs and the Clogs. The a cappella work songs of the plantation slaves, and the poly-rhythms of their patting juba and Ring Shout dancing allowed for a freedom of meter, and spawned a new approach to the European dances. White songwriters of the minstrelsy era began to borrow on black free-rhythmic ideas, thus transforming European musical traditions. The second element was the use of humor and mimicry. As Afro-American dance often imitated the natural environment, birds, animals, and other people were all subject to representation, often in a lighthearted whimsical, caricatured manner. The third element was uninhibited improvisation. Used in the early Ring Shouts, as well as early Jig and Cakewalk competitions, improvisations are at the heart of jazz vernacular movement and led directly to the creation of Swing dancing. Swing dance improvisations are still generally based on jazz vernacular movements (moves like the Suzy Q, Slow Boogie, or Shimmy), but with a high degree of unconformity. Basically, as long as it works with the music, anything goes! Author and dance critic, Edward Thorpe, expresses it beautifully when he explains:

> ... with Black dance the concern is not with the self-conscious presentation of something "beautiful" for the onlooker to observe, but almost wholly with what is felt, what emotion is being experienced by the dancer himself. (Thorpe, 1990, 13)

Swing is all about your connections—the connections between you and the music, and you and your partner. Honing your own creative instincts and interpretative skills allows you the freedom to express your inner joy through Swing dancing. It's not about impressing onlookers. It shouldn't matter who's watching—Swing dance is an expression of your soul.

## Rhythm, Humor, and Improvisation

In a 1941 *Life* magazine article on theatrical dance, specifically on the career of Fred Astaire, writer Lincoln Barnett offered clear examples of the difference in the "feel" between European and Afro-American music. For an idea of the European straight tempo style, Barnett suggests reciting "very rapidly, without taking a breath" these lines of the British poet, Lord Byron:

> The Assyrian came down like the wolf on the fold,
> And his cohorts were gleaming in purple and gold;
> And the sheen of their spears was like stars on the sea,
> When the blue wave rolls nightly on deep Galilee.

Then, Barnett suggests contrasting that with the percussive feel of the African American style. He offers American poet Vachel Lindsay's verse, *The Congo*, as an example of that style. In Barnett's words: "Swing it":

> Fat black bucks in a wine-barrel room,
> Barrel-house kings, with feet unstable,
> Sagged and reeled and pounded on the table,
> Pounded on the table,
> Beat an empty barrel with the handle of a broom,
> Hard as they were able,
> Boom, boom, Boom,
> With a silk umbrella and the handle of a broom. (Barnett, *"Fred Astaire: He Is the No. 1 Exponent of American's Only Native and Original Dance Form,"* 74, 76)

The use of syncopations—unstable restless rhythms—is the first key element that led to swing music and dancing. At the heart of the Afro-American musical tradition, it was one of the important ingredients in the creation of ragtime music and then jazz. Jazz music, in turn, was one of the important ingredients of Swing dancing.

Los Angeles musicologist Paul Chipello explains that jazz music always consists of "syncopated" rhythms, and those syncopations refer to strikes or attacks on weak beats in music and dance movement (Personal interview). The songs of the minstrels were upbeat and syncopated; the popular minstrelsy genre launched the careers of composers such as Daniel Emmet, James Bland (the first successful black songwriter), and Stephen Collins Foster, who reportedly performed in blackface when he was as young as nine years old. Stephen Foster is generally regarded as the first composer of American popular music. His songs, such as the traditional standards "My Old Kentucky Home," and "Oh Susanna," were featured in many of the traveling minstrel shows and became familiar to most Americans. In 1847, Foster sold "Oh Susanna" to a music publisher for the price of $100. And while the publisher would have subsequently made huge sums of money on the hit tune, Foster himself never received a penny more for it. Copyright protections and "royalty" fees for songwriters were not established until the following century (Larry Starr and Christopher Waterman, 2003, 25, 43).

To what extent minstrel music directly effected the development of jazz can be debated. However, along with African American work songs and spirituals, the minstrel shows also gave white audiences "catchy tunes" and the musical rhythmic ideas that helped prepare them for jazz—and subsequently, for the big band era of swing music.

The second important element of Afro-American dancing that led to minstrelsy's vernacular jazz steps, and on to Swing, was its pervasive usage of humor and mimicry. Throughout Africa, dancers use masks to represent the birds and animals that are prevalent in their regions. It is common for animal masquerade dancers to change from one animal to another, from a snake to a leopard for instance, in the course of an African dance drama (Felix Begho in a collection of essays in Welsh-Asante, 1997, 179). This type of mimicry requires an enormous range of body movements and the use of all parts of the dancer's body—not just the arms and legs, but also the torso and hips. Mimicry can be an attempt at serious representation, but can also be wildly fanciful and capricious. It has produced such dances as the "Buzzard Lope," the "Pigeon Wing," and "Beat The Mule" (which may have led to the Buck dance)—but it was also applied (in a humorous mocking spirit) to people. Nineteenth-century black slaves imitated and grossly caricatured the formal dance styles and movements of their white masters. Ironically, white entertainers then imitated those same parodies in their stage and traveling minstrel shows.

As white minstrel men in blackface toured the country, white audiences often believed the minstrels were authentic representations of African Americans. Giordano comments:

> In reality, the caricature of the African American was completely derogatory and stereotypical. (2007, Vol. 1, 152)

This typical minstrel poster, circa 1900, shows that Al G. Field's white performers (depicted in circles at the top of the poster) "blackened" their faces to perform as "Doc Quigley's Dancing Professors." As derogatory and offensive as they were, such performances exposed American's to cross-cultural dance blends. (Library of Congress.)

Many Northern whites had never actually seen plantation slaves before. A glimpse of African American culture and of the lifestyles of the "enslaved Negroes" (however bogus) was a welcome curiosity, especially when presented, as it generally was, in the safe, lily-white environment of the blackface minstrel show. For a small admission fee, of twenty-five cents, the horrors of slavery vanished under a fanciful veil of song and dance. It was an imaginary setting, where plantation life was joyous and filled with laughter and fun (Barbara S. Glass, 2007, 125–126).

In the humorous minstrel shows, American citizens could forget their concerns about the welfares of the slaves. They could lose all feelings of guilt. There was no brutality and no suffering on the stage-set minstrelsy plantations. Whites could revel in black culture without actually experiencing a black person, and the grotesque stereotypes of African Americans ran rampant.

Author Eric Lott uses the phrase: "love and theft" when referring to blackface minstrelsy. The word "theft" (as opposed to the "borrowing" of the black inventions and cultural performances) makes sense here, as it must be acknowledged that minstrels posing as black men profited from their source material while prohibiting the black entertainers from actually performing themselves (Lott's book is titled, *Love and Theft: Blackface Minstrelsy and the American Working Class*, 1993).

The third and perhaps most important ingredient in African American dance, which also defines the original style of Swing dancing, is the tradition of uninhibited improvisation. This bold and careless device takes away the prim and proper and infuses the dance with individual expressions of euphoria. The concept of "the individual" is important here because while social Swing is a partnered dance and there are moments of close embrace, there are also moments of distance and space. Sometimes partners hold both hands (open position Swing) or one hand (a send past); then there are release moments where the dancers let go of both hands and move on their own (breakaways), allowing for personal expression, spontaneous responses to the music, and the freedom to dance from the heart.

These three Afro-American dance elements (percussive rhythms, humor and mimicry, and uninhibited improvisation) helped define the genre of minstrelsy. But they were also important elements in the development of the Lindy Hop—the original style of Swing, and have remained defining characteristics of Swing dance in general.

### Minstrels Jim Crow and Master Juba

Certain people will always stand out in a community, regardless of the time and place in which they live. Sometimes their success is fleeting (the 15 minutes of fame pattern), but sometimes their mark is so indelible that it is written about in annals of history for years, decades, and even centuries. Such is the case with two nineteenth-century dance entertainers, Jim Crow and Master Juba. Renowned for their solo Jig styles, they were pioneers of American minstrelsy, and served as catalysts toward the creation of Swing dancing.

Thomas Dartmouth Rice ("T. D." Rice, "Tom" Rice, or "Daddy" Rice) was a white, nineteenth-century actor credited with popularizing the black-faced minstrel shows on the American stage. Rice created and portrayed a black character named "Jim Crow"; his character became so popular that its debut is often used to mark the official beginnings of the minstrelsy period in American theatrical history. In her essay, "Black Minstrelsy and Double Inversion, Circa 1890," historian and scholar Annemarie Bean defines two distinct stages in the development of minstrelsy:

> Early minstrelsy is defined from the purported (as opposed to the documented) first minstrelsy performance of "Jumpin Jim Crow" by T. D. Rice c. 1828 to the beginning of the Civil War in 1860. "Late minstrelsy" is defined as post–Civil War minstrelsy. (Bean in Elam and Krasner, 2001, 189)

The story of how T. D. Rice came to create the character of Jim Crow varies according to different sources, and some dispute the story altogether. However, historians generally agree that the character was based on an old deformed "Negro slave." Purportedly, the slave was owned by a man with the surname of Crow, who owned property behind a theater where Rice was performing at the time. It was customary that slaves took their names from their owners, so the decrepit slave called himself "Jim Crow." Rice watched the curiously awkward movements of the slave going about his duties tending to the stable and the yard. In Jim Crow, Rice saw the makings of an entirely new character, never before seen on the theatrical stage.

In a 1881 *New York Times* newspaper article on the subject of Jim Crow and Tom Rice, author Edmon S. Conner (a professed observer of Jim Crow himself) described the slave's crooked shoulders and the left leg deformity that caused a "laughable limp." Conner writes:

> He [Crow] used to croon a queer old tune with words of his own, and at the end of each verse would give a little jump, and when he came down he set his "Heel a-rockin'!" He called it "jumping Jim Crow." (Conner in Stearns and Stearns, 1994, 39–40)

Tom Rice toyed with the slave's song and fooled around with the slave's movements. When he blackened his face and became the singing/dancing Jim Crow, his all-white audience reportedly went wild. After the first performance, he was called back onto the stage "twenty times." The Jim Crow song contained several verses of lyrics, but Rice's refrain (that would have been repeated a number of times in the song) went as follows:

> Wheel about, turn about
> Do jis so,
> An, ebery time I wheel about
> I jump Jim Crow! (Stearns and Stearns, 40)

The Jim Crow song became a hit, both in the United States and Britain, and made Rice a celebrity in the field of minstrelsy. The song has been preserved, but there is no film footage of Rice's performances, so it's hard to imagine what the Jim Crow dance actually looked like. Most dance scholars suggest it was a blend of Jigs and shuffles; however, those terms conjure up an array of images and can be interpreted entirely differently by different dancers. It may have been a dance known, in Swing jargon, as "Truckin'." Swing dancers use this term in highly stylized individual ways, but the various movements: Jigs, shuffles, turns, and jumps could all be easily incorporated into a version of Truckin'. However, there is also a good argument to be made that Tom Rice was, instead, dancing a version of "Break-a-Leg," another, entirely different early Swing dancing move.

Break-a-Leg requires holding the weight back over your base left leg, and then extending the heel of the right leg forward. As the weight is shifted forward, the dancer drops forward (sometimes dramatically) over the front right foot. As legendary Lindy Hopper Frankie Manning explains it, "It's like you're walking and one of your legs gives way. You have to quickly change the weight so you don't put weight on the injured leg." During a personal visit to see Manning in November 2009 (he was 94 at the time and recovering from hip surgery), he demonstrated the footwork while seated in a chair in his living room. Break-a-Leg would seem an obvious choice in mimicking lameness, and the whole effect of the move would suit the stylized characterization of an elderly person with a limp. However, regardless of whether Jim Crow's dance was more like Truckin' or Break-a-Leg, Tom Rice created a dance step used by the original Lindy Hoppers, and then subsequent Swing dancers. Rice's dancing Jim Crow character spurred on the development of minstrelsy and definitely contributed to the later development of Swing dancing.

JIMMY CROW.

Tom Rice/Jim ("Jimmy") Crow, sheet music, circa 1834–1847, shows a typical derogatory image of this famous song and dance character from minstrelsy. Interestingly, Crow was often illustrated in the "Truckin'" (or "Break-A-Leg") Swing-like dance pose shown here. Movements of this sort paved the way for Swing dancing, and were immediately absorbed into the Lindy Hop, the original style of Swing. (Brown University Library.)

The name "Jim Crow" later became a derogatory epithet for African Americans; the name was eventually attached to the U.S. segregation laws that lasted until the 1960s. But for much of the nineteenth century, Jim Crow set the bar for success in the world of minstrelsy. As Historian Ken Emerson puts it:

> Minstrelsy swept the world in the 1830s and 1840s much the same way rock and roll did almost 100 years later. In the same way that Elvis Presley electrified the world so did Daddy Rice when he did "Jump Jim Crow" on the London stage. (*The American Experience*, pbs.org., "Stephen Foster," Special Features)

Inspired by the success of Tom Rice, white minstrels in blackface became increasingly popular. Solo minstrel performances soon led to group productions; Daniel Decatur Emmett and his blackface troupe, the Virginia Minstrels (circa 1842), are generally credited as being the first organized group. These demeaning and crude depictions of blacks, tailored specifically to entertain white audiences, continued in an increasingly insensitive manner. Dressed in flamboyant baggy costumes, or sometimes in tattered rags, the minstrels donned outlandish wigs and performed clownish songs and dances. Northern blacks were often featured as more educated and dapper than their Southern slave counterparts, but all blacks in general were represented as "happy darkies" foolishly satisfied with their subservient societal role.

After the Civil War, authentic black minstrel companies were making appearances on the minstrel circuit; however, they were still fronted by white managers in order to get bookings, and for their own protection (Stearns and Stearns, 1994, 43). Prior to the Civil War, in fact, black entertainers were as a rule banned from performing in minstrel shows. However, there was one well-documented and famous exception: a dancer named "William Henry Lane."

Known as "Master Juba," William Henry Lane was by all accounts a dancing phenomenon. In the 1911 book *Monarchs of Minstrelsy*, author Edward Le Roy Rice writes of Master Juba: "the world never saw his equal" (48). Critics noted the "extraordinary command he possessed over his feet," and wrote about Lane's footwork as if it was entirely different from what other minstrels were dancing at the time. As minstrelsy was developing and its entertainers were becoming world famous, Master Juba was acknowledged as the best of the best (Marian Hannah Winter, in Paul Magriel, 1948, 50).

Young Master Juba studied under a teacher, a dancing coach, who undoubtedly helped him achieve the grace and ease of his steps. His purported teacher was an "Uncle Jim Lowe," who, unfortunately, seems to have disappeared into obscurity. So did Lane's dancing talent surpass his teacher's? Or might Uncle Jim Lowe have been the greatest dancer of all time? Either way, William Henry Lane was clearly a remarkable talent. Critics of the time, when describing his dancing, mention his flexibility, his elasticity and ability to spin. He could also, reportedly "tie his legs into knots" and "fling them about recklessly" (*Illustrated London News*, 1848, "Juba at Vauxhall," 77).

William Henry Lane's life remains somewhat of a mystery. Many historians contend that he was a free-born Negro from Providence, Rhode Island, who grew up in lower Manhattan, New York, in an area called Five Points. This was an American slum, a community of brothels, breweries, and dance houses, where Irish immigrants and free blacks lived side-by-side, sharing their cultures and mixing their dances. English author Charles Dickens visited New York in 1842 and toured this notoriously rough neighborhood as inspiration for his writing. In his *American Notes for General Circulation*, Dickens describes a dancer that he himself witnessed in a Negro dancing cellar, performing to thunderous applause:

> Single shuffle, double shuffle, cut and cross-cut; snapping his fingers, rolling his eyes, turning in his knees, presenting the backs of his legs in front, spinning about on his toes and heels like nothing but the man's fingers on the tambourine. (Dickens, 1868, 40)

Dance historians generally agree that the dancer described by Dickens was Master Juba. Evidence lies in the fact that when Lane performed in London he was advertised as "Boz's Juba" (Boz was used as a common nickname for Charles Dickens). Lane reached a pinnacle of success in 1848 when he toured England with a group of white minstrels called "Pell's Ethiopians" and received top billing over the lot of them. Marshall Stearns adds, in referring to Master Juba, "At a time when white men in blackface were making fortunes imitating the Negro, the real thing must have been a revelation." He adds:

> Lane's dancing had a rare authenticity. He was apparently *swinging*—relatively speaking—naturally and effortlessly. (Stearns and Stearns, 1994, 47)

The quality of "natural authenticity" is at the very heart of the jazz dance vernacular. While the European social dances were created in the Protestant–Victorian cachet of refined elegance and the heavenly ideal of grace, all the jazz vernacular steps that eventually led to Swing dancing were created from the earthly expressions—the joys and hopes, as well as the pain and sorrows, of that particular experience of being African American in the era of slavery in the United States.

While Henry Lane passed away in 1852, by most accounts in his twenties, minstrel group shows continued to grow in popularity throughout the decade. However, although there were a few black entertainers (other than Lane) who managed to break into minstrelsy during that decade, it wasn't until after the Civil War, and the emancipation of the slaves, that African Americans organized their own companies (Robert C. Toll, 1974, 198–199). American historian Linda Dahl notes that the minstrel circuit (especially for black entertainers) was a difficult way to earn a living. The traveling was "constant," and the pay was "short." Minstrels had to competitively fight for jobs, especially in the rural areas, and their audiences in those towns were "poor, unlettered" and "often drunk and demanding" (Dahl, 1984, 10).

When the larger touring shows pulled into a town, the entire minstrel company would stage a parade; their brass bands led the way, wailing the syncopated music of a military march—a style that music scholar Jack Wheaton notes would later be called *Dixieland* (1994, 61). The shows themselves generally followed a standard three-set format. The first set offered comedic songs and jokes. The second set, called an *olio*, featured novelty acts and performances by solo "star" performers, and the final set was a narrative skit that included music, dancing, and burlesque.

The first set would culminate in a "Walk-Around," which was a circular strut by members of the cast, reminiscent of the Ring Shout. In the show's finale, the Walk-Around was often repeated again, sometimes with challenge dances, which were competitions where the performers would try to "outdance" each other. In late minstrelsy, these Walk-Around challenges gave rise to a number of specific movements (and specific dances like the Essence and the Cakewalk), some of which were incorporated into the original style of Swing dance, the Lindy Hop.

## The Essence and the Cakewalk

The creative combustion of cultural diversity and talent, the whole explosive mix, that produced the American form of entertainment known as "blackface minstrelsy," also produced specific new dances that kept the journey toward Swing dance progressing.

The "Essence of Old Virginia" is often regarded as minstrelsy's most famous dance. It was a gliding, mobile dance, well suited for "on stage" productions. When the Buck dance at some point began to "travel" (perhaps conforming to performance choreography, or enabling minstrel performers to enter or exit the stage more easily), the dance got an expanded name: the Mobile Buck. The Mobile Buck in turn may have led to the creation of the Essence, which was certainly a traveling dance incorporating slides and glides along with its shuffles. Historian Zita Allen suggests that the dance may have looked a lot like Michael Jackson's "Moonwalk" (PBS, *Free to Dance*, "From Minstrel Show to Center Stage," 2001) and ragtime composer Arthur Marshall is quoted as saying this about the Essence:

> If a guy could really do it, he sometimes looked as if he was being towed around on ice skates . . . the performer moves forward without appearing to move his feet at all, by manipulating his toes and heels rapidly, so that his body is propelled without changing the position of his legs. (Marshall, from Stearns and Stearns, 1994, 50)

This description certainly does suggest the Moonwalk. Interestingly, it was not uncommon for Swing dancers to incorporate the Moonwalk into their repertoire of moves in the 1990s, and "slide steps" have long been popular with Swing dancers.

In the late nineteenth century, several all-black minstrel companies were successfully touring in the United States and overseas. A number of black performers emerged from these productions as stars, including Billy Kersands, who by all accounts was an expert at the Essence. Known for his unusually large mouth, which could stretch open wide enough to accommodate objects such as billiard balls, and even cups and saucers, Kersands could also peel off a dozen vests while gliding across a stage, dancing a great Essence (51).

As black minstrel companies gained acceptance, white minstrel shows took off in a new direction. The white productions became larger and more lavish, and they dropped the satirical plantation skits so degrading to the African American. But, oddly enough, the black minstrel companies began to adopt those same old worn-out routines and portrayed themselves in the same stereotypical character roles as their white predecessors had. Black minstrels still blackened their faces. They also used white greasepaint on their lips to make them appear larger and more caricature-like. Winter explains that these black minstrels corked up "as black as possible" to satisfy their audiences, who were used to seeing "Negro minstrels" as they were depicted by white performers (Winter, in Magriel, 1948, 60).

Historians have pointed out, however, that for all the degrading and racist aspects of the genre, black minstrels did learn the ins and outs of show business, which helped launch their careers in later theater productions. They became booking agents, producers, and even big stars. Bill "Bojangles" Robinson, for example, got his start making $5 a week plus board in the minstrel show "The South Before the War" (D. D. Livingston, "Taps for Bill Robinson," *Dance Magazine*, 1950). And minstrelsy facilitated increased acceptance of black vernacular dance styles with white audiences and the public at large. Barbara Glass sums it up nicely when she writes this, regarding African American minstrel performers:

> ...they gradually transformed its format into a showcase for their talent and a vehicle for their cultural arts—a monumental achievement. (2007, 124)

The three elements of the Afro-American tradition, the rhythmic complexities, the humor and mimicry, and the individual improvisation and expression were built on and fine-tuned in the years of the black minstrels. The competitive Walk-Around, especially, led to improvisations, which were repeated, further conceptualized, and eventually turned into jazz steps that could be named and recognized. One of the original dances of the Southern plantations that found its way onto the minstrelsy stage, into vaudeville (the genre which followed minstrelsy), and then into widespread popularity was a dance called the Cakewalk.

When slaves got a peek at the balls and cotillions held in the "Big Houses" on the Southern plantations, they saw white men formally strutting about in dapper attire. They watched white women in floor-length gowns, holding their skirts and petticoats up off the ground, tiptoeing up stairs and daintily stepping this way and that. They saw formally dressed white couples strolling arm in arm in the gardens, and dancing together in the European social styles. When the parties were over, the slaves entertained themselves by mocking the movements of the party guests. They tipped their imaginary top hats, bowed and curtsied to each other, and strutted and preened in parody of what they had witnessed.

In general, plantation owners were humored by such behavior. Eventually, at the encouragement of their employers, slaves staged parades on the front lawns of the "Big Houses." The slaves dressed up in their master's old clothes and danced in the same elaborately exaggerated manner they had practiced. Humorous mimicry was in full play. They high-stepped and pranced, while their masters laughed and applauded from the comforts of their large and shaded front porches. These slave parades became a festive tradition at Southern "jubilees" (large parties on the plantations), and became increasingly competitive. Percussive rhythms and impromptu improvisations were added to the parodies and, eventually, the most high-stepping, best dancers were awarded homemade cakes by the plantation masters. This gave the dance its name, "the Cakewalk." It is often reported that the expression "That takes the cake!" originated with these parades. (The saying may have actually come from Ireland, where giving cakes as prizes was a common tradition dating back long before this time.)

After the Civil War, authentic black minstrel companies added and adapted Cakewalk moves to their shows, usually in their finale Walk-Arounds. As one of the early Savoy Ballroom Lindy Hoppers, Al Minns, explained it, "When the Cakewalkers got on the stages, they started kicking their legs up higher. And that's when the Cakewalk dance really caught on" (Minns' interview on "Eye on Dance" television series, *Rhythm's the Name of the Game*, 1981).

In the late nineteenth century, dancers of all ages, black and white, began dancing the Cakewalk to syncopated show tunes and marches, and Cakewalking contests began appearing everywhere, often with

Dancers performed the Cakewalk at the 1901 World's Fair (Pan Am Expo) in Buffalo, NY, as the dance craze was at its height. The Cakewalk broke color barriers, blurring the lines between black and white entertainment, and was immediately absorbed into the Lindy Hop, becoming a permanent part of Swing dance vocabulary. (Photo by Hulton Archive/Getty Images.)

cash prizes. From its humble beginnings as a slave plantation dance, the Cakewalk became a national fad. It broke the color barrier as the first African American dance accepted in white society ballrooms, although it should be noted that blacks were generally prohibited from entering those ballrooms. Nonetheless, the Cakewalk brought new societal respect for black entertainment in general and paved the way for the ballroom dance crazes that were soon to follow.

# 3

# Ragtime, Jazz, and
# Swing Dance Gets a Name

New York City in the 1890s was a bustling metropolis filled with theaters, entertainment venues, and music halls. On 28th Street, home to the music publishing industry, the rumblings of the energized city floated up from the sidewalks through open windows of rehearsal halls and piano rooms. The street noises clamored and clanked, like a kitchen full of pots and pans banging together in musical harmony.

They called it "Tin Pan Alley," an area where careers were launched, stars were born, and dreams were realized. Singers and composers flocked to 28th Street to audition new material for song publishers, and everyone was singing and dancing to a new musical craze called "ragtime."

The rhythms of "rag" were loose and syncopated. Music scholar Paul Chipello explains that ragtime meant, literally, "ragged time," as piano players—both black and white were holding, bending, and syncopating beats. The player's left hand kept a steady 2/4 beat (Chipello describes it as a "boom-chick, boom-chick" rhythm), while the right hand "ragged" around it, blending in weak beats and syncopated melodies full of jazzy rhythms (Personal interview).

By the end of the nineteenth century, although minstrel shows were declining in popularity, the exuberant Cakewalk was sweeping the nation. *The Creole Show*, an "all Negro" musical production opened in New York in 1889, featuring women performers (a new trend) as well as men dancing the Cakewalk. Women brought fresh improvisations to the dance, and new possibilities—suddenly the Cakewalk could be performed by "couples" as a "partnered" dance. But it was the dance team of Bert Williams and George Walker, two Afro-American male "eccentric" entertainers, who helped turn the dance into an international craze. Brilliantly talented Cakewalkers, Williams and Walker became one of the highest paid acts in musical theater.

Authors Donald D. Megill and Richard S. Demory reflect on the cross-influences of the Cakewalk and ragtime music, and suggest that whichever came first—the dance or the musical "rags"—both fads paved the way for the development of jazz (1989, 5). As ragtime piano songs blended with the brass bands of minstrelsy, a new sound emerged. It was seasoned with the flavors of New York, (with its ragged Tin-Pan Alley tunes), and Southern spices from New Orleans, (in the syncopated marches of the Dixieland bands). Jazz music was born from this savory mix of North and South, piano and brass. And from this point forward, from the music of jazz, it's a short hop, skip, and a jump to swing music and to the pioneers of the Lindy Hop style of Swing dancing.

## The Animal Dances and the House the Castles Built

The exact origin of the word "jazz" is unknown and, although its beginnings are often marked by the recordings of the "Original Dixie-land Jass [sic] Band" of 1917, no one can say for certain exactly what year it first appeared. But one thing is sure: This brassy, swingin' age of jazz marked the dawning of a new-found freedom, especially for women. Corsets were a thing of the past. Hair was bobbed short. Long cumbersome skirts were out, and the newly attained "ability to move" was celebrated. For healthy exercise, and simply for the fun of it, dancing was *the* thing to do.

The Cakewalk had always emphasized the solo, expressive style of the "individual." So when the twentieth century brought back the European custom of partnered dancing, it was "modernized," allowing for free movement and individual expression borrowed from Cakewalking. Women draped themselves like swooning maidens on their partners, and couples wrapped their arms around each other's waists and over each other's shoulders. Everyone was grinding and wriggling to dances with animal names in their titles. On the sheet music for Jos M. Daly's "Turkey Trot Song" (1909), the title is prefaced with the claim: "The most talked about dance in the world today."

(Daly had also previously composed the lesser-known "Chicken Reel.") The Bullfrog Hop dance movement was spelled out in its lyrics: ". . . Then you drop like Johnny on the spot. That's the Bullfrog Hop." Interestingly, "Johnny's Drop" is a step that remained well known to Lindy Hoppers into the twenty-first century. The Grizzly Bear, a dance stemming from Irving Berlin's popular creation, caught on with the public in the 1911 Ziegfeld Follies show. The dance featured lumbering, bear-like movements; the dancers were supposed to shout out periodically "It's a bear!" But the "Grizzly Bear" was one of literally hundreds of animal dances. The Bunny Hug, Kangaroo Dip, Possum Trot, Monkey Slide, etc., didn't have much staying power, but for a short time were the dances everyone was doing. And many of the vernacular Afro-American movements spotlighted in these dances were further developed.

These animal dances all had specific steps that needed to be "learned," which in turn created a trendy new profession: the American Ballroom dance instructor. Dance teachers like Irene and Vernon Castle were suddenly in demand as everyone wanted to learn the newest steps. The incredibly popular animal dances, however, were not accepted by all segments of society. Many considered the movements too "suggestive," and there was a backlash against them. Moral character was deemed "in jeopardy on the dance floor" and crusaders against cheek-to-cheek dancing raised their voices and preached loudly against it (Catherine Gourley, 2007, 55). The Castles taught the popular dances but refined them, taking out the grinds and wriggles, making them acceptable to polite society elites and calming the voices of the anti-dance crusaders. Author Eve Golden points out that unlike many of the professional dancers of the time, the Castles danced with an air of wholesome sophistication, which made them exceedingly respectable. They were clean-cut, married, and socially accepted. Their New York dancing school, Castle House, opened in 1913 with sponsorship from the city's upper crust. They offered classes and dances, served up along with sandwiches, cakes, chocolates, and tea (Golden, 2007, 49, 87).

Irene and Vernon Castle discarded the animal dances from their roster of classes as being awkward and unrefined. Instead, they created new dances or "tamed" old ones. Thanks to their endorsement, everyone wanted to learn (among a myriad of other dances): the One Step, the Two Step, the Tango, and Irene and Vernon's own "Castle Walk."

Irene and Vernon Castle, famous for "taming" the more scandalous trendy dances, still emphasized the "fun" of Social dancing and popularized the concept of the social dance hall as a respectable venue where men and women could socially dance together. (1913 photograph. Library of Congress.)

Aside from dancing talent—and their obvious grace and charismatic charm, which led to their success—the Castles had two important assets that contributed to the continued popularity of partnered dancing. The first was their ability to recognize, and later to create their own, dances with mass appeal. The public masses were clamoring for excitement and joy in their everyday lives, and the Castles' philosophy was that dancing should be easy, and above all else, fun. In their 1914 *Modern Dancing* book, Vernon breaks down the basic step of their Castle Walk, stresses its "ease," and then adds:

> It sounds silly and is silly. That is the explanation of its popularity. (Castle and Castle, 47)

Irene Castle in 1956, reminiscing back on she and Vernon's career, stated:

Ballroom dancing is supposed to be fun. I think one of the reasons so many people liked the dancing Vernon and I did is that they could see we were having a grand time together. (Donald Duncan, *Dance Magazine*, "Irene Castle in 1956," 87)

And while the Castles may have "watered down" the more authentic jazz vernacular steps, they couldn't discard them altogether, as slow drags, struts, and bent-knee kicks had already been absorbed into the mainstream, where they remained popular. In fact, there's a good case to be made for the Castles actually giving those vernacular movements a broader audience. This may be due, in large part, to their second important asset: their brilliant musical arranger and orchestra leader, James Reese Europe. Europe, an African American, became a super-star orchestra leader of the New York society set, providing dance bands of all sizes for club dates and society parties. In 1910, he formed the Clef Club, a chartered organization that served as New York's booking office and trade union for black musicians. Europe's own orchestra (made up of Clef Club members with their collective understanding of rhythm breaks and syncopations) helped the Castles set the latest dance trends. Music scholar Gunther Schuller asserts that together, Europe and the Castles created many of the popular sounds and styles that helped initiate the jazz age. Schuller examines Europe's recordings of such songs as "Castle House Rag" and sums it up nicely when he writes:

Europe could take a polite salon piece and make it swing. . . . In summary, James Europe was the most important transitional figure in the pre-history of jazz on the East Coast. (1986, 249)

The association between James Reese Europe and Irene and Vernon Castle produced new dances and trendy steps that celebrated Afro-American rhythm and movements, yet were acceptable to polite white society and kept them in the mainstream. Although the swing era came much later, Schuller hints that Europe paved the way for swing music, describing his syncopated melodies as being, "smoothed-out ragtime tunes," which must have been "electrifying to dance to" (Schuller, 1986, 248).

Europe signed with one of the largest sheet music publishing companies and produced vast numbers of compositions, many of which included the name "Castle" in their titles. Eve Golden's engaging book *Vernon and Irene Castle's Ragtime Revolution* points out that 10 of James Reese Europe's 15 songs published in the spring of 1915 related to Castle dances, including "Castle House Rag," "Castle Maxixe," and "Castle Perfect Trot" (2007, 70).

Scott Joplin is generally considered the most important figure in ragtime; his well-known 1899 ragtime composition, "Maple Leaf Rag" was the first piece of sheet music to sell over a million copies. ("The Entertainer," another of Joplin's early twentieth century songs, gained renewed popularity in 1973 when it was featured in the major motion picture, *The Sting*.) But a later jazz age pianist, James Price Johnson, is credited with creating the highly skilled ragtime piano style known as *stride*. Johnson, a professional piano player by his early teens, toured with James Reese Europe's Clef Club Band in his twenties, and was an influential piano instructor to Fats Waller. He also wrote music; one of his best-known compositions is "The Charleston," the song that helped define the jazz age. Schuller writes of James Price Johnson:

> His greatest contribution was to recast the rhythms of ragtime into a more swingin' steadier jazz beat. (1986, 216)

It's clear that in these pre-jazz years, the lines between ragtime, jazz, and "swingin'" music were somewhat blurred. But one of the lasting legacies of Irene and Vernon Castle was that their Castle House ballroom marked the beginning of the respectable public dance venue, where couples and singles could go to dance to popular music. Prior to Castle House, dance halls were located in rough neighborhoods and were deemed "disreputable and dangerous" for decent women. Yet there were no other places to social dance at the time, with the exception of formal private functions. Inspired by the success of Castle House, the top New York City hotels began clearing away tables, laying down hardwood floors, and hiring dance orchestras to play ragtime music. An assortment of upscale public dance venues opened downtown and uptown (in Harlem), and in various other metropolitan areas around the country.

While social dance flourished in New York, Broadway theater shows from 1900 to 1920 were short on African American talent, as the best black entertainers were touring the South in vaudeville productions.

Vaudeville shows were productions spotlighting a variety of specialty acts (comedians, acrobats, singers and dancers, etc.). The money performers could earn in vaudeville was far superior to what they could make in a show segment on the Broadway stage (Stearns and Stearns, 1994, 140–141). Yet, during those same years, a great migration was underway in the United States, as African Americans moved north to escape the segregation and prejudice prevalent in the South. In 1921, one successful New York show (often called "a musical breakthrough," "a phenomenon," even), spotlighted African American talent and changed the face of American theater. With music and lyrics by Noble Sissle and Eubie Blake, *Shuffle Along* brought a new jazzy dance style to the stage and electrified its audiences. Advertised as "The World's Greatest Dancing Show," it may well have been. Alan Dale, in *The New York American* on May 25, 1921, writes that he was "enthralled" by the dancers in the show:

> How they jiggled and pranced and cavorted, and wriggled and laughed
> ... every sinew in their bodies danced. (Dale, quoted in Nathan Irwin
> Huggins, 1971, 289)

With *Shuffle Along*, vernacular African American dance was back in the spotlight, with all its texture, vigor, and style.

## The Renaissance and Rent Parties of Harlem

By the time of *Shuffle Along*, New York in the 1920s was bursting with swingin' jazz, and the jazz age was ready to swing. There was an innovative spirit in the finger snappin', toe tappin', danceable rhythms there, and nowhere was that energy more concentrated than in the piano bars, the clubs, and cabarets of uptown Harlem.

New York's Harlem, in those years, was a city in flux. Originally named by Dutch settlers after Haarlem, in the Netherlands, a real estate boom and bust had devastated exclusive white European neighborhoods and triggered white flight from the area. At the same time, a steady stream of African Americans was trekking in. They brought with them more jazz vernacular dances, and new blends of music, which had been emerging and developing in the vaudevillian South. This period of time, the 1920s through the 1930s is known as the "Harlem Renaissance," as literature, art, music and dance of the highest quality were created and flourished there. It was a town of highbrow culture by day, and lowbrow culture by night in the piano bars and cabarets. Jazz was right at home in the new Harlem. The area, however, was an expensive place to live. Even before the Great Depression, lodgers had to come up with creative ideas to pay their rents. The "rent party" emerged as a way to make ends meet and have some fun at the same time. Renters would charge guests between 25 cents and $1 to enter their homes and enjoy some of the best entertainers the city had to offer; performers included Fats Waller, who may have epitomized the Harlem style better than anyone else. Waller's early recordings showcase his stride piano style, learned from James Price Johnson, which he honed at rent parties. The 1978 Tony Award–winning revue, *Ain't Misbehavin', The Fats Waller Musical Show*, is a salute to Waller's music and includes his composition "This Joint Is Jumpin'" (lyrics by J. C. Johnson and Andy Razaf), which gives listeners a taste of the Harlem rent party:

> The piano's thumpin
> The dancers are bumpin'
> This here spot is more than hot
> I mean this joint is jumpin'

There was a general feeling among the musicians of Harlem that something extraordinary was happening there. While their music was often dubbed socially unacceptable by both whites and well-educated blacks in the area, there was no denying its genuine and ultimate appeal. And Harlem's stride piano compositions and ragtime riffs were pushing a new music and dance craze into the mainstream: the Charleston.

Norma Miller, one of the original Savoy Lindy Hoppers, lived in Harlem in the 1920s, and got her first taste of the Charleston as a child at the rent parties her mother hosted. She writes this about the rent parties:

> . . . the admission price was twenty-five cents, and the money she raised would be used to pay the rent. Mama would sell pigs feet, peas and rice, and jump steady (another name for bootleg whiskey). Guests would flock to our apartment, and dance the famous Charleston, which I learned by watching them. (Miller and Jensen, 1996, 20–21)

Miller often became the entertainment herself at those parties, dancing the Charleston for her mother's party guests in exchange for ice cream treats (21). Frankie Manning, another original Savoy Lindy Hopper, also lived in Harlem as a child, and he accompanied his mother to rent parties in their neighborhood. He recalls watching the party guests dance "Slow Drags," the "Black Bottom" and the "Mess Around" to slow tunes. But the up-tempo numbers inspired a lot of individual improvisation and lots of Charleston (Manning and Millman, 1997, 25–26).

The Charleston is a dance of debatable origins. Anthropologists and dance historians have pointed out that the basic step is an exact replica of an old African Dance, the Ashanti "Ancestor Dance," and that its variations often mirror a Haitian dance called "La Martinique" (Melville J. Herskovits, 1958, 146; Katherine Dunham, "The Negro Dance," 1941, 999). Many sources suggest that it was black dockworkers in Charleston, South Carolina, who created the Afro-American version of the dance and gave it its name. However, a 1927 *Time* magazine article reports:

> Australians swear that this knee-wagging, hip-smacking, arm-swinging dance, commonly thought to have originated in the U.S. with Carolina Negroes, started as a war dance in the Australian hinterland. ("Science: Lost Found," March 28, 1927)

The dancing Whitman Sisters were purportedly dancing the Charleston on the vaudeville circuit in the early 1900s, and Henry "Rubberlegs" Williams (so nicknamed because of his loose-legged dancing style, called "Legomania"), was the documented winner of a 1920 Charleston contest in Atlanta, Georgia. But when a black chorus line of young dancing men, known as "the Dancing Redcaps," danced the Charleston in unison in the 1923 Broadway show, *Running Wild*, to James Price Johnson and Cecil Mack's "Charleston" song, that's when it caused a sensation. Suddenly the dance was propelled into mass popularity. Although the Black Bottom, the Shimmy, and the Texas Tommy were also dance crazes in this decade, the Charleston proved its own lasting power by being revived many times over (Stearns and Stearns, 1994, 111–112).

In 1923, Fletcher Henderson's 10-piece swingin' orchestra was hired at Club Alabam, marking the beginnings of New York's big jazz bands.

Henderson's orchestra is credited as creating new sounds in Charleston dance music, which pushed the jazz age toward the big band era of swing. Louis Armstrong joined Henderson's band in 1924; it is generally agreed that Armstrong, or "Satchmo," came to epitomize the essence of jazz. His fluid improvised trumpet solos have been described as "elegant" and "profound," and his musical innovations became the model for the entire vocabulary of jazz music. Armstrong's raspy, gravelly (yet at the same time silky and passionate) singing voice, combined with his horn-playing skills and his natural showmanship, catapulted him to the height of fame. His unique and timeless style have made Armstrong an undisputed jazz icon.

There were a host of other musicians congregating in New York at this same time who could definitely "swing it." In Henderson's band, for example, Louis Armstrong played alongside such musical greats as Charlie Green, Buster Bailey, and Coleman Hawkins. Paul Whiteman's Jazz Orchestra played in downtown New York. And long before he'd organized his own band and been given the nickname, "Count," William Basie had a steady job at an upscale elegant piano club in Harlem. One of the greatest of the jazz composers, Duke Ellington, was playing to a mostly white audience at Harlem's Cotton Club. In fact, although the entertainment in Harlem was entirely black, most of the city's "club clientele" was white. As original Savoy Lindy Hopper Norma Miller puts it: "At night, Society came to Harlem, they called it slumming" (Miller and Jensen, 1996, 27). Regardless of what they called it, and for whatever reasons they came, the people poured in. The spotlight was on Harlem. During this time, prior to the big band era of swing, the city was becoming a world capital for musical entertainment, housing a glorious array of top-notch bands and musicians.

Uptown in Harlem, dancing on the off-beats to slow blues and up-tempo rags became the every-night norm. And it was there, in that city, at that particular time—during the Harlem Renaissance—that new entertainment venues began to emerge. A whole host of cabaret clubs and piano bars, plus larger dance clubs and ballrooms, launched the careers of many of the great jazz musicians. The jazz musicians, in turn, lay down the musical rhythms—the smoothed-out rags and the improvised swingin' solos, the "hot licks," that made dancers want to get up out of their seats and step onto the dance floor. The musicians didn't just "set the stage" for it, they drove the emergence of Swing dancing.

In this 1946 photograph, jazz icons Louis Armstrong (right) and Duke Ellington are shown in a studio session, recording together for the first time. Both of these musicians were among an array of musical greats who honed their skills in the various nightclubs and ballrooms of New York City in the 1920s. (AP Photo.)

## Lindy Hops the Atlantic

The entire decade of the 1920s was defined by innovation and accomplishment. As skyscrapers began dotting the skylines, metropolitan cities emerged. Roadways were built, and the automobile became the American family's everyday mode of transportation. Radios broadcast news and entertainment into people's homes, and motion picture advancements brought the "talkies" into theaters (Al Jolson's *The Jazz Singer* was a box-office hit). There were important discoveries and developments in the fields of archeology, science, and medicine. Amidst the vibrancy of it all, flappers in fringe garters and pearls jubilantly waved their arms and kicked their legs in the frenzy of the free spirited Charleston. Celebrated were the "daring" novels by writers like Hemingway and F. Scott Fitzgerald, and on May 20, 1927, Charles A. Lindbergh electrified the nation with his solo transatlantic flight from New York to Paris. Lindbergh, nicknamed "Lucky Lindy" may have never been a dancer himself, but it was his heroic accomplishment that gave Swing dance a name.

The year was 1928. The city was Harlem, New York. The venue was the Manhattan Casino, which later became known as the Rockland Palace. Prior to World War I, James Reese Europe had held concerts there, and Vernon and Irene Castle had performed there. Frankie Manning describes the building as being, "a very big ballroom, more like a giant arena," and he explains that "besides dances, they held special events, such as boxing matches there" (Telephone interview). In June 1928, the Manhattan Casino was host to a dance marathon, in which 80 couples had signed up to compete. An offshoot of the Charleston's popularity, the dance marathon was an endurance competition where entrants danced until they tired and had to quit or until they literally dropped from exhaustion. The popular marathons were being staged all over the country: in New York there were at least two unrelated competitions going on at the same time. The *New York Times* reported that 29 couples were competing in a marathon at Madison Square Garden that started on June 10, and suggests there was also a "Dusky Derby" going on in Harlem (June 16, 1928). A *Time* magazine article also mentions both competitions, noting that the Harlem marathon was for "Negro couples," and that Bill "Bojangles" Robinson acted as the event's master of ceremonies and competition judge (July 9, 1928).

The Harlem marathon, held at the Manhattan Casino, hosted 80 couples and lasted for 18 days. It came to an end on July 4, at 4 AM, with four couples still on the floor, when the Board of Health shut it down (the Board also stopped the event at Madison Square Garden). Those four couples, who split the $5,000 in prize money, included two of Harlem's best-known and most talented dancers: George "Shorty" Snowden and Mattie Purnell (Stearns and Stearns, 1994, 315). It should be noted that the details of these two separate marathons are reported with slight variations by the different media sources. There are discrepancies as to the number of contestants in each, and in the amounts of prize money awarded. Some sources suggest it was "six" couples splitting the Harlem purse, and that the "police" halted it; *Time* magazine even mentions that a marriage ceremony may have occurred between two of the contestants during the event ("Dance to License Bureau," July 9, 1928, 27). A *New York Times* newspaper article concurs, noting that a crowd of "over 300 persons" gathered to watch as:

Team No. 18, of the Harlem negro dance marathon, got a marriage license at the Municipal Building shortly after noon yesterday. (27)

This same article also notes that one couple had been eliminated from the Harlem Derby the previous night and that only "eight couples remained." The elimination occurred because the male dancer had "failed to keep at least one hand on the arm or waist of his partner," as the rules specified he must (*New York Times*, June 29, 1928).

In general, the rules in all marathon competitions were the same. Couples danced for an hour, and then had 15 minutes to rest before starting up again. Although, as the hours stretched on, it wouldn't really have been dancing—it was more like dragging along and taking turns napping while holding each other up. In the evenings, larger audiences came to watch the events and cheer on the contestants. Sometimes the audiences threw spare change to couples who still had enough strength to dance "shine" steps or tricky moves; sometimes there were mini-contests within the marathon events where prizes of "$5 or $10" would be offered to the liveliest dancers. Shorty Snowden, by all accounts, liked to outshine his competitors. A *New York Times* article of June 21, 1928, reported that:

> . . . the sixty-second hour of Harlem's dance marathon at Manhattan Casino drew to an end last night . . . All the prizes offered for fancy stepping and other competitions during the evening were won by George Snowden and Mattie Purnell. ("14 Couples Survive Eleven Days' Dance," 27)

The article documents that Snowden and Purnell were rewarded for their "fancy stepping" during this particular marathon. As the story goes, a reporter covering the Harlem Derby watched at least one of the mini-competitions. As Snowden broke away from his partner, and improvised a bit of stylized footwork, the reporter asked Snowden, specifically, what it was that he was doing. Snowden purportedly thought of Charles Lindbergh ("Lucky Lindy") who, the year before, had completed his successful solo transatlantic nonstop flight. Newspapers at the time had printed headlines like: "Lindy Hops the Atlantic." And, Snowden replied to the reporter, "I'm doing the Lindy Hop!" And that's how the dance got its name.

This story of George "Shorty" Snowden and the reporter has been told and retold for years throughout the swing community. Although the story's accuracy is sometimes debated, Frankie Manning's autobiography explains it in exactly the same way Snowden told it to Manning. In a February 2009 telephone interview, Manning added, "And at that time, there were a lot of old-timers around, and no one denied it." Manning's description generally matches the one that Shorty Snowden gave Marshall Stearns during their personal interview in 1959 (Manning and Millman, 2007, 79, 243, 245; Stearns and Stearns, 1994, 315, 394). And one New York music and dance critic, writing in 1930, gives strong credence to Snowden's story. Carl Van Vechten, who was known as much for his lavish, racially integrated Manhattan parties as he was for his writing, wrote about the Lindy Hop in his *Parties: a Novel of Contemporary New York Life*:

> The Lindy Hop made its first official appearance in Harlem at a Negro Dance Marathon staged at Manhattan Casino sometime in 1928. Executed with brilliant virtuosity by a pair of competitors in this exhibition, it was considered at the time a little too difficult to stand much chance of achieving popular success. The dance grew rapidly in favor, however, until a year later it was possible to observe an entire ball-room filled with couples devoting themselves to its celebration. (Van Vechten, 1930, 184–185; Quoted from Mindy Aloof, 2006, 101)

Charles Lindbergh's historic flight took place on May 20, 1927, and Shorty Snowden's Charleston marathon participation was in June of 1928. However, Lindbergh's heroic accomplishment had made him an overnight sensation, a national folk hero, and his name remained in the news in 1928. Nettie H. Beauregard, curator of the Missouri Historical Society, worked directly with Lindbergh in compiling a comprehensive guide to his numerous decorations and trophies. She writes:

> Never has an individual received such widespread adulation … The admiration and enthusiasm for Lindbergh is as great today as on the day of his epochal flight. (Beauregard, *Exhibition Guidebook*, 1935, 5, personal archive collection)

Many of the newspaper and magazine articles written by staff writers, correspondents, and even Lindbergh himself not only mentioned

National American hero Charles A. Lindbergh ("Lucky Lindy"), posing here with his plane "The Spirit of St. Louis," gained international acclaim with his 1927 nonstop flight from New York to Paris. That "hop" across the Atlantic is also credited as the inspiration behind the naming of the original style of Swing, the "Lindy Hop." (AP Photo.)

Charles Lindbergh's name, but also included the word "hop" or "hopping" in their headlines or first paragraphs. As early as May 11, 1927, for instance, one article read: "Lindbergh Starts East for Paris Hop" (*New York Times*, 3). The following year, on June 11 (a week prior to Snowden's marathon competition), a *New York Times* article on Mexico's leading flier, Captain Emilio Carranza, described Carranza as becoming "more like Colonel Charles A. Lindbergh" in his everyday methods. The article's headline read: "Carranza Secretive on Washington Hop" (21).

It's quite interesting to note that, according to the newspapers, as Shorty Snowden was competing in the Charleston marathon, Lindbergh was definitely in New York City. He arrived at New York's Curtiss Field in June, and reportedly stayed in town into July, testing "junkers" and flying "new craft" on the field. Over the Fourth of July holiday, Lindbergh spent time at the home of New York politician,

F. Trubee Davison (*New York Times*, June 24, 1928, 24; *New York Times*, July 3, 7). Also, Fox Movietone Newsreels featuring Lindbergh were in general release at theaters in New York at the time. For instance, in March 1928, *40,000 Miles with Lindbergh* was circulating in the area (*The Record-Post*, "Captain Charles A. Lindbergh in Fox News Reel," July 7, 1927; *Catskill Mountain News*, "Lindy Onscreen Friday-Saturday," March 23, 1928).

All of this points to the fact that Charles Lindbergh's name could easily have been on Shorty Snowden's mind when he spoke to the reporter. Frankie Manning suggests that the reporter was a Fox Movietone News reporter, as Snowden himself recalled in his interview with Stearns. Unfortunately, few of the Movietone clips from that period still exist. Without film documentation, it is difficult to imagine the exact footwork pattern witnessed by the reporter. Snowden could only explain that his breakaway was made up of "fast" fancy footwork that no one had seen before, and that it seemed dazzling and new (Stearns and Stearns, 316). Dance instructors have generally agreed that Snowden's "breakaway" move in the 1928 marathon was probably some eight-count pattern (based on the rhythm of Charleston), which became the Lindy Hop's basic step.

The George "Shorty" Snowden story may be impossible to prove with 100 percent certainty, but it certainly is a great story—and adds intrigue and allure as to how the dance was named.

# 4

# It Started at the Savoy

In the years of Prohibition (1920–1933), when it was illegal to sell, manufacture, or transport alcohol for consumption, many Americans flaunted their defiance of the law. As saloons were forced to close down, nightclubs, cabarets, and speakeasies quickly replaced them. And while these clubs advertised musical entertainment, and often dancing, they were also generally drinking establishments, with alcohol readily available. It is estimated that by the year 1929, there were 32,000 speakeasies in New York, twice the number of saloons prior to Prohibition (Spiller, Clancey, Young, and Mosely, 2005, 146).

Many of the theatrical people working on Broadway, as well as singers and musicians from all entertainment genres, gathered in the late-night clubs of Harlem. The clubs had such names as The Plantation Club, Yeah Man, Bamboo Inn, the Bamville Club—and were on practically every street corner. And they were all making music. The horns were jammin' with the reeds and strings. The piano players were cuttin' each other, tickling the keys in friendly games of one-upmanship. Soloists were mixing with orchestra musicians, honing the art of jazz improvisation. Staccato rags met Charleston riffs, and got shaken and stirred with the soulful sounds of torch songs and blues. And in this cocktail mix of talent and innovation, jazz musicians in the Harlem clubs created new music, smoother grooves that inspired a new smoother style of dancing.

On a small stretch of 133rd Street, between 7th and Lenox Avenues, the nightclubs reverberated with steamy hot jazz. With an abundance of clubs clustered tightly together, the street was known as "Jungle

Alley" and it played host to New York's best musicians and their fans, along with other patrons of the arts and lovers of good music. Jungle Alley clubs like Mexico's, the Catagonia Club, the Clam House, and The Nest stayed open all night, nourishing a musical environment ripe with creative energy and innovative spirit.

In Duke Ellington's autobiography, *Music Is My Mistress*, he noted that Mexico's was home to some of the best "musical challenges," duels between two or more musicians, to see who could outplay whom. The club became known for its after-hours jam sessions; in fact, Ellington called it "a real after-after-joint," as it was open into the mid-morning hours. And the musicianship was so outstanding that it prompted Ellington to add that if there had been tape recorders in those days, they would have captured for posterity "impossible things" (Ellington, 1976, 92–94).

Generally known as Pod's and Jerry's, nicknames referring to the club's owners, the Catagonia Club was another "after-after-hours joint." It was a racially integrated cellar speakeasy, jumpin' with music, singing, and dancing. Piano player extraordinaire, Willie "The Lion" Smith, had long-term employment there when he wasn't working somewhere else, and he always packed the house with musicians who jammed along with him, plus stage and screen celebrities (Mae West and Tallulah Bankhead were frequent patrons) who came to hear him play. Billie Holiday's first singing job in Harlem was there (she made $2 a night plus tips), and white musicians like Artie Shaw, Benny Goodman, and even the Dorsey Brothers and Charlie Barnet jammed there, too. Besides its "top and bottom," a drink of wine and gin that became a Harlem specialty, its menu offered red beans and rice, a variety of chicken dishes, and pig's feet, a Catagonia Club favorite (Kellner, ed., 1987, 285–286; Meg Greene, 2007, 24).

By all accounts, the Clam House (sometimes called "the Mad House") was the raunchiest of the "Jungle Alley" clubs. Its floorshow featured a long-standing singer, Gladys Bentley, who dressed in drag and performed an assortment of risqué, raspy-voiced, scat-style songs. Music critic Carl Van Vechten featured Bentley in some of his magazine articles. Van Vechten had long been interested in black music and the phenomenal sounds coming out of Harlem. He frequented the clubs, met the singers and entertainers of "Jungle Alley," and wrote about them. Before long, his white music-loving readers wanted to meet them, too. Gladys Bentley became a popular

Harlem celebrity, and later performed at several other nightclubs in New York. Van Vechten, himself, was a regular patron of a larger club called The Nest, which opened in 1923 in the basement of a brownstone apartment building, purportedly one of Mae West's favorite spots. Garvin Bushell, a musician who played at The Nest in the 1920s, recalled that the club owners were "local boys," on good terms with the police department. While liquor flowed freely there, The Nest was never raided because, according to Bushell, a lot of money was paid to the local cops to keep them "looking in the other direction." Bushell also remembers that the club's floor show was a tongue-in-cheek production with a cast of characters, in bird costumes, all dancing and singing in unison, "Where do the birds go every night? To the Nest! To the Nest!" (Bushell and Mark Tucker, 1998, 49–50).

## Gangsters, Revues, and the New Smooth Sound

Like Montmartre in Paris was for its artists, Harlem in New York became a cultural center for its local musicians. But it also became the place to be, and be seen, by white jazz enthusiasts from outside the area. Harlem in the twenties was easy to get to, well lit, and safe for late-night revelry. Singer Ethel Waters remembers:

> In those days, Harlem was anything but an exclusively Negro section . . . The district was swarming with life—men, women and children of every shade of color. (Waters, 1989, 123–124)

Many of the Harlem nightclubs were "black and tans," racially mixed, as more and more of New York's white socialites streamed into the area seeking nightlife entertainment and "adventure." And in the hedonistic heart of the jazz age, as flappers danced, drank, and scoffed at the law, Harlem became an around-the-clock party. Scandal was in vogue. Bootleggers illegally manufacturing and smuggling alcohol were viewed as professional entrepreneurs. White socialites drank at ringside tables watching black entertainers. And as the white jazz enthusiasts and elites continued to pour in, so did their money. Before long there were businessmen, and gangsters, willing to gamble on the new trend. Organized crime moved into Harlem. Mob bosses openly strutted around town, cavorting with politicians and debutants alike. Large entertainment venues were opened, not just catering to white patrons—but catering to white patrons only.

Owney Madden was one of the notorious gangsters who cashed in on the Harlem cabaret scene. He took over a club at 142nd Street and Lenox Avenue, changed the décor to an exotic "jungle setting" meant to attract the white downtowners, and changed the name on the club's marquee to "Cotton Club." Madden's vision for success was simple: the audience was to be 100 percent white, while the floorshow entertainment would be entirely black. In the fall of 1923, with a lavish stage revue including a full orchestra, singers, dancers, and a chorus of high-kicking glamorous showgirls, his soon to be "world-famous" club made its grand debut. Madden's formula worked, and many nightclubs were subsequently based on his model. However, while sparkling with sophisticated glitz, the Cotton Club owed much of its success to the hiring of a new orchestra in 1927, Duke Ellington and the Washingtonians. The club's all-white audiences were craving energetic, dazzling jazz, and Ellington served it up hot. His band was an instant hit. And when CBS radio decided to broadcast "live" nightly sessions from the Cotton Club, Duke Ellington gained national attention and, eventually, international fame.

As mobsters and gangsters were admired, even idolized, in the Roaring Twenties, Owney Madden drove around Harlem in a chauffeur-driven, bullet-proof Duisenberg. He reportedly had financial interests in other unnamed New York nightclubs, and he controlled most of the city's illegal liquor trade. However, unlike some of the more notorious gangsters from other cities, Madden avoided publicity. He was photographed only twice: each were police arrest pictures (Stanley Walker, 1933, 107; Ralph Giordano, e-mail interview). In the mid-1930s, after Prohibition was repealed and as a group of Italian mobsters was allegedly encroaching on his territory, Madden left New York. But his Cotton Club moved downtown, where, in a new more accessible location, it successfully prevailed throughout the decade.

The opening of the downtown Cotton Club included an extravagant revue featuring both Cab Calloway and Bill "Bojangles" Robinson. Another act on the show's playbill was "Whyte's Maniacs," which featured the fast, flying footwork of Whitey's Savoy Lindy Hoppers— with dancer and choreographer Frankie Manning. In a telephone interview with Manning, he admits that while he'd already danced professionally at various theaters and nightclubs, his Cotton Club job made him finally "feel professional" because it was such a "first-rate, big-time club." Manning acknowledges being aware of the Cotton

This photograph of the Cotton Club was taken circa 1936–1937, when Whitey's Lindy Hoppers were performing there. Note that the illuminated marquee billed them as "Whyte Maniacs." Cab Calloway and Bill "Bojangles" Robinson were the show's headliners. (Photo by Frank Driggs Collection/Getty Images.)

Club's mob affiliation: "They were so well organized, though," he reports, "that they hired people to run the club's operations. Herman Stark was the stage manager when we performed there, and he did a good job of managing all the entertainment. If you didn't know, going in, that there were mob ties to the Cotton Club, you'd never guess it" (April 6, 2009).

The Wilkins brothers owned two separate nightclubs in New York. LeRoy Wilkins owned a club at 135th Street and 5th Avenue called LeRoy's (where Count Basie got his first steady Harlem gig), which was for the middle-income Harlemite. His brother Barron owned the predominately white-only Exclusive Club at 134th Street and 7th Avenue. With a strict dress code, and affordable only to the wealthy, the Exclusive Club was exactly as its name implied: exclusive. Al Jolson and Joan Crawford were among a host of celebrity regulars, and Duke Ellington's band worked there in the early 1920s. Barron Wilkins had previously owned a string of nightclubs in the city, and was a prominent citizen of Harlem. His life was cut short however, in 1924, when Julius Miller, a local gangster known as "Yellow Charleston," gunned him down near his club. It was generally suspected that Miller bootlegged liquor for Barron Wilkins' club. However, when Miller was executed for the murder the following year, he was still claiming to have shot Barron Wilkins "in self-defense." So the association between the gangster and the Exclusive Club remained unclear (*New York Times*, "Yellow Charleston Pays Death Penalty," September 18, 1925, 14).

Connie's Inn was opened in 1923; it was first a deli, where Fats Waller worked as a delivery boy. Dutch Schultz, another Harlem gangster, known for running the numbers racket, was part owner of the club. Schultz had an affinity for jazz music and an eye for great talent. And by the late 1920s, the club's floor shows, *Keep Shufflin'* and *Hot Chocolates*, with songs by Andy Razaf and Fats Waller, and the musical genius of Louis Armstrong on horn, went on to become Broadway revues.

The floorshows of New York's nightclubs became increasingly lavish and grand. Small's Paradise, one of the larger clubs (taking up a good amount of real estate on 7th Avenue) hosted full-out presentations. Black-owned and managed, the club had first opened in 1917 as Small's Sugar Cane Club. It was so successful that its owner, Edwin Small, expanded in 1925. He named his new club Small's Paradise, the club was also known as "Harlem's Home of Mirth and Music." Along with a Chinese and American menu, there were singers belting out the blues, an array of stunning chorus girls kicking up their heels, and a cast of talented waiters who danced the Charleston and roller-skated, all while spinning their trays. The club was racially integrated, although it had a reputation of catering to its white clientele and its exorbitant prices kept the average Harlem resident out. Norma Miller's autobiography notes that she supported herself for awhile in the 1940s by producing dance revues at Small's Paradise (188). Another interesting note is that basketball star Wilt Chamberlain owned the club for a brief period in the 1960s. He renamed it: Big Wilt's Small's Paradise and hired Ray Charles as its house entertainer.

By the late 1920s, Louis Armstrong and a host of other remarkable musicians onstage in the nightclubs of Harlem were featuring free rhythmic ideas, improvisations, and a relaxed, new way of playing. Jazz historian Ernie Smith suggests that as band drummers began whisking wire brushes across the snare drums, they achieved a more flowing, constant, rhythm. Rhythms in general were becoming "more fluid," as bandleaders replaced their tubas and banjos with upright basses and guitars. Frankie Manning agrees, adding, "The tuba and banjo sounds were more up and down in their feel. The bass and guitar gave a more strumming, smoother feel to the music." In the 1930s, the new sound would come to be known as "swing." Manning explains, "Swing dancing is done to swing music ... It's very smooth, and it flows." When the music first began to swing, dancing evolved right along with the music. That's when the Lindy Hop was born (Smith in Miller and Jensen, 2006, xiv; Manning PBDA video archives 1995; Manning in Ken Burns' *Jazz*, Episode 4, PBS, 2000).

## New York Ballrooms and the "Home of Happy Feet"

While the nightclubs and cabaret musicians of New York were developing the musical sounds of swing, dance aficionados who wanted a full night of dancing, rather than a floorshow, would have headed for one of the city's public ballrooms. New York City's Grand Central Palace opened in 1911, and was most likely the first public ballroom to offer social dancing on a large scale. As Irene and Vernon Castle were actively promoting partnered dancing and dance studios sprouted up everywhere, Grand Central Palace was designed to accommodate over 3,000 dancers (Giordano, 2007, Vol. 2, 30).

One avid ballroom dancer who saw the Castles perform there was inspired to open his own dance hall. Dreaming big, and obtaining the financing to make his dream a reality, Louis Brecker, who referred to the Castles as his "dancing idols," opened his Roseland Ballroom in Philadelphia in 1918. The following year he opened his second Roseland—this one in New York City, on the corner of Broadway and 51st Street. New York's Roseland Ballroom held its grand opening on New Year's Eve, 1919, with appearances by Flo Ziegfeld, Billie Burke, and Will Rogers. With a strict policy of segregation (the customers were white), and room for 1,250 couples, the opening night was a complete sellout (Lon A. Gault, 1989, 283–289).

When Fletcher Henderson's band played at Roseland in 1924, Louis Armstrong was in the brass section. Musician Coleman Hawkins, also in the band, recalls that the audience went wild for Armstrong and wouldn't let him sit down. He reports, "They made him [Armstrong] play ten choruses of 'Shanghai Shuffle.' " That year, Roseland Ballroom was the most popular dance venue in New York (Quoted in Ken Burns' *Jazz*, Episode 5, PBS, 2000). Fletcher Henderson's band had previously played at Club Alabam, which was also a popular Broadway dance hall by the early 1920s. Another New York venue, the Audubon Ballroom, is generally credited as playing host to the first dance marathon in 1923. Some of the other popular dance halls in New York were the Renaissance Ballroom, the Bluebird, Venetian Danceland, the Dunbar, the Outhammer Ballroom, the Golden Gate, the Alhambra, and Brooklyn's Rosemont. By the mid-1920s, numerous sumptuously decorated, large-scale ballrooms were opening across the country. But the most important ballroom in the development of the Lindy Hop was undeniably the Savoy Ballroom, which opened March 12, 1926, on Lenox Avenue between 140th and 141st streets—taking up an entire city block.

The Savoy Ballroom was known as "The Home of Happy Feet," a phrase attributed to actress Lana Turner. She purportedly called it that on one of her visits to the ballroom, and the name stuck. Many celebrities visited the Savoy, from movie stars to Broadway entertainers to politicians and statesmen. Clark Gable, Joan Crawford, Tyrone Powers, Mickey Rooney, and Marlene Dietrich were all Savoy customers. Winston Churchill was a patron there at least one evening, and Joe Louis and Sugar Ray Robinson were regulars. But it wasn't just celebrities who flocked there. Young and old, rich and poor, black and white (the interracial mingling there, with blacks and whites freely dancing together, was unprecedented in any other ballroom in America)—everyone went to the Savoy. They gathered together there not only to hear the best of the best swing bands, but also to watch the dancers. The ballroom became known for having the most remarkable dancers—the Lindy Hoppers. Trumpeter Bill Dillard recalls that when he played the Savoy, "Every night there would be two or three busloads of tourists coming there" (Dillard in the film, *The Call of the Jitterbug*, 1988).

While there is evidence that the Savoy managers were disinterested at first, perhaps even hostile, in recognizing the original dancers, they eventually gained enormous appreciation for the Lindy Hoppers and for the dance that was bringing so much praise and acclaim to their ballroom. When celebrities were in the house, management would clear space on the floor and have the Lindy Hoppers put on a show just for them. The Lindy Hoppers were eventually allowed free admission to the ballroom, and were allowed to practice there during the day while the bands were rehearsing. The best dancers would spend their afternoons in the ballroom, and then go back again every night. It was a way of life. Frankie Manning says that he was "lucky enough to live two blocks from the Savoy." But he quickly corrects himself, "I shouldn't say that because," he pauses, "I actually lived *at* the Savoy Ballroom! I used to go home to eat and sleep, that's all" (Manning, PBDA video archives, 2005).

The Savoy Ballroom was also sometimes referred to as "the Track," perhaps because in its early history it was used as a racetrack for dog racing. But Frankie Manning points out that when ballroom dancers moved counterclockwise (on the "line of dance") around the Savoy's elongated floor, doing a fast Peabody for example, they were reminiscent of a group of racecars or horses on a track, racing around the ballroom. So, the flow of the ballroom traffic may have produced the nickname. A third possibility for the nickname is that in the 1930s, racetracks were seen as glamorous—as the epitome of high-status social venues, and a

The Interior of the Savoy Ballroom—where two bandstands provided continuous music and the musicians played "for the dancers." The Lindy Hop was developed at the Savoy and from there was introduced to the world. (Courtesy of Photofest.)

"track" of moving bodies around the ballroom would have inspired visions of highbrow sophistication (Stearns and Stearns, 1994, 316; Manning and Millman, 2007, 70).

Unquestionably the most elegant ballroom in Harlem, the Savoy was *the* place to go for a first-class celebration of music and dance, the height of sophistication for a public dance hall. The large marquee in front advertised the evening's bands, and tickets were sold at a booth out front. The street-level entrance welcomed visitors into a spacious lobby, with a sparkling cut-glass chandelier hanging from the ceiling. There was a coat-check room down a flight of stairs, and from there patrons would climb two flights of shimmering marble stairs lined with mirrors to enter the ballroom. A dress code kept gentlemen in jackets, and women were always dressed to impress. The dance floor at the Savoy, constructed of layers of maple and mahogany wood, was encircled by a railing and was, by all reports, enormous—taking up one half of the entire ballroom. The other half of the room was a carpeted lounge area, decorated in luxurious hues of blue and gold. A soda fountain served snacks and soft drinks (after Prohibition, beer was available as well, but hard liquor was never served), and patrons could sit at tables

Drummer/bandleader Chick Webb is credited with propelling Ella Fitzgerald—the velvety-voiced songstress of swing—to stardom. During the 1930s, Webb's band was considered to be the Savoy Ballroom's "house band." (Courtesy of Photofest.)

and chairs, or in booths lined up under the windows along Lenox Avenue.

The Savoy boasted two side-by-side bandstands, featuring two 12- or 13-piece bands. On the northern side was bandstand number one, the larger of the two, where the "house musicians" played. Chick Webb was at the Savoy more than any other band, always on the number one bandstand. The music played continuously. When it was time for Chick Webb's band to take a break, a second band on the southern side would join in. Both bands would play the same song until Chick Webb's band faded out, and the second band took over. The second band might be the Savoy Sultans, or Teddy Hill's Band, Jimmy Rushing, Buddy Johnson, Tiny Bradshaw, or any one of the over 250 bands that played at the Savoy.

Bands that played the Savoy were never paid much money to perform there. So, the more famous bands, such as Duke Ellington, Cab Calloway, or Count Basie, were only booked for one-nighters or short-term engagements. But playing the Savoy could instantly "make" a lesser-known band's reputation; getting a gig at the Savoy Ballroom was every band's dream. However, Frankie Manning points out that the bands were hired specifically to cater to the dancers, so, "if a band played and people didn't dance, that band was gone!" The Savoy Ballroom featured live music for dancing every night of the week; but *dancing* didn't mean patrons standing around swaying to the rhythms, it meant footwork that was synchronized with the music and full-out, energized, explosive Lindy Hopping. It has long been rumored that the entire dance floor had to be replaced every three years from the constant wear and tear. As Frankie Manning has often mentioned, the ballroom floor would look like it was "getting into the mood" because it bounced up and down with the dancers, too (Manning, PBDA video archives, 1995).

The most electrifying evenings at the Savoy were the "battles of the bands," when the house band would compete against a visiting guest band. Manning estimates that 2,000 people could dance at the Savoy "without anyone getting kicked"; however, on some of the "battle" nights, gigantic crowds turned out. In 1929, for instance, the first of the Savoy's "battle of the bands" attracted a crowd estimated at 5,000. And in a well-advertised duel between Bennie Goodman and Chick Webb in 1937, it was reported that thousands entered the ballroom, while thousands more were turned away. Goodman and Webb had many identical arrangements of the same songs, so it was easy to compare them as they played. No prizes were handed out, but patrons got to form their own opinions of who had "won" the battle.

"And do you know who won that battle between Goodman and Webb?" Manning asks. Then he answers the question himself: "In my opinion, it was the dancers. Because for eighty-five cents, for *eighty-five cents*, we got to experience an electrifying night!" Interestingly, however, it's often noted that Guy Lombardo's band broke all attendance records for a single-night appearance at the Savoy; until that is, the night Glenn Miller played there at the height of his popularity (Manning, PBDA video archives, 1995; Manning and Millman, 2007, 62–63; Gault, 1989, 241). There is also mention of a night, in 1935, when the guest appearance of boxer Joe Louis brought a crowd estimated at "more than 50,000" to the ballroom. The police were "compelled to call in special reserves" to disperse them (The Savoy Ballroom's 25th Anniversary Booklet, 1951, written by Savoy Staff, accessible at www.savoyballroom.com).

## Behind the Scenes

Moe Gale, the white owner of the Savoy, spent little time in his ballroom. Instead, he concentrated his efforts in running a kind of hiring agency for bands. He booked musicians into theaters, nightclubs, and touring shows around the country, and is credited with "discovering" the singing group, The Ink Spots, and supervising their rise to fame. He left the daily running of the Savoy Ballroom to his black manager, Charles Buchanan, who oversaw everything from employee matters to payroll and policy issues. Norma Miller describes Mr. Buchanan as "a tall; distinguished West Indian with cropped graying hair and a professional air." Buchanan eventually became part-owner of the ballroom (Miller and Jensen, 1996, 39).

There were dance hostesses at the Savoy who were hired to dance with male patrons who felt shy and unsure. At first, they could be hired at three dances for a quarter; later on the price rose to a quarter per dance. Helen Clarke reports that when she started working as a Savoy hostess, there were about 50 girls employed, and that they had to follow the strict rules set forth by Mr. Buchanan. In 1990, Clark participated in a panel discussion sponsored by the

New York Swing Dance Society titled, "The Savoy Ballroom Remembered." She said:

> You had to come on time . . . There was no fraternizing with the musicians, and no leaving the place with anyone. And a wardrobe mistress always checked our dresses to see if we looked all right. (Crease, "The Savoy Ballroom Remembered," *Footnotes*, Fall, 1990, 4)

There were also bouncers at the Savoy who kept the ballroom "trouble free," and who were notorious for taking their jobs seriously. Trumpeter Buck Clayton played with Count Basie's band at the Savoy, and he remembers that the bouncers there were more "severe" than anywhere. Clayton describes the bouncers in his autobiography:

> If you were wrong they would throw you out of the Savoy twice . . . Many a trouble-maker had to go to Harlem Hospital with broken legs or arms after an encounter with those Savoy Ballroom bouncers. (Clayton and Elliott, 1989, 109)

Sunday afternoons, from 3 to 5 PM, were for young people at the Savoy. Live bands started in the afternoon and stayed right on through the evenings. Dance exhibitions and "opportunity contests" were often held on Sundays. (Norma Miller recalls that she danced in the ballroom for the first time during an Easter Sunday matinee.) Monday night was "Ladies Night," when every woman who arrived with a paying male customer got in free. Tuesday wasn't usually a busy night, so it became the hangout night for a group of Savoy regulars who gave themselves the name, the "Savoy 400 Club." According to Norma Miller's autobiography, "They all wore yellow and green corduroy jackets with '400 Club' on the back." Frankie Manning adds that it was not an exclusive club. It's often assumed that the club was open only to expert dancers or wealthy patrons, but in Manning's words, "Anyone who filled out the registration form could join." In addition to the corduroy jacket, club members got reduced admission on Tuesday nights.

Cynthia R. Millman, co-author of Manning's autobiography, points out that the 400 Club was created in 1927 by the Savoy management as a marketing tool to boast that it had "400 members." According to New York's wealthy socialite Mrs. William Astor, that was the perfect number of guests to "fill a ballroom." Wednesday night at the Savoy Ballroom was usually set aside for fraternal organizations; Thursday night was

"Kitchen Mechanics' Night." The Kitchen Mechanics were the domestic workers in New York—the cooks, nannies, and housekeepers who traditionally had Thursdays off. By Thursday night, they were ready to dance, and they showed up at the Savoy in droves. Friday nights, like Wednesdays, attracted a "society crowd" and was geared for social clubs or fraternal parties. Frankie Manning recalls that there were a lot more Foxtrots and Waltzes played for the dancers on those nights. He himself didn't attend the club on too many Friday nights: as he puts it, "The other nights at the Savoy were more swinging." Saturday was the biggest night, when the Savoy Ballroom was packed with dancers and non-dancers alike all crowding the floor. The biggest dance competitions took place on those "packed out" Saturday nights (Miller and Jensen, 1996, 109–110; Manning and Millman, 2007, 66).

## The Original Dancers

There is no question that George "Shorty" Snowden was the original king of the Savoy. He won most of the weekly dance competitions and was by all accounts an amazingly "inventive" dancer. Both Frankie Manning and Norma Miller agree that he created a number of dance steps that became popular Lindy Hop moves, including the step that bears his name. Count Basie gave Snowden lasting recognition for that step in his 1938 recording of "The Shorty George."

Dancing the Shorty George requires walking forward as if your knees have been cinched together by a tight rubber band. Your elbows stay high, but your hands are lowered and your fingers point at the floor. Evocative of everything swing dancing represents—humor, fun, and intentionally awkward "grace" paired with skillful coordination— the Shorty George caught on. It became a standard swing step, not only in the Lindy Hopper's vocabulary, but in stage and film choreography as well. It was danced by the likes of Fred Astaire (in *You Were Never Lovelier*, 1942), the Andrew Sisters (in *Buck Privates*, 1941), and Spike Lee's Lindy Hopping cast in *Malcolm X* (1992), to name a few examples. Frankie Manning choreographed the dance sequences in *Malcolm X*; he has danced his wonderfully fluid version of the Shorty George move as part of the Shim Sham line-dance routine time and time again at Swing dancing events all around the world.

George "Shorty" Snowden is also featured in *After Seben*, a Paramount Studios short subject film released in 1929 that provides the earliest look at the Lindy Hop, still in its infancy, on film. Three couples recruited from the Savoy Ballroom demonstrate their dancing skills, accompanied by the Chick Webb Orchestra. Snowden, along with Mattie Purnell (his dance partner during the marathon in which he named the Lindy Hop), are the third couple to perform. The influence of the Charleston is obvious in all three couples' routines; however, Snowden can be seen moving from closed to open position, dancing the breakaway, which has been documented as a root-source, key maneuver that led to the Lindy Hop. Jazz historian and film archivist Ernie Smith notes that the filming of *After Seben* actually took place in 1928, the year prior to its official release date (Miller and Jensen, 1996, xx). It is remarkable footage, and clearly documents Snowden and Purcell's early confidence and prowess as dancers.

Mattie Purnell was George "Shorty" Snowden's first partner. But she was not his only partner—he also danced with Pauline Morse in the late 1920s. As Frankie Manning explains, Snowden later danced with a third partner as well, named Bea Gay, whom everyone called "Big Bea." Shorty Snowden was somewhere between 5' 1" and 5' 4" tall. "But," Manning says, "'Big Bea' must have been 6' 2"!" (Manning, PBDA video archives, 1991). One of their signature moves was where Bea went back-to-back with Shorty, linked arms with him, and then rolled him up onto her back. The 1937 short film clip *Ask Uncle Sol* gives a good look at this comedic move. Overall, Snowden is remembered as a dancer who could shine with any partner and who could "outshine" early dance competitors in speed, fancy footwork, and finesse.

Shorty Snowden is also credited as the first to organize a group of Lindy Hoppers. He formed a six-couple team and took them out of the Savoy to work professionally at other clubs. They worked at the Paradise Restaurant in New York's Times Square, where they joined the Paul Whiteman Orchestra in performing for an entirely white audience, as well as at Small's Paradise in Harlem, among other gigs. Snowden's legacy is remarkable. As one of the early creators of the Lindy Hop, he named the dance, left a signature step that bears his name, and organized the first professional team of swing dancers. Yet Swing dance historian Terry Monaghan points out that for all his "key innovations," Snowden's name remains surprisingly unknown. However, Monaghan adds this positive remark, around which all swing dancers can rally:

Fortunately, the stubborn persistence of the Lindy tradition suggests that not only will it survive long enough to be taken seriously, in the way that George Snowden would have wished for, but that his diverse legacy will finally be adequately acknowledged. (Savoyballroom.com)

By the late 1920s, there was a whole slew of original Savoy dancers with nicknames like Speedy, Blackjack, Shoebrush, and the Sheik—dancers who were definite standouts, but whose real names have sadly disappeared over time. However, several other early stars of the Savoy Ballroom are well remembered, such as LeRoy "Stretch" Jones, who Manning has always described as a tall, elegant dancer and one of his first idols. With a smooth and graceful style, LeRoy "Stretch" Jones was sometimes referred to as the "Fred Astaire of Lindy Hop." His partner (his "Ginger Rogers") was Beatrice Elam, known as "Little Bea" because of her small 5' stature. Getting their start in Shorty Snowden's dance troupe, Jones and Elam were both early professionals. Snowden also hired a brother and sister duo, Freddie and Madeline Lewis, who Manning knew later as Savoy Ballroom regulars.

Robert "Rabbit" Taylor was a quick-footed early member of Whitey's Lindy Hoppers before Manning was asked to join. Another of both Frankie Manning and Norma Miller's early Savoy idols was George T. Ganaway, known as "Susquehanna" (named, perhaps, after the flowing Susquehanna river in central New York State), and by a second nickname, "Twist Mouth" George. Both Manning and Miller credit "Twist Mouth" George Ganaway with inventing the "twist" step that the women do on counts one and two of Lindy Hop's basic step. Ganaway claimed that he taught it to his partner Edith Matthews, and she was the first to show it and popularize it. It was also Twist Mouth George who pulled Norma Miller into the Savoy Ballroom to join him in a dance exhibition (when she was a young teenager dancing on the sidewalk outside the ballroom). In her autobiography *"Swingin' at the Savoy,"* Miller explains that the nickname "Twist Mouth" came from Ganaway's tilted, crooked smile. She writes, "His hat was cocked to the side of his face where the twist was, and he had the longest legs I had ever seen" (38).

All in all, it was this vibrant assemblage of swingin' musicians and supremely talented dancers, united together at Harlem's Savoy Ballroom, that gave birth to the Lindy Hop. The Savoy was much more than a music and dance hall. It was the spawning ground of an important piece of American artistic culture—Swing dancing.

# 5

# Whitey's Lindy Hoppers

Every swing dancer can understand the feeling, that first impression of walking into a ballroom when the floor is filled with dancers, the music is wailing, and the drums are pounding out a beat that sets your soul on fire—you're amazed and wowed by the energy of it all. The band members are in sync like finely tuned machines, and the soloists are reading each other's minds, one taking over where the last one left off, like separate puzzle pieces of some grand orchestral plan. You step onto the dance floor with a partner and, suddenly, you're part of that same plan, in that same creative musical moment—and every part of your body starts swinging. Lindy legend Frankie Manning described those evenings as "electrified," and he enjoyed talking about them. But sometimes he'd stop talking abruptly, finding no words to adequately depict the energy of it all. In those instances he often closed his eyes, shook his head, and whispered under his breath, "Those were swingin' nights."

Frankie Manning was 19 years old when he and his friends went to the Savoy Ballroom for the very first time. The year was 1933. He headed up the steps that led to the dance floor, and in his own words:

> . . . I could hear this swinging music coming down the stairwell, and it started seeping right into my body. I got to the top step, went through the double doors, and stopped for a moment with my back to the bandstand, taking it all in. When I turned around and faced the room . . . well, I just stood there with my mouth open. The whole floor was full of people— and they were *dancing*! (Manning and Millman, 2007, 62)

Manning and his friends had previously danced the Lindy Hop at the Alhambra Ballroom and at the Renaissance Ballroom, which they referred to as "the Reny." Occasionally, they ventured into the Dunbar or the Audubon Ballrooms. But the Savoy was in a league all its own. It was the most elegant, most sophisticated, and classiest of all the ballrooms, and it had a reputation for being where the "best" dancers went. At first, Manning and his friends were intimidated about going there. As Manning has often explained it, "You started off at the Alhambra ... elementary school. Then you went to the Renaissance— that was high school. And when you got to be really good you graduated to college, which was the Savoy Ballroom" (Manning talking to Robert Crease in *Footnotes*, 1987, 1; Manning talking to Judith Mackrell in *The Independent*, "Jumping Jive Revived," April 22, 1988, among many sources for this quote).

On his first trip to the Savoy, Frankie Manning witnessed some of the best dancers showing off their moves in "the corner." According to a 1936 article in the *New York Post*, the Savoy management set aside the "north end of the ballroom" for the wilder Lindy Hoppers, to protect the shins and ankles of the other guests (Archer Winsten, *New York Post*, "Wake of the News," May 7, 1936, 21). That area, on stage right of house band's number one bandstand, became the designated area for what came to be referred to as "Cats Corner." It was where the flashiest and most accomplished dancers could have their moments in the spotlight, and a delighted audience of onlookers could "ooh and awe" them. Manning and his friends learned their Lindy Hop by watching the best dancers, honing their observational skills, and then experimenting with moves. It wasn't long, however, before Manning was showing his own moves and his own style in the Cats Corner jams. He quickly became one of the best dancers at the Savoy Ballroom, and ultimately one of the best Swing dancers of all time.

The elite dancers who joined in on the Cats Corner jams were constantly perfecting their moves and creating new ones. Their Lindy Hop performance skills blended with their social dance abilities (which helped further develop the dance), and made them a very marketable commodity. Audiences at the Savoy loved to watch them, and the dancers loved to be watched. Herbert White, a former prize-fighter and WWI sergeant, who was employed at the Savoy as a bouncer, took special interest in the Lindy Hopping youngsters. Known as "Whitey" for an approximately two-inch streak of white in

Weekly dance competitions at the Savoy Ballroom constantly pushed the early Lindy Hoppers to reach for higher acrobatic heights, and brought busloads of tourists to the ballroom to watch. This photograph was published in *Life* magazine on December 14, 1936. The caption explains that, thanks to audience applause, these competitors won a prize and are giving an encore exhibition for the (mostly white) crowd. A nearby photograph of the Ballroom's marquee shows that the "Maple Leaf Pinochle Club" was being welcomed, and touts the Lindy Hop contest. (Photo by George Karger/Pix Inc./Time Life Pictures/Getty Images.)

his hair (which he often highlighted with white shoe polish), he was the first to organize the Lindy Hoppers into professional groups. Originally, Whitey chose 9 or 10 couples and got them performance jobs at various clubs, social functions, and wealthy socialites' parties. Eventually, however (using a variety of names but known collectively as Whitey's Lindy Hoppers) his dancers gained worldwide recognition, performing in a variety of venues, including nightclubs, hotels, theater shows, and major motion pictures.

Dance historian and author Cynthia Millman notes that Whitey had, at one time, been employed at Barron Wilkins' nightclub as a dancing waiter. He had also previously trained dancers at Ed Smalls' Sugar Cane Club, on upper 5th Avenue (the club later moved and became

Small's Paradise). So, not only did White have an eye for talent, he also had the skills necessary for coaching and organizing the dancers (Manning and Millman, 2007, 262; Winsten, *New York Post*, May 7, 1936, 21; Bruce Kellner, 1987, 344).

Over the years, Whitey has been referred to as a "legendary character," a "guru," "a thug," even "a semi-gangster." But, by all accounts he was an excellent organizer and a charismatic leader. Judy Pritchett, Lindy Hop historian and Frankie Manning's long time girlfriend and confidant, notes that Herbert "Whitey" White got to know all the young dancers at the Savoy and he picked out the best, most reliable dancers. She adds:

> They were invariably delighted to make a few dollars doing what they loved. (Pritchett, *Archives of Early Lindy Hop*, savoystyle.com)

From the time Frankie Manning became one of "Whitey's Lindy Hoppers," in 1934, Whitey had a tremendous impact on Manning's career and his life's course. Manning always regarded Whitey as a mentor and a friend, and had fond memories of the man. In the "Acknowledgments" section of his autobiography (2007, 17), after he "thanks" his own mother, who adored dancing and used to take him to rent parties and social events in Harlem (but accused Frankie of being "too stiff" on the dance floor), Manning then "thanks" Herbert "Whitey" White.

Another of the early Savoy Lindy Hoppers, Norma Miller, always felt a strong sense of loyalty to Whitey. She notes in her autobiography that while he took "control" of her life, she wouldn't have traveled the world as she did if he hadn't chosen her as one of his dancers. He gave her the chance "to put the Lindy on the map" and gave all his Lindy Hoppers, in Miller's words: "A sense of destiny" (Miller and Jensen, 49, 56; Telephone interview).

Ruth Reingold Ettin, another of Whitey's Lindy Hoppers, started dancing at New York's Savoy Ballroom in 1936 (a few years later than Manning and Miller). She was one of three couples selected by Whitey to dance at the Apollo Theatre, and she recalls, "Whenever we saw Whitey, we'd all run and hug him." And while she didn't socialize with him outside of the Savoy Ballroom, or the rehearsal hall (she recalls a room down the street from the Savoy with a Victorola and mirrors where her group would practice), she adds, "Whitey was like a father to me." Ettin also reports that it was Whitey who choreographed her group's Apollo routines, and that "he was an excellent choreographer" (Telephone interview).

Shorty Snowden's early Lindy Hoppers, and those employed under Herbert White, were the true pioneers of Swing. There were no old movies to peruse for dance step ideas, no routines to recreate, no guides or booklets to follow, no teachers to help them execute new moves. They were the innovators. They created the basics, the original guidelines and vocabulary of Swing dancing, and with Herbert White at the wheel, they drove into unchartered territory—introducing their new American folk dance, the Lindy Hop, to the world.

## Ambassadors of Swing

Under the auspices of Herbert White, a select group of Lindy Hop dancers worked throughout the United States as well as internationally. They traveled to Great Britain (for a royal command performance at the London Palladium), France, Ireland, Switzerland, New Zealand and Australia, and even to South America. Through the years Whitey's troupes worked under a variety of names, such as "Whyte's" Hopping Maniacs, "Whitey's" Hopping Maniacs, Whitey's Lindy Hoppers, Whitey's Jitterbugs, and Whitey's Congeroo Dancers. It was common for Whitey to have several of these groups performing in different cities at the same time. In 1936, for instance (the same year that Frankie Manning's troupe was hired at the famed Cotton Club), a second group of Whitey's dancers was performing at the Harlem Opera House, and a third team that had been touring with Ethel Waters got a booking at the Paramount Theater, in Los Angeles. Those dancers on location in Los Angeles were then hired to dance in the Marx Brother's Hollywood movie, *A Day at the Races*.

Released by MGM studios in 1937, *A Day at the Races* features one of the best-filmed Lindy Hop routines ever captured on the silver screen. The dance scene opens with Harpo Marx playing a piccolo—when suddenly the swing music kicks in and four teams of Whitey's Lindy Hoppers jubilantly swing out to the song "All God's Chillin' Got Rhythm," performed onscreen by vocalist Ivie Anderson. The segment is filmed at a variety of angles and is exceptionally well edited. It features wide-shots of the troupe, highlighting the ensemble aspect of Lindy Hopping, as well as closeups of individual dancers' faces and feet. The Lindy Hoppers in *A Day at the Races* include Leon James with Norma Miller, Johnny Innis with Dot Miller (Norma Miller's sister), Snooky Beasly with Ella Gibson, and George Greenidge with Willamae Ricker.

The undisputed best look at Lindy Hopping on screen, however, appears in the 1941 movie *Hellzapoppin'* (Universal Pictures), which was loosely based on the Broadway musical of the same name. The musical play debuted at the 46th Street Theater on September 22, 1938, and ran for 1,404 performances, a theatrical record at the time. It was described in its program notes as "A free-for-all vaudeville revue." The movie *Hellzapoppin'* followed the same basic concept, with the Lindy Hoppers being among a number of acts featured in brief spotlighted segments (Steven Suskin, 2006, 71; Hal Erickson, 2000, 28).

The routine in *Hellzapoppin'* is generally considered to be the epitome of Swing dancing, a summit which may, perhaps, never again be equaled. For the movie's filming, Herbert White hired four couples (the top six current Harvest Moon championship Lindy Hoppers, plus two additional dancers). The dancers in *Hellzapoppin'* include Billy

Lindy Hopper Frankie Manning performs "the snatch" with his partner Ann Johnson on the set of the 1941 movie *Hellzapoppin'*. Harlem Congeroo Dancers (from left to right): Billy Ricker, Ann Johnson, Frankie Manning, Mickey Jones, Willamae Ricker, and Al Minns, William Downes. The choreography, along with the talent and precision of the dancers (and the way in which they were filmed), made the Lindy Hop routine in *Hellzapoppin'* an onscreen masterpiece. (Courtesy of Cynthia Millman.)

Ricker with partner Norma Miller, William Downes with Frances "Mickey" Jones (whom Norma Miller refers to as: Mickey Sayles), Al Minns with Willamae Ricker, and Frankie Manning with Ann Johnson. Frankie Manning choreographed the number, although he has always humbly asserted that he didn't think too much choreography was actually needed. The dancers already knew the moves, but Manning put the segments together so the couple's separate routines flowed from one to the next, and worked well with the music that was chosen for the scene. With bodies flying through the air in a spectacular display of aerial showmanship, there is raw frenzy in the *Hellzapoppin'* routine. But the brute strength and power of the air steps is balanced by delicate interplay, and finely tuned coordination, between the dancers. Manning's innovative choreography along with the dancers' athleticism and break-neck-speed dancing (which often prompts viewers to ask, "Are they dancing in real time; are they really dancing that fast?"—Yes!), combine to create a dazzling two-and-a-half minute display of sheer explosive joyous energy. In sum, *Hellzapoppin'* is the consummate onscreen masterpiece of the Lindy Hop.

While all the individual accomplishments of the various members of Whitey's Lindy Hoppers were important to the development of Swing dancing, some of the dancers were standouts, either for their exceptional abilities or their resurgence in later years as dancers, teachers, and historians.

"Stompin' Billy" Hill along with his partner, Norma Miller, were two notable examples of Lindy Hoppers selected by Whitey to go on tour to Europe. They were joined by Edith Matthews (Twist Mouth George's partner, who had first introduced the twisting motion into the basic Lindy swing-out), and Leon James, who was a remarkably dynamic dancer. In 1935, Edith Matthews partnered Leon James in the first Harvest Moon Ball competition, and they were crowned the Lindy Hop champions. James was well regarded for his flashy performance skills, and it is his vibrant facial expression that shines in a camera close-up in *A Day at the Races*.

Frieda Washington gets credit for performing the first aerial in Swing dance with Frankie Manning, and Willamae Briggs Ricker was considered one of the most versatile of all the women of Whitey's Lindy Hoppers. But it was Ann Johnson who danced with Manning in the *Hellzapoppin'* routine, and he always called her a "solid, fearless dancer." He explained that during air steps her legs would be wiggling this way and that way, but that she always managed to land solidly on her feet—"like a cat" (*Never Stop Swinging*, 2009, among a variety of sources for this quote).

Another accomplished member of Whitey's Lindy Hoppers, "Long-Legged George" Greenidge, was an early friend of Frankie Manning's who was responsible for creating a number of specific Lindy Hop variations, including "the Turnover" and the "Long-Legged Charleston" steps. John "Tiny" Bunch was unique in that, despite being 6′ 4″ tall and weighing 350 pounds, he was a graceful light-footed dancer. Bunch's partner was Dorothy "Dot" Moses who, at 90 pounds, got her nickname because "she looked like a little dot." According to Frankie Manning, "John 'Tiny' Bunch looked like King Kong throwing Dot around!" (Manning, PBDA video archives, 1991).

Norma Miller was one of Whitey's best and most charismatic dancers, appearing in numerous stage and screen productions (including *A Day at the Races* and *Hellzapoppin'*). As well as performing in Europe, she danced across America on tour with vocalist Ethel Waters. But one of the most remarkable aspects about Norma Miller was that she never left show business. As popular music styles changed in the 1950s and swing sounds gave way to bebop and rock and roll—Miller continued to make her living as a dancer. During those years, when Lindy jobs became hard to come by and other members of Whitey's Lindy Hoppers were retiring from performance life, Miller organized her own Jazz company and went right on dancing. She employed Chazz Young, Frankie Manning's oldest son, as one of her Jazz dancers, encouraging him in his own successful career as a Jazz, Tap and Lindy dancer. *Jet* magazine, in 1959, notes that bandleader Cab Calloway took his Cotton Club Revue, which included the "Norma Miller Jazz Dancers," on a seven-week tour of South America (May 14, "New York Beat," 63).

Always a brassy, energized dynamo, Norma Miller has been featured in numerous documentaries, including the Ken Burns PBS documentary *Jazz* (along with Frankie Manning). She appeared in the motion picture *Malcolm X*, and won an Emmy nomination for her choreography in the 1993 CBS television movie, *Stompin' at the Savoy.* Also a talented comedienne, Miller appeared often in *Sanford and Son*, the Redd Foxx television sitcom. She has continued to travel extensively in the twenty-first century as a dance teacher and Lindy Hop historian, imparting her knowledge and expertise to a new generation of Swing dancers. Her love for the Lindy and her remark-able autobiography, which chronicles her life-long enthusiasm for dance in general, have made her one of the icons in the world of Swing. (Lindy Hop preservationist Mickey Davidson continues to showcase Miller's choreography on tour.)

Later members of Whitey's Lindy Hoppers include the only white couple ever to be invited to join: Harry Rosenburg and Ruth Reingold Ettin. Whitey matched them together as dance partners for his Apollo Theater shows. Frankie Manning recalls that "Ruth and Harry were two of the top dancers." He adds, "And I don't mean the top *white* dancers. I mean two of the top dancers, period!" (Telephone interview with Manning, March, 2009).

Al Minns had just turned 18 when he and his partner, Mildred Pollard (later known as Sandra Gibson), entered the Harvest Moon Ball compe-tition of 1938. Sandra Gibson was always beautiful, but she was also so physically strong that she could have worked for the New York Police Department. "They wanted to make a *cop-a* out of me," she says. Afraid to do aerials herself, she liked to pick up her male partners, brute strength, and throw them around. The climax of her 1938 Harvest Moon Ball routine with Al Minns featured Minns jumping up into her arms. As the music stopped they both stood there grinning widely holding that final pose. The judges were obviously impressed: Minns and Gibson won first place in the competition! Gibson was later nicknamed "the Boogie Woogie Queen" for her sensuous hip-shaking boogie. Minns developed a crazy legs style of dance (his nickname was "Rubberlegs"), which became his trademark (Gibson in *The Call of the Jitterbug*, 1988; Robert Crease's interview with Gibson in *Footnotes*, April–June, 1987, 1).

In the 1950s and 60s, Al Minns teamed up with Leon James to tour college campuses with Marshall W. Stearns. Stearns served as a moderator as the trio presented a historical look at the development of Jazz dancing. Jazz historian, author, and college professor, Marshall Stearns, is credited with getting study courses in jazz added to univer-sity curricula. In 1952, with his own enormous personal collection of jazz records and music publications, he founded the Institute of Jazz Studies at Rutgers, which developed into one of the largest collections of jazz material in the world—a treasure trove of archival material for researchers and historians (Robert Walser, 1999, 195–196).

Stearns's superb book, *Jazz Dance*: *The Story of American Vernacular Dance*, originally published in 1968 and co-written with his wife Jean, is a captivating history of dance. Interestingly, however, both authors rely on Al Minns and Leon James as sole sources for their Savoy Ballroom material and for Lindy Hop in general. Unfortunately, and for reasons one can only speculate about, it seems that neither dancer mentioned the name "Frankie Manning" to the Stearns. It is also interesting to note that Manning was adamant that Minns and James had "stretched the truth" in some of the stories they related to the Stearns (specifically in their tales of *The Jolly Fellows* gang and gang warfare at the Savoy). In any event, Marshall and Jean Stearns' book is a remarkable achievement, and Leon James and Al Minns were certainly devoted ambassadors of Swing, touring and educating audiences in the early vernacular dances. In 1958, as participants in Rhode Island's Newport Jazz Festival, they attracted an audience of 400, and, according to one *New York Times* writer covering the event, they "stole the spotlight from the major programs of the festival." Minns and James also performed for a 1961 "Dupont Television Show of the Week," in which they are featured demonstrating "1920s styles of dancing," including the Lindy Hop. The two men partner each other in the Lindy Hop segment, and even perform an aerial together (John Wilson, *New York Times*, "Lecture on Dance Steals Jazz Fete," July 6, 1958, 50; "Dupont Television Show," accessible on YouTube.com).

Al Minns and Leon James also appear in *The Spirit Moves*, a documentary produced and directed by Mura Dehn, which was filmed on location at the Savoy Ballroom circa 1950. Dehn set up a camera in one corner of the Savoy and documented dancers doing a variety of dance steps—from vintage moves to popular styles of the time—tracing the history of jazz dancing. Dehn was a Russian émigré who moved to the United States in 1930 and devoted much of her life to the study and documenting of Afro-American dance. In the 1960s, her Mura Dehn Jazz Ballet Company joined forces with the Pepsi Bethel Authentic Jazz Dance Theater (Pepsi Bethel was one of the Savoy Ballroom dancers featured onscreen in *The Spirit Moves*) and in 1969, both the Bethel and Dehn dance companies toured Africa as cultural emissaries for the U.S. State Department.

Pepsi Bethel (nicknamed "Pepsi" by his grandmother, after his favorite soft drink), became one of Whitey's Lindy Hoppers in the early 1940s. With a long professional career in dance, he later taught Ballet dance for students of the Alvin Ailey American Dance Center, and "authentic Jazz dance" at New York's Clark Center. Bethel used the term "authentic Jazz," to differentiate the Afro-American style of Jazz from the Broadway-stage style of Modern dance, also called "Jazz." In an interview in the *New York Times* in 1978, Bethel noted that the hardest thing for his classically trained dance students to learn was the relaxed loosening of the knees, as well as the shameless "freedom of movement" so essential to the "jazz character." He too was an important ambassador of dance, encouraging interest in and preservation for the Lindy Hop style of swing (Bethel's interview with Mark Deitch, *New York Times*, August 6, 1978, 12, 16).

## The Legacy of Frankie Manning

Frankie "Musclehead" Manning was born in 1914, and the entire swing world mourned his passing in 2009, at the age of 94. Beloved by Swing dancers around the globe, his accomplishments as a dancer, historian, and ambassador of Swing have been unparalleled. As one of Whitey's early Lindy Hoppers, Manning was a phenomenal, multi-talented dancer. (His nickname developed from onlookers noticing that the top of his head moved when he was thinking about great Lindy Hop material and planning his jam circle moves at the Savoy Ballroom. His friends would chant, "Go, Musclehead, go!" as he swung out onto the floor.)

Manning was the chief choreographer for Whitey's dance troupes, and when Decca Records released Jimmy Lunceford's 1935 arrangement of "Posin'," the song's musical "breaks" (moments where the music briefly "stops") inspired Manning to try something new. He coached the other dancers to hit those same breaks, stopping at exactly the same time the music did. That led to his subsequent creation of ensemble choreography, synchronized Lindy Hopping routines (Manning, PBDA archives, 1991).

The energy in a lineup of Lindy Hoppers all "swinging-out" at the same time is one of the most captivating elements of Swing dance as a performance art. But besides the creation of ensemble choreography, Frankie Manning also created the first aerial in Swing dancing, a move he called "Over-the-Back," which added a whole new dimension to the Lindy Hop and Swing dancing in general. He has often told the delightful story of how that first aerial came about. The year was 1935, and Shorty Snowden had challenged some of the younger Lindy dancers (the "new upstarts" at the Savoy Ballroom, of which Manning

Whitey's Lindy Hoppers performing ensemble choreography at the Moulin Rouge, Paris, France, in 1937. Billed for this tour as "Whyte's Hopping Maniacs" the dancers included (from left to right): Frankie Manning and Naomi Waller, Billy Williams and Mildred Cruse, Lucille Middleton and Jerome Williams. (Courtesy of Chazz Young.)

was one) to a dance competition duel. In a well-publicized contest at the Savoy, Snowden's three best couples would go up against three couples of Savoy newcomers. Manning practiced all week with his partner Frieda Washington on a new move. Manning had seen Shorty and Big Bea do a particular lift many times: Bea lifted Shorty onto her back and carried him around. It was a comical move, with Shorty riding upside down on Bea's back, kicking his legs in the air. Manning thought about getting Frieda up onto his back, and then flipping her clear over from there. No Lindy Hopper had done anything like that before. When he asked Frieda about it, she boldly agreed to give it a try. Practicing with a mattress, after many falls and unsuccessful attempts, they could finally perform the aerial flawlessly.

On the night of the competition, the Savoy Ballroom was packed. The energy level was high; everyone wanted to see if Snowden, the unofficial "King of the Savoy," and his teammates could prevail as champions. In the dance-off, the dancers alternated turns, one of

Shorty's couples would dance, followed by one of Whitey's. Frankie Manning and Frieda Washington were the last couple to dance. Manning remembers that things seemed to be going just right, he and Frieda were connecting well, and everything felt good. He whispered to her, "Should we go for it?" She whispered back, "Let's do it!" They turned back to back, linked arms, and Manning threw her over his back and she landed *WHOOM*, right on beat with the music. There was a moment of hushed silence, and then suddenly, "it was as if the entire Savoy rose up as one," Manning recalls. "Everyone was yelling and shouting and carrying on." That's when Frankie Manning realized he'd done something very special.

Manning couldn't say who officially won the competition; when he and Frieda landed that first aerial, there was mass pandemonium. But he remembered that Shorty Snowden asked him later, "So, where did you get that step?" Manning responded truthfully (much to Snowden's surprise), "I got that step from you!" Shorty had no idea what he was talking about, so Manning explained how he took Big Bea and Snowden's lift one step further. Snowden thought about it for a minute and responded, "Oh yeah, I guess you could do that," to which Manning replied, "I know I could. I just did!" (In Manning's retelling of the story, he usually throws back his head and laughs at this point.) But then, on a more serious note, he generally suggests, "Snowden would have eventually thought of the aerial himself." Manning always ends the story by adding, "I just felt lucky to have thought of it first" (PBDA video archives, 1991, among many sources).

A plethora of new aerials were quickly created which brought added excitement to the ensemble performance routines. Countless acrobatic steps and aerial maneuvers made their way into Swing dancing, and new aerials are still being created in the twenty-first century. But history has recorded the fact that it was Frankie Manning (along with Frieda Washington) who first gave Swing dancers wings.

Manning retired from dancing in 1955, and spent the next 30 years working for the United States Postal Service. But in 1986, dancers Erin Stevens and Steven Mitchell from Pasadena, California, flew to New York and persuaded Frankie to give them private Lindy Hop lessons. This reignited Manning's career. From that time forward, as the resurgence of Swing dance blossomed, Manning was at the forefront of the movement as a dancer, choreographer, and teacher, carrying the torch for all the Lindy Hoppers of his day. A true ambassador of Swing dance, he traveled constantly with the selfless goal of spreading the joy of the Lindy Hop. Moved and inspired by his stories of the Savoy Ballroom, and by his remarkable dance abilities (well into his eighties, Manning could still throw a partner over his shoulder; into his nineties, his footwork was still awe-inspiring), dancers the world over called upon him to teach in their communities. He continued to be in great demand even into his nineties, traveling an average of 40 weekends a year (Chazz Young in the television documentary *Frankie Manning: Never Stop Swinging*, Cohen, 2009). Manning's gentle manner and wonderful personality were legendary (everyone who met him commented on his disarmingly egoless and humble spirit), and Swing dancers everywhere adored him. His infectious laugh, his always-positive attitude, his excellent speaking ability, his seemingly tireless sharing of his life stories (his memories remained intensively clear to the end), and his genuine love of the dance moved and inspired Swing dancers everywhere. And while Frankie Manning couldn't live forever, thanks to Lindy Hoppers the world over, his legacy will.

On May 21, 2009, Swing dancers converged upon the Manhattan Center in New York City for a memorial weekend tribute to the late Frankie Manning (organized by Elliott Donnelley, David Jacoby, Tena Morales, and Buddy Steves, along with advisors Cynthia Millman and Judy Pritchett). The event had originally been planned as a celebration of Manning's 95th birthday; however, he died of pneumonia just weeks shy of the party. The event went on as planned, but as a celebration of Manning's life and as a testament to his Lindy Hop legacy. The tribute began with the showing of a made-for-television documentary by Julie Cohen, *Frankie Manning: Never Stop Swinging* (Swing Bud Productions, 2009), which follows Manning's dancing career from its beginnings through his becoming a Lindy Hopping legend into the twenty-first century. Later in the weekend, the attending audience was treated to a full-show stage production that loosely followed the chronology of Frankie Manning's life as outlined in his autobiography. It was a spectacular show, culminating in a reenactment of the *Hellzapoppin'* routine, which prompted Norma Miller to point out, was still as "timely a routine" as the day Manning choreographed it (Personal interview after the show). There were live band dances on Thursday through Monday evenings during the event. And while an earlier funeral and church service had been held on May 2, a second memorial service (appropriately titled *Celebration of a Dancing Life*) was conducted on

May 22 at Manhattan's Fifth Avenue Presbyterian Church, during which family members, fellow dancers, and close friends gave speeches that moved the audience to both laughter and tears. Swing music from the Bennie Powell and Frank Wess Quintet brought Lindy Hoppers to their feet, dancing in the aisles, in a spontaneous and heartfelt loving display. After the memorial service, the dancers exited the church and paraded behind a brass band, in a New Orleans–style jazz funeral procession (waving handkerchiefs and parasols, and carrying photographs of Frankie Manning) to Central Park. There, under the warm sunshine, on a glorious New York afternoon, the George Gee Orchestra played in the Naumburg Bandshell—and everybody danced.

## It's All There . . . in Black and White

Much has been written about the power of music to cross racial lines, to break cultural barriers and build bridges, and to unite people around the globe, but in the 1920s and 1930s, racial segregation and prejudice were a fact of American life. It was a common occurrence: the musicians played their hearts out and the audience applauded and cheered. But at the end of the night, when the members of the all-black touring band packed up their instruments and exited the theater, they couldn't get a room for the night. If there were no black-owned restaurants in town, they couldn't get a hot meal. The hotels didn't want them, and they weren't allowed in the local diners.

"It was heartbreaking," says dancer and entertainer Delilah Jackson of her touring in the South. "You couldn't even get a sandwich. They'd tell you to go back in the kitchen and somebody with their dirty hands, a dishwasher, would hand you a sandwich to eat and you'd have to eat it by the roadside" (Jackson in *The Call of the Jitterbug*, 1988).

Whitey's Lindy Hoppers also encountered racial prejudice on the road. During the years of the Great Depression, group members were well paid for their performances and well respected for their talents in Europe, where racial prejudice wasn't much of a problem. But traveling in America, they discovered that—especially in the South—it was a whole different story. In Frankie Manning's autobiography, he recalls segregation signs posted on drinking fountains that said "colored" and "white." He could spend his money shopping at a Woolworth's Department Store, but he wasn't allowed to sit at the store's lunch counter. Touring in the South with singer Sarah Vaughan, he remembers stopping at a local diner for lunch, where he couldn't get service for a sandwich, not even to go (37, 211). Similarly, Norma Miller recalls touring with Ethel Waters in a caravan of vehicles, including two chauffeur-driven Lincolns and a tour bus carrying the show's musicians, dancers, and specialty acts. Because of the "race" issue, they couldn't get service at a hamburger stand on the road. Miller shakes her head and speaks with heartfelt eloquence, "We weren't some scruffy people on the highway . . . we were the biggest show out there. Ethel Waters could have bought the whole darn block. And we couldn't get a hamburger!" She goes on to explain how she and the other entertainers coped with the hatred and the prejudice: "We steeled ourselves. We grew armor!" (Miller in *The Call of the Jitterbug*, 1988).

Europe offered a haven for black musicians and entertainers, a more color-blind environment, and many chose to pursue their careers overseas. Singer, dancer, and actress Josephine Baker, one notable example, relocated to France and became an international star. Coming back to New York, after a decade of being revered in Paris and acclaimed throughout Europe, Baker was turned away from the St. Moritz Hotel. To worsen matters, the hotel staff explained that Baker's Italian husband and her French maid, both fair-skinned, could lodge there, but that she, Josephine Baker herself, would have to stay elsewhere (Gottschild, 2002, 31).

Right on through the 1940s, discrimination and racial segregation plagued the music and entertainment business. In 1941, as white clarinetist and bandleader Artie Shaw embarked on a 32-stop tour through the South, he was requested to "shelve" his black horn player "Hot Lips" Paige. A *Time* magazine article on the subject explained:

> The South can take all-negro bands like Cab Callaway's and it doesn't mind small mixed combinations; against a Negro in a large white band it tends to draw the color line. ("Music: Artie Shaw on Tour," September 22, 1941, np)

Instead of leaving Paige at home, however, Artie Shaw cancelled the tour. Like most of the jazz and swing era bandleaders, Shaw helped break down racial divides by hiring his musicians on the color-blind basis of talent. Saxophonist bandleader Charlie Barnet also persisted in crossing racial lines throughout his career. Barnet led the first white band to play at Harlem's Apollo Theatre, with unprecedented success. A 1942 article in *The Billboard* reported:

> Barnet is one of the few paleface maestri making regular stops in colored locations and theaters, preferring to play for the hep sepia swing addicts. ("C. Barnet's Sepia Circuit," December 5, 1942, 20)

And while bandleader Benny Goodman took the first racially mixed band on tour, Barnet always insisted on hiring the musicians he most admired, regardless of color. Benny Carter, jazz saxophonist, was one of the many black artists to work in Barnet's bands. He recalls that during the swing era in New York, white musicians often went uptown to Harlem to sit in with black bands. "We welcomed them and enjoyed the jamming," Carter explains, "but we couldn't go downtown and join them." The uptown and downtown music scenes were firmly segregated, and a racially integrated band was socially taboo. However, by the time Benny Goodman's mixed bands began to tour, they met with such great success that things did noticeably begin to change. Once big money was involved, agents and promoters got onboard, prompting jazz critic and producer John Hammond to comment: "It is amusing to note that commercial success has a magnificent way of eliminating color segregation" (Carter and Hammond quoted in Ross Firestone, 1993, 80, 201).

In Harlem, at the Savoy Ballroom, Whitey's Lindy Hoppers were insulated from much of the racial prejudice that permeated American culture at the time. The Savoy was the first integrated ballroom in America, and Frankie Manning has often reported that, at the Savoy, no one cared if you were black, white, green, or blue. All anyone wanted to know was, "Can you dance?" But, in 1937, Manning and his friends were turned away from midtown Manhattan's Roseland Ballroom, where they had gone one evening to hear the Fletcher Henderson band. The bouncer at the door denied them entry because of the color of their skin. Manning never forgot the experience, although he is generally quick to add, "It just rubbed off us. We just walked right back to the Savoy, and had a great evening." It is worth noting however, for the record, that in 1999 a huge party was organized at the Roseland for Manning's 85th birthday, and the ballroom's management made an official apology for the incident. An autographed pair of Frankie Manning's dance shoes was added to a display case alongside those of Fred

Astaire, Savion Glover, and Gregory Hines (Manning, PBDA archives, 1991; *Never Stop Swinging*, 2009, among other sources).

While "color" made no difference at the Savoy, Ruthie Reingold Ettin and Harry Rosenburg, the only two white youngsters to become Whitey's Lindy Hoppers, were never photographed with the rest of Whitey's dancers. In fact, Ruth Ettin recalls being "moved out of the way, to the sidelines, when the photographers came around." It was too controversial to show white dancers as part of a mixed-race dance team. Ettin also notes that sometimes, in live performances, she would hear the audience gasp and whisper, or even yell out loud, "Hey, they're white!" (Telephone interview; Ettin in *Never Stop Swinging*, 2009).

Dance historian Ralph Giordano points out that "racially mixed" scenes, those involving blacks and whites onscreen together, were commonly edited out of movies. For example, many Americans didn't get to see Whitey's Lindy Hoppers dancing in the Marx Bros. movie *A Day at the Races*. The entire production number was routinely censored out of the film because Harpo, who is white, is shown "mixing" with the Lindy Hoppers (Giordano, 2007, Vol. 2, 93).

In 1981, early Savoy Lindy Hopper Al Minns commented that he, for one, understood why black dancers were often left out of films and didn't get their deserved Hollywood acclaim, "It was all a matter of money!" (*Eye on Dance* television series, "Third World Dance: Tracing Roots," 1981). Jazz historian Ernie Smith concurs, stating:

> ... movie moguls were not about to jeopardize box office revenue by defying long-entrenched prejudices. Performances by black dancers and artists were generally inserted as specialty numbers in otherwise all-white films which made it easy for local censors to remove racially objectionable sequences at whim. (Smith, *Dance Research Journal*, "Recollections and Reflections of a Jazz Dance Film Collector," 1983, 47)

It is impossible to guess how many spectacular performances ended up on the cutting room floor because Hollywood was slow to recognize black dance as a legitimate art form worthy of showcasing. Thankfully, however, there are many wonderful performances that did make it onto the silver screen. Ernie Smith, an authority on jazz music and dance, amassed an outstanding film collection, which not only included Hollywood major motion picture clips, but also very early and very rare examples of black Jazz dance.

Over time, there has been an ever-increasing appreciation of the tradition of black dancing, and recognition of its profound influence on American art forms. Since the years of slavery, minstrelsy, the jazz era, the creation of the Lindy Hop and the big band era of swing, racial divides continue to be broken in America, and mutual respect between people of all colors has increased dramatically.

In November 2008, the first African American president of the United States was elected into office. When Frankie Manning was asked for his reaction to that milestone, he responded, "I have lived a long time, and I have never envisioned this happening in my lifetime. But since it did happen in my lifetime, I want to thank the Lord for letting me see this come to pass. It's a wonderful thing for the world" (Telephone interview, March 2009).

# 6

# Swingin' in Hollywood

At the Savoy Ballroom in Harlem, New York, there was a bond between the dancers that transcended race, creed, income levels, age, and even fame. Frankie Manning and Norma Miller have always agreed that celebrities went there because the dancers never hounded them for their autographs or crowded around them. It didn't matter how much money someone made, or how famous someone was, at the Savoy it was all about dancing. As early Savoy Lindy Hopper Ruth Ettin explains it:

> All we wanted to do morning noon and night was dance . . . that was the bond between us. (Pritchett, *Archives of Lindy Hop*, savoystyle.com)

While Ruth Ettin and her partner Harry Rosenburg were the only white dancers actually hired as Whitey's Lindy Hoppers, there were many other white Swing dancers who frequented the Savoy. As those dancers traveled to other cities and danced in other ballrooms around the country, they exposed new groups of Swing aficionados to the Lindy Hop style of Swing dancing they'd encountered at the Savoy. One such dancer was Ben Mankofsky. Born in 1919, Mankofsky learned to Swing dance at the Savoy Ballroom in the mid-1930s. As the depression years ended, he relocated his window drapery business from New York to Chicago, where he became a regular dancer at the Aragon Ballroom. He is featured in a 1944 *Chicago Daily News* photograph Swing dancing at the Aragon with his wife at that time (Florence Mankofsky), on a night when the Harry James Orchestra played and "seven thousand jammed the North Side Ballroom." The newspaper points out the Mankofskys were "distinctly 'in the groove' to the sweet tunes of the James trumpet" (Chicago *Daily News*, photo caption, July 15, 1944; Telephone interview with Mankofsky).

Another white dancer who learned to Swing at the Savoy Ballroom, and then took his dance moves cross-country, was Solomon Rudowsky, later known as Dean Collins. Rudowsky grew up in Newark, New Jersey, with one brother and three sisters (who reportedly pushed him to learn dancing at an early age). As a teenager, he frequented the nightclubs of Harlem, and he learned to Lindy Hop by watching dancers at the Savoy. When he moved to California in 1936, he began honing his dance style in the nightclubs of Hollywood. Small framed and limber, Rudowsky dazzled the eye with his fast and agile footwork. He could propel himself into a multitude of spins, turning on a dime like a spinning toy top. He quickly established himself as one of the best dancers in the Los Angeles area. But he had trouble finding performance work. Deciding that his name was perhaps stifling his job opportunities, he decided to legally change it. Solomon Rudowsky became "Dean Collins." His widow, Mary Collins, notes that her husband's last name was never "Cohen," as is sometimes mistakenly written. She adds that her husband chose the name Dean Collins after he found a lost wallet belonging to a man with that name (Telephone interview).

Collins got his first lucky break when he was hired—not as a dancer, but as a choreographer—for the 1940 RKO motion picture *Let's Make Music*. Thinking he was interviewing for an $11-a-day job as a dance extra on the film, Collins was completely surprised when RKO hired him instead, for $100 a day, to choreograph the movie's dance scenes. Thanks to that job, Collins went on to work in a slew of Hollywood motion pictures in the 1940s (Dean Stewart, *Los Angeles Times*, "Dean Collins, Remembering Swing Dancer's King," August 5, 1984; reprinted in *Dance Action*, March, 1988, 12–13).

## Dean Collins and the Hollywood Dancers

Dean Collins, by many accounts, was a dancer with fast feet, fast fists, and a "short temper." His widow Mary Collins explains that, while he was easy enough to get along with, he was quick to defend himself. "He stood up for himself. He wouldn't let anyone take advantage of him." Collins's niece, Alycia Keys, agrees with that sentiment and adds: "He stood up for his family too. He was always a verbal tiger." Keys, who lived intermittently with her aunt and uncle throughout her youth, refers to Collins as "Uncle Dino" and remembers him as being "super intelligent" and "cunning"—especially when playing cards and shooting pool (Telephone interviews with Mary Collins and Alycia Keys).

The importance of Collins in the overall history of Swing dancing cannot be overlooked. He is credited not only with bringing the Lindy to California, and with being a remarkable dancer whose prowess is showcased in many motion picture musicals, but also with organizing a group of youthful dancers in Los Angeles—honing their Swing dancing skills and distinctive style and then promoting their talents with feisty persistence. Many of those dancers went on to perform in Hollywood movies themselves. And because the motion picture industry had a tremendous influence on popular styles of music and dance, Collins's style affected a whole new generation of Swing dancers.

"Dean was our Swing dance guru!" exclaims Jean Veloz, one of the Hollywood dancers who socially danced and performed with Collins in the 1940s. She explains that when Collins began organizing, promoting, and hosting Swing dance competitions at various nightclubs and restaurants in the Los Angeles area, a close-knit "clique of dancers" followed him and participated in the contests. Veloz was a frequent contest winner, and she proudly recalls, "I won $15 in prize money one night, which was a lot of money at the time!"

Jean Phelps Veloz (her maiden name is Phelps) remembers that because Lindy was all the rage then, everyone wanted to see it. The clubs would regularly be packed with spectators eager to watch the competitions, and there were often celebrities on hand as well. One night, after winning a dance contest at The Hollywood Café (the same club where she met Dean Collins for the first time), Veloz was invited over to the table of movie star and dancing phenomenon, Gene Kelly. "That was a big thrill," she gushes. "Gene Kelly introduced himself, congratulated me on my win, and then complimented my dancing abilities. Talk about inspiration!" (Telephone and personal interviews).

By the early 1940s, Jean Veloz and her brother Ray Phelps were two of the best Swing dancers in the Hollywood area. They often partnered each other in dance competitions and were a tough duo to beat. Ray

This photograph was taken on the set of the 1941 movie, *Buck Privates*. Dean Collins and his dance partner Jewel McGowan are pictured in the center (the identities of the other dance couples are uncertain). This was one of the many films that hired Collins for both his dancing skills and for his ability to provide a group of his dancing friends. In *Buck Privates*, Collins and McGowan have a brief onscreen solo, which spotlights their wonderful style. (© Universal Pictures / Courtesy of Photofest.)

Phelps recalls those days with great pleasure and suggests that he always did well in the contests because of his sister. He explains:

> ... she'd give the biggest smile in the world, and throw that arm up in the air—and she had 'em! (Ray Phelps in *Legends of Swing*, On Tap Productions, 2009)

A petite blond dancing dynamo, Jean Veloz developed a captivating style of Swing that brought her special attention and opportunities in Hollywood. Although she and her brother Ray grew up in Santa Maria, California, Veloz was first exposed to Swing dancing in Hollywood. In her own words:

> I went to Hollywood to visit my cousins and they took me to the clubs. I'd see these kids dancing, and I started learning some of the moves.

Then I'd take those moves back to Santa Maria with me and teach them to my friends. (Telephone interview)

When Veloz won a Swing competition at an American Legion auditorium in Santa Maria, circa 1939, she was inspired to better her dancing skills. A few years later, when she won first place in a competition in Hollywood at the American Legion Stadium (beating out over 500 other dancers), her life was changed. Her prize was a card in the Screen Actors Guild, along with a cameo appearance in the Hollywood motion picture *Swing Fever* (released by MGM in 1943). In *Swing Fever*, Jean Veloz dances with two partners, Don Gallager and Lenny Smith, trading off and taking turns with them both at the same time. The Kay Kyser Orchestra is featured on the bandstand during the scene, playing the song "One Girl and Two Boys." Veloz gives a marvelous dancing and acting performance. The SAG card enabled her to work in other movie productions, and her single-parent mother, who had always encouraged her children to dance, moved the Phelps family to Hollywood. While Ray served overseas during World War II, Jean continued to dance, performing in more than 20 Hollywood films.

Jean Veloz gives much credit to Dean Collins for molding the look of her Swing dance style. In 1945, Veloz and Collins were partners in the Warner Bros. movie *A Horn Blows at Midnight*. It should be noted that Collins's regular partner (for 11 years) was Jewel McGowan, who worked with him in numerous movies. McGowan was also a remarkable dancer, renowned for her "swivel"—a pronounced twisting action, on counts one and two of her basic step. A few of The movies that Collins and McGowan danced together in include *Buck Privates* (1941), *Springtime in the Rockies* (1942), *Always a Bridesmaid* (1943), and *Living It Up* (1945).

Irene Thomas was another Lindy dancer influenced by Dean Collins in the early 1940s. Thomas was one of the most innovative of the female dancers in the Hollywood group. Sliding, jumping, and experimenting with leg locks and body isolations, she was a "highly improvisational" dancer who mixed her Tap dance and Swing skills. One of her original variations, frequently seen in the Swing scenes of the early Hollywood films, is the women's leg-locking Quick Stop or, "the Drop," as Thomas used to call it. "I was ad-libbing one day and I just came up with that move," Thomas explains. "I used to dance it with Eddy Markwell, who was 6' 2". It really showed when I did 'the Drop' with him!" Another of Thomas's signature moves can be viewed

Jewel McGowan frequently partnered Dean Collins, in films of the 1940s. This photograph exemplifies their iconic, stylized look. Note the counterbalance between them, his "pike" body positioning, and her remarkable deep "swivel." (Courtesy of Mary Collins.)

in a simulated rainstorm scene in the movie, *The Powers Girl* (United Artists, 1943). While Dean Collins (holding an umbrella) dances with Jewel McGowan, Irene Thomas swings past her partner, Bob Ashley, and does what she calls a "Fanny Bump," or "Fanny Push," in which she deliberately juts her fanny out and then immediately resumes twisting forward again on the basic. That Fanny Bump became a popular women's Lindy styling step. Thomas also performs a "Fanny *Slide*," accelerating with tremendous momentum between her partner's legs in that same dance scene. She recalls that the movie director put a wet soapy patch of fabric on the seat of her underpants so she could keep the momentum going. It worked well. She skids the entire width of the pavilion on her backside. This is much like the slide maneuver performed by Whitey's Lindy Hoppers Frankie Manning and Ann Johnson in the 1930s and early 1940s. An article in *Life* magazine, accompanied by photographs, spotlights Manning and Johnson doing a Fanny Slide at the Savoy Ballroom ("Harlem's New 'Congeroo' Gives Girls A Workout," June 16, 1941, 49–50). Manning and Johnson also perform the same move in the 1941 movie *Hellzapoppin'*. But the umbrella scene in *The Powers Girl* put a whole new spin on things. Irene Thomas exclaims, "We were all soaking wet, and I had to rehearse that slide over and over again!" (Telephone interview).

Chuck Saggau was part of the Dean Collins group and worked in numerous films of the 1940s. He first started dancing at the Hollywood Palladium on Sundays; that's where he recalls first meeting Dean Collins. While he didn't participate in the Swing dance contests, he did get a lot of extra work in movies, including *Home in Indiana* and the short film, *Swinging on a Teagarden Gate* (with Jean Veloz), among others. One of Saggau's favorite movie experiences, however, was working in the 1943 Busby Berkeley film *The Gangs All Here* (20th Century Fox), in which he Swing dances with the lanky comedic actress Charlotte Greenwood and gets to speak a few lines. He notes that he rehearsed the scene with Greenwood for a couple of weeks before filming and, "during that time, she learned to Swing dance pretty well!" Chuck Saggau's wife Sally points out that Charlotte Greenwood liked to kick up her legs. "She had this way of kicking her legs out, kind of sideways, and then way up high," Sally recalls. I'm sure she wanted to get those kicks into her dance number." In their dance scene in *The Gangs All Here*, Greenwood does perform her high kicks, while Chuck Saggau darts underneath her legs, and does a flurry of solo Swing steps of his own (Telephone interview with Chuck and Sally Saggau).

The scene in *The Gangs All Here* shows off Chuck Saggau's dance talents as well as Greenwood's gangly flexibility and comedic abilities. But it's a short film made in 1944 (which also features Saggau) that is often viewed as the pinnacle of Swing dance comedy on film. *Groovie Movie* is a tongue-in-cheek, faux-documentary that traces the history of swing dancing. It's a campy classic, a comedy, produced and narrated by innovative filmmaker Pete Smith. He made a series of short, quirky films for MGM between the years of 1931 and 1955 that chronicled popular fads of those years. Along with Chuck Saggau, Jean Veloz, and Irene Thomas, the cast of dancers in *Groovie Movie* includes Arthur Walsh, Bob Ashley, Lenny Smith, and Kay Vaughn Smith. While the dancers demonstrate various Swing maneuvers, Pete Smith provides his own signature brand of zany satirical narration for the film. It's a magical mix of phenomenal dancing, and clever, comical entertainment.

Early California Lindy dancer Jean Phelps Veloz danced in a slew of 1940s Hollywood films. She is shown here (on the right) with her brother Ray Phelps at the Casa Manana ballroom, in Culver City, CA., dancing one of the signature moves of the Hollywood-style of Lindy, "the Drop." Jean and Ray continued dancing together over the years, so Phelps Veloz "wasn't too rusty" when she found herself back in the spotlight again during the 1990s Swing dance revival. (Courtesy of Jean Veloz.)

The all-white cast-members of *Groovie Movie* (with the exception of two black youngsters who share an onscreen moment in the film), were protégés of Dean Collins and danced on the Hollywood club circuit with him. They performed many of the same variations, and all danced in the same style—a smooth, slotted style of Lindy, which is attributed to Collins and which, later, became known as West Coast Swing. During the resurgence of Swing in the 1990s, this pre–West Coast style was labeled "Hollywood Style" by Swing dancers Sylvia Skylar and Erik Robison, who brilliantly recaptured the look and feel of it, and the name stuck. "Smooth Lindy," and even "LA Style" (as in "Los Angeles") were other names used to describe that particular style of Swing, and *Groovie Movie* became an important resource guide for students seeking to learn it.

## East vs. West

Interestingly, the word "Lindy" is never mentioned in *Groovie Movie*. Instead, the Swing dancing in the film is referred to as Boogie Woogie or Jitterbug. But Jean Veloz asserts, "We all called it 'Lindy,' though." She doesn't recall that she, or any of her dancing gang, used the term Lindy Hop. "It was just 'Lindy,'" she verifies.

The use of the term "Lindy Hop" was prevalent on the East Coast throughout the 1930s and 1940s. But in California, the Lindy dancers called what they were doing "Lindy," or "Jitterbug" (a term that became extremely popular, throughout the entire nation, for describing any sort of Swing dancing). Jean Phelps Veloz remembers that she started using the word "Lindy" in the early 1940s, when she began associating with Dean Collins. Before that time, she called everything she was dancing simply "Swing." Early Hollywood Lindy dancer Chuck Saggau also recalls that he originally referred to everything he danced as "Swing." "Just 'Swing,'" he states. He too picked up the word Lindy when he started hanging out with the Dean Collins group. "We never really took dance lessons," Saggau explains, "we all just learned from each other. And we started calling what we were dancing, 'The Lindy'" (Personal interview with Veloz; Telephone interview with Saggau).

Mary Collins was married to Dean Collins from 1964 until his passing in 1984. She asserts that her husband referred to his style of dancing as "the Lindy," and that he first learned the Lindy Hop at the Savoy Ballroom in New York, and subsequently "smoothed out" that style. Years later, the California smooth style of Swing became known as "West Coast Swing" and in fact, West Coast Swing became California's "official" state dance in 1988. The style is sometimes credited to Dean Collins, but according to Mary Collins (and many others who knew him), "Dean never called his style 'West Coast Swing.'" She suggests that "the term 'West Coast Swing' may have been created later by dance instructors, as a way of differentiating it from other Swing styles, like Jitterbug or East Coast Swing" (Telephone interview).

Jean Phelps Veloz always thought it was perfectly natural that the Swing terminology of California would be different from that of New York. She explains:

> Dancers from New York danced the Lindy very differently from the style that we were used to. Whenever we met dancers from New York, we saw

it right away. Their basic step moved in a circular pattern rather than on a straight-line slot. (Personal interview)

Early Hollywood Lindy dancer Irene Thomas concurs: "There were distinct differences between the styles of the East and the West Coasts." In 1946, Thomas left Los Angeles and moved to New York. She admits that "I tried to Swing dance in New York, but it was too different. I really couldn't dance with anyone there" (Telephone interview).

The difference between the New York Savoy-style "Lindy Hop" of the 1930s and the Hollywood "Lindy" of the 1940s is threefold. The first difference is in the movement of the basic. The Lindy Hop, as it was socially danced at Harlem's Savoy Ballroom (and is sometimes referred to as the Savoy-style), moved in a circle, often broadening into an oblong elliptical floor pattern. Lindy Hoppers generally stayed "squared off" to each other as they rotated their eight-count basics clockwise. The early California dancers, on the other hand, dancing Lindy in the style popularized in 1940s Hollywood films, moved their basics in a straight-line slot. So the movement of the basic in the two separate styles differed noticeably in shape. Dancers have always adjusted their styles and movements to match their dance environments, and it is generally agreed that slot dancing developed out of spatial restrictions and concerns. A circular basic worked well on a spacious floor, such as the one at the Savoy Ballroom in New York, but on the small and often over-crowded dance floors of the intimate Hollywood clubs, the slotted-style made good sense. Dancers could line up, shoulder to shoulder, and move past each other without getting in each other's way. Another influential force in the development of slot dancing involves choreography for stage and film: slot dancing is ideal for showing profiles of every dancer in a scene, all at the same time.

A second difference between the two styles involved body positioning, the basic stance for balance, style, and interplay with a partner. The original body positioning of the East Coast Lindy Hop was vertical, and the earliest Savoy dancers (like George "Shorty" Snowden) danced upright in the style of the 1920s Charleston. However, as the music changed and Lindy Hoppers began bouncing to the "new" swingin' sounds of the 1930s, they bent their knees more and struck a forward, "over your haunches" stance. Frankie Manning is credited, circa 1934, for taking the Lindy Hop "horizontal," leaning forward from the waist and stretching the leg back for a long-legged line (Manning and Millman, 2007, 80–81). The Lindy dancer of the West Coast struck the exact opposite position. The Hollywood-style required counterbalance between the partners, an "anchoring back," with both partners leaning away from each other. Dean Collins danced in what is often described as a high diver's "pike position," but his group of California Lindy dancers, for the most part, danced more upright and vertically than their East Coast counterparts.

Thirdly, both the Lindy Hop, and the West Coast Lindy, had many of the same variations in common. But there were a few specific moves at the heart of, and peculiar to, each style. The Lindy Hop retained more Charleston at its core, in fact, Frankie Manning suggests in his autobiography that Charleston became so absorbed into the Lindy Hop (with variations such as Hand-to-Hand, Squat, Side-by-Side, Flying Charleston, Back or Tandem, to name a few) that he didn't think of it, originally, as being a separate dance. It was all Lindy Hop (49). The Hollywood Lindy didn't utilize much Charleston, but instead played heavily on a six-count variation, later called "the Sugar Push," in which the leader (in open position) blocks his partner from walking past him on the slot. Another specific move for the Savoy-style Lindy Hopper, the "Swing Out," was used to break away from closed to open position, moving through a piece of the basic called "the face-off." In the Hollywood-style of the dance, that "Swing Out" was replaced by a straight "Send Out" of the follower onto the slot. Also, the Lindy Hoppers' "circular" basic step was replaced on the West Coast by a specific move that Dean Collins created, which was later called "the Whip." (The Whip eventually became one of the basic vocabulary steps of West Coast Swing.) The whipping action in the early Lindy was a shoulder twist for the leader and a strong push out, or "whip" (on counts 5–6 of the eight-count basic), which propelled the follower right back onto the slot where she began.

## The Big Band Era of Swing

Early Hollywood Lindy dancer Jean Veloz often declares: "Timing is everything!" And for the Swing dancers in the Los Angeles area in the late 1930s and early 40s, that is clearly the case. They were in the right place at the right time, with the right skills, when the big band era of swing officially got underway. Hollywood producers and choreographers celebrated the "new fad" with scripts loaded with Swing dancing scenes and situations.

Bandleader Benny Goodman is credited with being the lightening rod that sparked the big band explosion, catapulting swing into national prominence. In the early 1930s, America's major ballrooms offered mostly "sweet" sentimental sounds of orchestras such as Ted Weems, Lawrence Welk, and Sammy Kaye (although Latin bands were also in demand because Tangos and Rumbas were popular with dancers). But as the Great Depression was coming to an end, the country was ready for a brighter, more upbeat sound. Swing music had already been around for some time, but suddenly "hot" bands that played swing with a driving danceable beat were becoming popular.

In 1934, "Let's Dance," a network series on NBC radio hit the airwaves. The program hired three bands: the Kel Murray band (known for its bright, "sweet" sound), Xavier Cugat's "Latin" Orchestra, and Benny Goodman's "hot" swingin' band. Broadcast live from coast to coast, "Let's Dance" was a three-hour weekly program staged to simulate an imaginary ballroom. As the bands performed, listeners could dance in the "no-cost" comfort of their own living rooms. On the West Coast, the "Let's Dance" series was heard three hours later than in New York. That time difference meant that, in California, teenage audiences were tuning in to Goodman's "hot" new sound, and his band developed a youthful following. When Goodman embarked on a cross-country tour in the summer of 1935 (which reportedly met with "lukewarm reception" from audiences in Ohio, Michigan, Wisconsin, Colorado, and Utah), teens in Los Angeles eagerly awaited his arrival. And on the historic night of August 21, 1935, at the corner of Third and Vermont inside a ballroom called The Palomar, over 2,500 enthusiastic young fans gathered to see the band play live. *Los Angeles Times* writer Don Heckman interviewed Benny Goodman 50 years later, in 1985. Goodman recalled The Palomar event:

> We started out rather modestly, sticking to the softer arrangements. But, except for a few kids down in front, the crowd wasn't very responsive. After a while I said, "Well, forget it! If we're going to flop, we might as well play our kind of music." (Don Heckman, *Los Angeles Times*, "50 Years Later, Goodman Recalls Birth of Swing," Part VI/Wednesday, August 21, 1985, 2)

Bunny Berigan could blow a trumpet with a cool clear tone. Gene Krupa could drive his rhythms on the drums to a feverish pitch, and Fletcher Henderson could work his magic on a song—arranging it in a simple harmonic manner that gave it soul and made it "swing." With Goodman's gleaming clarinet at the helm, the band began swingin' the house with its hottest sounds, and the crowd went wild. As Goodman himself describes it:

> To our complete amazement, half the crowd stopped dancing and came surging around the stand . . . That first big roar from the crowd was one of the sweetest sounds I've ever heard in my life. (Goodman in Firestone, 1993, 149)

In reality, years before Goodman had even formed a band, there were plenty of bands that were swinging (Teddy Hill, Chick Webb, and Fletcher Henderson, to name a few). Legendary Lindy Hopper Frankie Manning comments: "It was when Fletcher Henderson was hired as an arranger for Benny Goodman, that Goodman truly started to swing" (PBDA video archives, 1991). In fact, Benny Goodman himself credited Henderson's arrangements for providing his popular "new" sound, and the main collection of Goodman's music charts were purchased directly from Henderson (Starr and Waterman, 2003, 129).

Nonetheless, as history records it, Benny Goodman's performance at The Palomar in 1935 gave birth to the era of swing. And while he clearly borrowed on Henderson's genius, it should be pointed out that Benny Goodman was an extremely talented bandleader and jazz improviser, who enlisted a remarkable assortment of talented musicians into his bands (breaking down racial barriers in adding black musicians, such as Teddy Wilson, Lionel Hampton, Charlie Christian, and Cootie Williams to his smaller ensembles). Benny Goodman took Henderson's "hot" swingin' sound and made it his own. His Palomar performance struck a chord with white audiences across the country, and he was quickly crowned the "King of Swing" by the national media.

The time was suddenly right for swing music and Swing dancing to take center stage. Hotels, nightclubs, and ballrooms in many major cities began providing national radio hook-ups, broadcasting their musical entertainment live. Jukeboxes installed in soda fountains, restaurants, and nightclubs all over the United States, were stocked with records and they, in turn, encouraged record sales. The music industry thrived as more "hot" bands developed loyal followings and record companies began selling records as never before.

By the year 1938, the mainstream media had become fully aware of the swing phenomenon and countless numbers of newspapers and magazine articles referred to it. *Life* magazine devoted 10 pages to the subject in an article titled, "Swing: The Hottest and Best Kind of Jazz Reaches Its Golden Age." The article was accompanied by photographs of numerous big band musicians, and reported that:

> ... as of August 1938, Swing is the most popular kind of popular music ... Jitterbugs are the extreme swing addicts who get so excited by its music that they cannot stand or be still while it is being played. (Aug. 8, 1938, 50–60)

A newspaper headline of 1938 reads, "Higher Soars the Swing Fever: The Business of Jam Jive and Jitterbug Seems to Suit the Temper of the Times." The accompanying article asserts that, while some may frown upon it, "swing is thriving" (Gama Gilbert, *New York Times*, Aug. 14, 1938, 6). Two of the most popular songs of that year were swing tunes: the Andrew Sisters "Bei Mir Bist Du Schoen," and Ella Fitzgerald and Chick Webb's "A Tisket A Tasket," and two cartoons created in 1938 (released the following year) attest to the popularity of the swing fad. *Jitterbug Follies*, written and directed by Milt Gross for MGM, and *I'm Just a Jitterbug*, by Walter Lantz for Universal Pictures, are delightful short films featuring animated characters in Swing dance situations. A number of documentary newsreels covering Swing competitions were produced that year, including footage from the annual Harvest Moon Ball. And Hollywood feature-length films of 1938, with scenes spotlighting Swing dancing, include RKO's *Radio City Revels*, 20th Century Fox's *Hold that Co-Ed*, and Paramount Picture's *College Swing*.

## Where They Danced

By the late 1930s, America's ballrooms were hiring "hot" big bands, such as Tommy Dorsey, Jimmy Dorsey, Chick Webb, Artie Shaw, Count Basie, and Glenn Miller. In the Los Angeles area, along with the large dance halls, there were also a number of intimate clubs that hired smaller ensembles and encouraged dancing. Jazz writer Floyd

Levin, for instance, heard a Dixieland band perform at The Hangover in the mid-1940s, and he recalls " ... the smiling dancers whirling around the postage stamp–sized floor. ... " There was an old stuffed moose head hanging over the club's bar, and Levin comments, "I think that moose was smiling too!" (Levin, 2002, 6, 7).

Bandleader Louis Prima owned a club called The Jitterbug House and Billy Wilkerson, publisher of *The Hollywood Reporter*, opened the Café Trocadero on Sunset Blvd for the upscale crowd (with "chateau-briand" on the menu). The Hollywood Café was a favorite spot of early Lindy dancers Ray Phelps and Jean Veloz (Jim Heimann, "Those Hollywood Nights," *Los Angeles Times*, May 21, 2006, S18; Personal interview with Jean Veloz).

Nat King Cole's band was the house band at the 331 Club in the early 1940s, and the club's frequent jam sessions featured Cole himself on piano. Cole later graduated to The Trocadero and his own "King Cole Room" (Stan Britt, 1989, 10). Billy Berg, a white nightclub owner, owned the Capri Club, The Trouville, and a club named after himself: Billy Berg's. Charlie Parker and Dizzy Gillespie played their "new" bebop swing music at Billy Berg's in the mid-1940s, and Slim Gaillard played their frequently enough that his band was advertised in *The Billboard* magazine as "The be-bop barbarians from Billy Berg's Beanery" (4 STAR Records advertisement, April 13, 1946, 23). In 1947, Louis Jordan's band was in Los Angeles for a gig at Billy Berg's when Jordan was the victim of a knife-wielding attack by his own wife, Fleecie Jordan, over an extramarital affair. Hospitalized for gashes and stab wounds, Louis Jordan (and all the musicians in his band) were out of work for "about six weeks." The Jordans eventually divorced, and Louis later married Florence "Vicky" Hayes, the dancer with whom he was having the affair (Scott Knowles DeVeaux, 1999, 386; John Chilton, 1997, 132–134, 168; Aaron Izenhall quoted in Chilton, 134).

Club Trinidad, The Streets of Paris, and The Latin Quarter were a few of the other small clubs favored by the early Hollywood Swing dancers. There were also elegant supper clubs like the Cocoanut Grove, housed in the Ambassador Hotel in Los Angeles, where many of the best bands played. And there were civic halls like the Pasadena Civic Auditorium, which could handle gigantic crowds. But one of the largest, and most renowned clubs on the West Coast, was the site of Benny Goodman's Los Angeles triumph, The Palomar Ballroom.

Originally known as Rainbow Gardens, The Palomar Ballroom boasted a 16,000-foot dance floor and was open every night of the week for dining, floorshow entertainment, and dancing. In 1939, bandleader Artie Shaw set a house record there, pulling in a crowd of 8,753 dancers. Sadly, however, in October of that same year, an electrical fire broke out in the building. Charlie Barnet's band was featured in the ballroom at the time, and the fire was so fierce and spread so quickly, "the band members were not able to save their instruments or their music." The Palomar Ballroom, totally consumed by the flames, burned to the ground (Gault, 1989, 52–53).

The Hollywood Palladium opened its doors on Halloween night, October 31, 1940, replacing The Palomar as "the" place to dance in Los Angeles. A reported 10,000 attendees packed the house for that premiere night, which featured the musical entertainment of the Tommy Dorsey Orchestra with Frank Sinatra on vocals, along with Connie Haines and the Pied Pipers. Advertised as costing over $1 million to build, the Palladium was a state-of-the-art ballroom with spotlights and dimmers, and an enormous wood floor cushioned with cork for maximum dancing comfort. All the top dance bands played there in the 1940s, and it became world-renown as a star-studded center of entertainment. While suffering wear and tear during a decline of use in the 1970s and 80s, the Hollywood Palladium was utilized for dances during the resurgence of Swing in the 1990s. The ballroom was refurbished and continued to sponsor events into the twenty-first century (Gregory Paul Williams, 2006, 266; Gault, 73–77).

Located on Ocean Park Pier in Ocean Park, California, Casino Gardens was the venue where Dean Collins first exhibited his "contest-winning style," and was, by all accounts, "enormous." According to its own publicity, it could handle a crowd of 10,000, although *The Billboard* magazine puts the club's capacity at 7,500. In 1944, the ballroom was purchased by bandleader Tommy Dorsey, his brother Jimmy, and bandleader Harry James ("Loads of Dough for Orks," July 11, 1942, 21; "Dean Collins," *Dance Action*, 1988, 13; Gault, 1989, 113–114).

Casa Manana, in Culver City, near Los Angeles, competed with the Casino Gardens for patrons. Originally known as The Green Mill, and then as Frank Sebastian's Cotton Club, Casa Manana gained acclaim for hiring the country's top white, *and* black orchestras. Count Basie, Jimmy Lunceford, Duke Ellington and Charlie Barnet all performed there; in the early 1940s, Louis Armstrong and his orchestra did a series of significant live radio broadcasts from the ballroom.

One of the most architecturally exquisite ballrooms in the world, the Casino Ballroom on Catalina Island was constructed as the largest circular ballroom in the world. William Wrigley Jr., chewing gum magnate and owner of the Chicago Cubs baseball team, purchased the entire island of Catalina, off the coast of Southern California, in 1919. His 15,000 square foot ballroom was named the "Casino Ballroom," after the Italian word for "casino," meaning "gathering place." There was never any gambling at the Casino Ballroom but gather there, the dancers did! Steamships carried passengers from San Pedro (near Los Angeles) to the island, where sometimes as many as 6,000 dancers packed the Casino on summer nights (William Sanford White, Steven Kern Tice, 2000, 45–51, 136–142).

The magnificent Casino Ballroom on California's Catalina Island opened in 1929, boasting the largest circular dance floor in the world. During summer months, throughout the 1930s and 1940s, the ballroom played host to top-notch popular big bands every night of the week. (Courtesy of the Catalina Island Museum.)

Catalina Island's Casino Ballroom juts out over the water, offering spectacular views of the ocean and the picturesque harbor town of Avalon. (Courtesy of Tamara Stevens.)

Swing dance aficionado Jim Stevens lived on Catalina Island in the summer seasons from 1936 to 1940, and he recalls dancing in the Casino Ballroom "every night of the week to well-known bands like Bob Crosby, Kay Kyser, Hal Grayson, Jan Garber, and some lesser known bands like the Herbie Kay Orchestra." He describes the excitement of racing to the pier to greet the Big White Steamer as it docked in Avalon Bay, and diving for coins that arriving passengers threw into the water (as they disembarked the ship). Then, he spent those coins on his nightly admission ticket into the Casino Ballroom. The ballroom's maple, white oak, and rosewood floor with an under-floor of cork was, in Stevens's words, "the most comfortable dance floor in the world." And he explains:

> You could walk out the huge French doors, onto the ballroom's romantic balcony and feel the ocean breezes, and see the twinkling lights of Avalon Bay. Every night there was a magical experience. (Personal interview with Jim Stevens)

Stevens made special trips to the island in the mid- and later 1940s to hear bands like Les Brown with vocalist Doris Day, and he remembers seeing Stan Kenton play there in the early 1950s. During the 1990s

Swing revival, the Casino Ballroom played host to Swing Camp Catalina (see Chapter 10), one of the largest swing events in the world at the time and, into the twenty-first century, the ballroom continued to be the site of music and dance extravaganzas.

A beachfront Spanish-tiled ballroom in Balboa, California, called the Rendezvous Ballroom, attracted hoards of high school and college students from the 1920s through the 1940s. When the dance floor got so crowded there was no room to move, a new dance was born at the Rendezvous: a dance to swing music that could be done in place with couples dancing "on a dime," called the Balboa (see Chapter 7). While the Rendezvous completely burned to the ground in the mid-1960s, an older ballroom a few blocks away called the Balboa Pavilion continued to draw dancers for special events into the twenty-first century (Giordano, 2007, 103–104, 203–204).

The Trianon and The Aragon, two grand dancing palaces in Chicago that exuded the utmost in luxury, became models for popular ballrooms in Los Angeles in the 1940s. The Trianon Ballroom in Southgate, California opened its doors in 1941. Bandleader Horace Heidt later purchased The Trianon and reportedly inspired other big band leaders to own ballrooms of their own when it was publicized that he had made back his $100,000 investment purchase, and cleared an additional $40,000, in just one year of operating The Trianon (Jimmy Contratto, "From a Nightclub to a Ballroom," *The Billboard* magazine, January 10, 1942, 11; and Ronald D. Cohen, "Music Goes to War" in Roger W. Lotchin, 2000, 53).

In 1943, 25-year-old Swing dance promoter Harry Schooler took a 10-year lease on old ballroom in Santa Monica, California, refurbished it with a giant dance floor, and gave it a new name: The Aragon. Business bustled at The Aragon until 1947, when a fire destroyed an amusement pier near the ballroom and, at the same time, the Red Car, a transportation system that carried passengers to and from the ballroom, halted its operations. On the brink of financial ruin, the Aragon Ballroom hired the Lawrence Welk Band, which had been working for 10 years at the Trianon Ballroom in Chicago. The Lawrence Welk family moved to California, and the Aragon was back in business again. In the early 1950s, Los Angeles television station KTLA began broadcasting Lawrence Welk's programs on a weekly basis live from the Aragon Ballroom. And by the mid-1950s, 40 million viewers were watching "The Lawrence Welk Show" every Saturday night on ABC Television (Time.com, "Amusements: King of Swing Shift," 1943; Cohen, "Music Goes to War," in Lotchin, 1999, 53; Ian Frazier, 2001, 69).

## War Time Hollywood

By the early 1940s, swing was in "full swing," and the better-known big bands were kept consistently busy year 'round. With engagements at hotels, nightclubs and ballrooms, they also played for USO dances, Red Cross dances, and various benefit functions, in honor of military personnel. America's dance venues were at their lucrative peak, attracting capacity crowds, as servicemen and their supporters enjoyed nights out on the town—reveling in upbeat music, and dancing like there was no tomorrow.

During World War II, and even prior to the attack on Pearl Harbor, December 7, 1941, the State of California worked with the War Department on production of ships and warplanes for the country's weapons arsenal. In the Los Angeles area, 55,000 aircraft factory employees got off work after midnight. Most of them were young (the average swing shift worker was 21), and their average shift ran from 4 PM to 12:30 AM. "Swing shift dances" were designed as entertainment venues for defense workers when they clocked out of their night shift jobs. The dances were the brainchild of Harry Schooler, a Vega Aircraft worker who began producing and hosting after-midnight dances at the Elks Hall in Burbank, California, for his co-workers. His event immediately caught on. Years before Schooler opened his Aragon ballroom, he was a clever promoter of dancing events. He took his swing shift dances to the Long Beach Auditorium and to Casino Gardens, where he featured such regulars as Bob Crosby and Alvino Ray on the bandstand from 12:30 AM to 5 AM The "swing shift" dance concept caught on across the country (Kevin Starr, 2005, 221; Time.com, "Amusements: King of Swing Shift," 1943; Life, "Life Goes to a Swing Shift Dance," January 19, 1942, 86–89).

The Billboard magazine notes that Duke Ellington drew a record swing shift audience at Casino Gardens in 1942, and that "swing shifters" were solicited to attend the dances through the Swing Shift News, a circular distributed among California's shipbuilding and aircraft employees ("Loads of Dough for Orks," July 11, 1942, 21).

When Tommy Dorsey purchased the Casino Gardens in 1944, Harry Schooler was hired as an "idea man"; his job was to think up promotional gimmicks that would bring customers into the ballroom. There were gimmicks for most nights of the week, including Sunday nights, when Kaye's Jewelers gave six lucky patrons diamond rings (Peter J. Levinson, 2006, 210).

One of California's more unique clubs was a World War II phenomenon called, The Hollywood Canteen. Movie star John Garfield dreamed up the idea of a ballroom where servicemen could dance and be entertained without admission charges. He enlisted the help of his friend, Hollywood starlet Bette Davis, to help him with the project, and Davis immediately leased an old livery stable at 1451 Cahuenga Blvd, near Sunset Blvd. Together, they transformed the building into a Western-themed ballroom with large painted murals, and wagon wheel chandeliers. According to MCA's press materials, the Hollywood Canteen debuted on October 3, 1942, with a dance floor that accommodated an average of 2,000 servicemen and a snack bar that ran the entire length of the ballroom. Refreshments and snacks were complimentary (there was no alcohol served and all the food was donated by companies in exchange for publicity). Each night, a rotating staff of 300 volunteers ran the club. Top Hollywood movie stars gave up their free evenings to entertain the crowds. They danced with the military personnel, served food (even washed dishes in the kitchen), and signed autographs. All in all, it was a hugely successful enterprise. It brought publicity to those involved in funding the club. The press printed photos of the movie stars in attendance, which furthered the careers of the movie stars themselves, and the venue provided great entertainment for the servicemen. Los Angeles was a major departure point for young men heading into the Pacific, and an evening at The Hollywood Canteen would have no doubt boosted their spirits (Dennis McDougal, 2001, 95; Otto Friedrich, 1997, 108).

During World War II, while servicemen and war-effort personnel were abroad, pop culture in America was dramatically changing. Musical trends were leading away from big band dance music. Ballrooms closed down as fewer people went out dancing, and nightclubs began booking smaller bands. Vocalists crooning sentimental ballads grew in popularity, and listening to music trumped dancing to it. Then, partnered social dancing in the 1950s began to give way to the coming "new" trend of the 1960s—the individual solo dances.

# 7

# A Dance by Any Other Name ... (Various Styles of Partnered Swing)

As the swing craze gathered steam in the mid-1930s, and the Lindy Hop spread nationwide, many offshoot styles of the dance emerged. The "Lindy," which developed in California, was closest in similarity to the original Harlem style (see Chapter 6), but many other regions developed Swing styles of their own. All the different styles and specialty dances of Swing have much in common. They are all danced (mainly) to swing music and are all counted in either six or eight beat rhythms. And while they can all be choreographed, performed as show numbers, or danced competitively, they are primarily social dances—based on leading and following a partner (excluding line dances) without set routines. However, there are a few obvious contrasting elements amongst the styles, which are better understood when examining each of them separately.

## Lindy Hop (and "the Lindy")

The Lindy Hop, born in Harlem, New York, in the late 1920s, is the original style of social-partnered Swing dancing. With Afro-American roots, it was the creation of street dancers, night owls, men and women of the working class who toiled to survive, sang their music from the gut, and spoke their stories from the heart. The language of the Lindy Hop was never the "Queen's English." Unlike the formal Ballroom dances, it never attempted to be prim and proper, never cared about social acceptability. It is American slang; a dance of many moods and individual expression, but it is always meant to be at its essence, a joyful celebration from the soul.

Lindy Hop is an eight-count pattern of single steps and rhythmic shuffles. The Lindy Hopper dances a circular basic with slightly bent knees, swaying torso and hip motions, and uses the entire body (not just the arms and legs), for a flowing smooth line. There is a gentle bounce inherent in the dance, a "pushing down" toward the earth in an even-pulsing rhythm, indicative of Afro-American dance styles. The Lindy Hop can be the most show-stopping style of Swing, with lots of kicks and character moves. It can be danced at breakneck speed (viewable in vintage film footage of Whitey's Lindy Hoppers' routines, which continue to be cause for awe and amazement), but it can also be danced to moderately up-tempo, medium, and even slow bluesy tunes, with ease and natural grace.

An eight-count rhythm is the foundation of the dance. However, from its outset, the Lindy Hop also incorporated six-count rhythmic moves. Legendary Lindy Hopper Frankie Manning remembers that the first variation he learned in his earliest exposure to the dance was actually a six-count pattern called the "Jig." Danced in closed position, with both partners facing each other, the Jig is a simple kick pattern, which Manning points out can clearly be seen in the dancers' footwork in the 1929 short film, *After Seben* (Paramount) (Telephone interview with Manning, March 5, 2009; *After Seben* is viewable on YouTube.com). The combining of both eight-count and six-count rhythms in the Lindy Hop has always allowed for a vast variety of moves and syncopations.

A 1943 *Life* magazine article labels the Lindy Hop as America's "truly national dance." The article is evidence that, although the word "Jitterbug" was used extensively in the 1940s, the term "Lindy Hop" was also widely recognized at the time. The *Life* article includes a photo layout of dancers performing signature variations of the style, such as the "Jig-Walk," "Trucking," and the "Suzy Q." Stanley Catron and Kaye Popp (two Swing dancers from the 1943 Broadway musical *Something for the Boys*) are featured on the magazine cover and in the photo layout demonstrating "floor steps" and "shine steps." Two of Whitey's Lindy Hoppers, Leon James and Willa Mae Ricker, are featured demonstrating "air steps," and are described as: "superlative performers who have exhibited their art throughout the world" (*Life*, "The Lindy Hop: A True National Folk Dance Has Been Born In USA," August 23, 1943, 95–103).

Improvisation has always been an important element in the Lindy Hop. Skilled dancers play with phrases in the music, hear and respond to musical "breaks," and interplay with live swingin' bands, communing with the riffs and musical arrangements. There is general agreement among the musicians who played the Savoy Ballroom that the Lindy Hoppers helped the musicians "find their groove." Likewise, the early dancers at the Savoy agree that the musicians inspired them to perform moves, and syncopations, they never knew they had in them. As jazz critic and scholar Nat Hentoff eloquently explains it:

> Night after night, the dancers and musicians at the Savoy spurred one another on to greater heights and earthier depths—always with an attitude of elegance. (Hentoff quoted in Robert G. O'Meally, 1998, 287)

Duke Ellington credited bandleader Chick Webb's success at the Savoy to Webb's relationship with the dancers. In *Music Is My Mistress: Memoirs*, Ellington writes:

> ...The reason why Chick Webb had such control, such command of his audiences at the Savoy Ballroom, was because he was always in communication with the dancers and felt it the way they did. (1976, 100)

Legendary Lindy Hopper Frankie Manning agrees that Chick Webb played for the dancers. He would see what a dancer was doing, Manning explains, and he would "catch it" on the drums. Bandleader Louis Jordan, according to Manning, was another great communicator with the dancers. He would tailor his solos to fit what the dancers were doing, and the dancers would respond with rhythmic steps that matched what he was playing. In the 1988 film, *The Call of the Jitterbug*, musician Dizzy Gillespie emphasizes the trade off between the musicians and the dancers, and he comments: "The best music is the music that is written for dance. Dancing enhances music." Then, reflecting on what he had just said, Gillespie laughs and says, "Let me write that down, please!" (Manning in PBDA video archives, 1991; Ken Burns, *Jazz*, "Norma Miller and Frankie Manning," June 26, 1997, 15; Gillespie in *The Call of the Jitterbug*, 1988).

Overtime, as popular tastes in music moved away from swing, the Lindy Hop disappeared into relative obscurity—until its resurgence in the 1980s, when a whole new generation of Swing dance enthusiasts embraced it again.

## Jitterbug/East Coast Swing

The origin of the word "Jitterbug," used as a Swing dance term, may actually be impossible to trace. The old English etymology of "jitter" comes from "chitter," meaning a tremulous sound, or quaver, of the voice. "Chyttering" referred to quivering, as in shaking or shivering in the cold (Hensleigh Wedgwood, 1878, 147). In American English, "jitter" also refers to shaking and quivering, but it is often suggested that the word stems from a compound form of the two words: "gin" and "bitters," and that it refers to the condition of "the whiskey jitters"—the tremors and twitching of an alcoholic's craving for liquor. Liquor, in fact, is sometimes referred to as "the jitter-sauce." Bandleader Cab Calloway gives himself credit for originally coining the word, "jitterbug," during the mid-1930s, before it was a Swing dance term. In a 1957 issue of *Jet*, Calloway explains:

> Years ago I had a trombonist we called "Bug." He liked to hoist a few before playing to steady his nerves but he still shook a little every time he mounted the bandstand and finally "Bug" became "Jitterbug." (Nov. 28, 1957, 30)

Cab Calloway's "Jitterbug" song of 1934 refers to a man who drinks heavily at night and wakes up with the jitters every morning. And while there's no mention of dancing in that song, Calloway's 1935 short film, *Jitterbug Party*, does create a sense of association between the word "jitterbug," and social Swing dancing.

Benny Goodman is credited for popularizing swing music throughout white mainstream America in the mid-1930s and, suddenly, although Lindy Hoppers had been doing it for years, Swing dancing was a "new" craze, with a "new" name: "Jitterbug." Iconic Lindy Hopper Norma Miller states that the word "Jitterbug" was the "white word for the Lindy Hop" (*The Call of the Jitterbug*, 1988). White America immediately embraced the word "Jitterbug," and by the late 1930s and throughout the 1940s, mainstream media writers and announcers used it as a general term—in reference not only to Swing dancing but also to the Swing dancers themselves. A 1938 newspaper headline in the *New York Times*, for example, reads, "Swing Bands put 23,400 in Frenzy: Jitterbugs Cavort at Randalls Island . . ." (May 30, 13). And, in 1940, *Time* magazine reported on a patient at a neurologist's office who complained of "spells." Whenever the patient had caffeine or "took a nip of alcohol," he would lose control of his leg muscles and "leap like a jitterbug" ("Medicine: Family Dance," October 28, np).

Regional and specialty dances that developed in those years, like Shag and Balboa, were also often referred to by media sources as "Jitterbug." A 1938 newspaper article, for instance, reports that "Manhattan's jitterbugs turned out 6,000 strong," at a benefit dance ("to swing for charity"), and the jitterbugging audience was engaged in "the most tireless and violent shagging ever seen outside of Harlem" (*New York Times*, "Swing Carnival Held to Benefit Charity," June 13, 15). The various line dances that became popular in those years, like the Big Apple and the Shim Sham, were generally thrown into the pot of dances called the "Jitterbug" as well.

Lindy Hop legend, Frankie Manning recalls first hearing the word "Jitterbug" at a Harvest Moon Ball, "in 1935 or '36." As Manning puts it:

> One of the *Movietone News* announcers said, "Look at those Jitterbugs dancing!" But we were all doing the Lindy Hop ... Jitterbug was a word given to the Lindy Hoppers to describe what they were dancing. (PBDA video archives, 1991)

Although "Jitterbug" originally referred to any style of dance done to swing music, instructors eventually came to use the term to mean "six-count Swing," as opposed to the eight-count Lindy Hop. Danced with either single-time, double-time, or triple-time footwork, the basic step of Jitterbug can be stationary, or can move in a circular pattern. Many of Jitterbug's kicks and "character moves" are very reminiscent of the Lindy Hop, and all of its variations can be incorporated into Lindy Hop.

The term "East Coast Swing" was originally employed as a means of differentiating between the look of the Swing dancers on the East Coast and their West Coast counterparts. At some point, however, dance instructors began labeling a single time, "easier version," of Jitterbug as the "East Coast Swing." For dancers who had trouble with quick footwork and found the triple-step too challenging, East Coast Swing replaced triples with single (two-beat) steps. There are hundreds, if not thousands, of patterns that can be led and followed in East Coast Swing. Ideal for the beginning Swing student, it is an easy dance to gain proficiency in before attempting the more challenging footwork of the triple-time Jitterbug, or the more complex rhythms of the Lindy Hop or West Coast Swing.

## West Coast Swing

Proclaimed by the state legislature as "California's official state dance" in 1988, West Coast Swing is similar to the Lindy Hop in that it uses patterns of both six and eight-count rhythms. However, a distinctive characteristic is that, like the early Hollywood-style of the Lindy (see Chapter 6), it is danced in a straight-line slot. While the history of the Lindy Hop is well documented, and there is a general consensus amongst dancers and historians as to how that particular dance evolved, the development and evolution of the West Coast Swing is not as straight forward. In fact, in examining the links between the early style of Dean Collin's California style of Lindy, the smooth style of Arthur Murray's Sophisticated Swing, Western Swing (Country and Western), the Bop, and then, eventually, West Coast Swing (with a return to the Hollywood-style in the 1990s) there is much that is open to interpretation. This is due, in no small part, to the fact that California dancers went right on dancing through the years of World War II, and even through the decades of the fifties, sixties, and seventies—adapting the Lindy to fit the changing popular styles of music and dance. In New York, the Lindy Hop virtually disappeared like some forgotten notebook tucked away in a drawer. When the drawer was reopened in the early 1980s, the dance was brought back to life by the likes of Lindy Hop legends Frankie Manning and Norma Miller. But, in California, the Lindy never disappeared. Thanks to the efforts of local dancers who formed swing clubs and associations bent on preserving the California style, the Lindy developed and evolved— eventually turning into West Coast Swing, a dance that has its own particular vocabulary of movements.

West Coast Swing is often referred to as a "dancer's dance": as the follower's footwork only rarely "mirrors" the leader's footwork, "learning" the basics is a necessity. "Slinky" and "sophisticated" are words often associated with West Coast Swing, especially when it is danced at slow tempos. At faster tempos, the dance inspires such words as "slick" and "smooth." While the early Hollywood Lindy dancers utilized a "twist, twist" on counts 1–2 of the followers walking basic (reminiscent of the follower's part in the Lindy Hop), the twisting was replaced by a smooth "walk walk" on the followers' 1–2, sometime in the 1960s.

There is no consensus on when West Coast Swing actually got its name, although most of the early Hollywood Lindy dancers suggest it was in the decade of the 1960s. Prior to that time, they were still calling it "Lindy" or "Jitterbug." While West Coast Swing originated in California, many similar styles of slotted Swing evolved in other parts of the country and took on names and nuances of their own. In Texas, for instance, a Dallas variation of West Coast Swing is often called "the Push," while in Houston it's referred to as "the Whip." In the late 1950s, a similar slotted dance style emerged at the Club Imperial ballroom in St. Louis, Missouri. It became known as Imperial Swing, although it is also sometimes referred to as St. Louis Slot dancing. In Washington, DC, West Coast Swing's closest cousin is known as DC Swing, or DC Hand Dancing (which is danced with a one-handed hold, mainly in open position). And even particular styles of Bop and Shag share common character traits with West Coast Swing.

## Western Swing

In the American Southwest during the 1930s and 1940s, there were a number of dance bands that developed a uniquely western sound and style. Touring and playing for dancers at county fairs, country festivals, hoedowns, and barn dances, these bands played an eclectic mix of musical styles, giving them all a "country and western" twist; with steel guitars, harmonicas and fiddles, even banjos and mandolins. During the big band era of swing music, when rags, blues, and the sounds of jazz were added to their playlists—a phenomenon called "western swing" was born. Originally, the sound was labeled "hillbilly swing," or "country swing," even "Texas swing." However, by the mid-1940s, most everyone was referring to the sound as "western swing."

The term "western swing" refers to a style of swing music, rather than a style of dance. There is actually, no specific or unique dance that matches that label. However, sometimes a one-step version of East Coast Swing is referred to as "Western" or "Cowboy" Swing. During the disco era, this four-beat dance was also sometimes referred to as the "Manhattan Hustle." The label "western swing" is sometimes confused with California's state dance, the West Coast Swing, partly because the word "west" appears in both titles, and partly because the West Coast style adapts easily to country and western swing tunes. While most dance historians point out there is no documented "tie" between the two, West Coast Swing may have originally been called Western Swing, as a way of differentiating it from East Coast styles. One thing is certain, however. Many of the country and western swing bands, in the late thirties and forties, attracted huge dancing crowds. Bands like Bob Wills and His Texas Playboys, and Leon McAuliff and His Western Swing Band, for example, dressed in western attire and exerted their influence on popular fads. In 1944, *The Billboard* magazine asserted that a "hillbilly craze" was sweeping the nation (*1944 Music Yearbook, The Billboard*, April 24, 367).

Two of the most popular western swing artists during the 1940s were Spade Cooley and Bob Wills. Cooley mixed his hillbilly twang with a swingin' big band sound, and bandleader Bob Wills is credited for contemporizing western music by adding percussion to his studio recordings. Wills gave his tunes a driving danceable swing rhythm, which attracted young "swing crazed" fans. His song "New San Antonio Rose" (recorded by Bob Wills and His Texas Playboys in 1940, and titled "new" so as not to be confused with his earlier instrumental song of the same name) was a pop and country crossover hit. Musicologists Starr and Waterman point out that "the introduction of New San Antonio Rose sounds as though it could have been taken straight out of a Benny Goodman arrangement" (2003, 151).

In the Los Angeles area, country and western bands were featured in many of the dance clubs during the forties, and Swing dancers cross-mixed to some extent with Country and Western dancers. Early Hollywood Lindy dancers Jean Veloz and her brother Ray Phelps made occasional outings to California's mountain community of Mammoth in those years, where numerous country western clubs featured the sounds of live "cowboy" bands. The brother and sister duo cut a rug on the dance floors there, although, as Ray Phelps recalls, "We didn't dance Country and Western. We went there to Swing!" While the local mountain residents may have worn boots, Phelps remembers that he and Jean wore their regular "Swing shoes." Ray Phelps especially liked to "slide." He points out that one of his friends and fellow Swing dancers, Lenny Smith, went so far as to dance "in moccasins" so he could slip and slide on the dance floors (Telephone interview). A cowboy boot doesn't allow the slipperiness that a moccasin would, and the weight of a boot, as compared to a shoe, inspires stomping and heavy-heeled kicking. However, as dance styles are constantly affected by each other, and dancers consistently— either advertently or inadvertently—borrow steps and stylings from each other, it is likely that Country and Western dancing would have cross-blended, to some extent, with Swing dance maneuvers, and would have influenced Swing dancing in general.

By the 1950s, a young generation of bands began mixing the twangs of western swing with honky-tonk riffs and rhythm and blues, creating a new musical craze. Bill Haley and the Comets, whose 1954 hit song *(We're Gonna) Rock Around the Clock* helped launch the entire era of rock and roll, was originally a country and western band. According to dance historian Ralph Giordano, Haley described his own sound as "western jive" and his early bands were named "Bill Haley and the Four Aces of Western Swing," and "Bill Haley and The Saddlemen" (19). Buddy Holly, Jerry Lee Lewis, the Everly Brothers, and even the rock and roll icon from rural Tennessee, Elvis Presley, are a few of the other pop music stars who were exposed to and influenced by country and western music.

## Balboa

At the Rendezvous Ballroom on Balboa Island, in Newport Beach, California, a group of Swing dancers in the 1930s created a new dance modeled to fit the tightest confines of an overly crowded dance floor. Reportedly, the *Rendezvous* would get so jammed with dancers that "Swinging away from a partner" was forbidden by the management. So, dancers had no choice but to Swing in "closed position," which inspired a new dance with a regional name: the Balboa. It is generally assumed that the dance was a modified version of the Lindy, however, early Hollywood Lindy dancer Dean Collins maintained that "Balboa is a smooth version of a dance called Shag." An early master of the dance, "Mr. Balboa" Willie Desatoff, long asserted that the dance came from the Rumba, which suggests that there were other possible influences on the dance (Collins on *Bobby McGee's Dance Party*, 1982, viewable on YouTube.com). Regardless as to what extent the various influences affected its creation, Balboa caught on and was popularized all over the Los Angeles area. Most of the early Hollywood Lindy dancers appear to have learned it from each other at or about the same time they learned the Lindy.

The original Balboa dancers developed their own individual signature styles, but in general they all stayed in a tightly closed position, diaphragm to diaphragm, shuffled close to the floor in an eight-count rhythm, and varied their footwork with flashy syncopations. The Ray Rand Dancers, a performing troupe of early Swing dancers, are often credited as standardizing the dance, and giving it a clear-cut basic step. The Ray Rand dancers were Maxie Dorf, Mary McCaslin, Lawrence "Lolly" Wise, Lillian Arnold, Hal and Betty Takier, Gil Fernandez, and Venna Cascon. Organized by Ray Rand, the manager of the Diana Ballroom in Culver City, the group performed in nightclubs of the Los Angeles area and did movie work as well.

Hal Takier and his first wife, Betty Roeser, were part of the Ray Rand dancers performance group. They were two of the best dancers in the country in the 1940s, winning the Harvest Moon Dance Festival (1948) at the Olympic Auditorium in Los Angeles. (Photo by Michael Ochs Archives/Getty Images.)

Two styles of Balboa developed in California. The style often referred to as "Pure Bal," keeps partners tightly connected through the upper torso throughout the dance. Variations are performed from the knees down, with footwork syncopations, direction changes, and stylings. A second style of Balboa is labeled "Bal Swing." This style allows more physical space between partners, so actual Swing patterns along with spins and dips can be added within the context of the Balboa basic step. Either style works with slow, medium, or "up" swing tempos, but Balboa is generally recognized as "the" dance to employ for "crazy fast" rhythms of break-neck speed. A 1943 short subject clip titled *Maharaja* features Hal and Betty Takier, two of the Ray Rand dancers, in a remarkable performance, which combines pure Bal and Bal Swing, with lots of Lindy movements and aerial work as well (Soundies Dist. Corp. of America; viewable on YouTube.com).

Balboa continued to develop in California long after the big band era of swing was over. It survived through the efforts of Swing clubs and individuals who kept it alive in the sixties and seventies, enjoyed a resurgence in the nineties, and maintained pockets of mass popularity in the twenty-first century. Maxi Dorf, one of the original Ray Rand dancers, stressed his concern for keeping the dance alive when he spoke emphatically to two of his students in 1986, "I hope you can duplicate my dancing and carry it on!" (Dorf, PBDA video archives, 1986).

## Shag (Collegiate, St. Louis, and Carolina Styles)

There are three distinctly different types of Shag: Collegiate Shag, St. Louis Shag, and Carolina Shag. In the late twenties and early thirties, everything "collegiate" was popular. College students were seen as trendsetters in everything from fashion wear to social dancing. In one 1932 newspaper article, the "collegiate trend" is frowned upon as "a type of dancing in which the partners dance in an awkward position, with noses and foreheads touching." Another article lists the most popular dances of 1932 as "the shag, the shuffle and the Lindy hop," all "collegiate in style" (*New York Times*, "Bar Collegiate Dancing," August 16, 1932, 20; *New York Times*, "Students Set Pace in Dance Invention," July 21, 1932, 19).

The origins of the original Shag dance are hazy, but dance historian Peter Loggins notes that the word "shag" was used, in the late nineteenth century, to describe a "vaudeville performer" and suggests that, in his opinion, the dance may have some relationship to the "Turkey Trot." Its evolutionary course is unclear; however, by the late thirties, Shag was all the rage both on and off college campuses. It became so popular, in fact, that a 1937 *New York Times* article describes it as "the fundamental dance step for swing." There is a classic instructional film from that same year featuring dance instructor Arthur Murray teaching the Shag. (Peter Loggins notes that Murray recruited his Shag performance dancers from "New York's collegiate ballroom, Club Fordham.") In the film, Murray assertively counts the rhythmic pulse of the dance as a "slow, slow, quick, quick," and basic Collegiate Shag has continued to be counted in this same manner, as a six-count basic, identical to the rhythm of East Coast Swing. All variations in East Coast Swing are adaptable to Collegiate Shag. It should be noted, however, that Shag employs single, double, and triple rhythms, and some versions of the dance (also called "Collegiate") do use an eight-count basic (*New York Times*, Crowther, "From the 'Turkey Trot' to the Big Apple,'" November 7, 1937, np; Murray in *How to Dance the Shag*, Skibo Productions Inc., 1937; Loggins, "The History of Collegiate Shag," collegiateshag.com).

For the "closed position" of Collegiate Shag, dancers join with their partners in a Ballroom holding position. This dance, however, never strives for Ballroom elegance or refinement. Instead, Collegiate Shag exudes youthful exuberance. Its bouncy hops and purposefully gawky, whimsical style give it a fun-filled flair. Good examples of Collegiate Shag on film are RKO Pictures *Bachelor Mother*, and Columbia's *Blondie Meets the Boss*—both Hollywood feature films of 1939.

St. Louis Shag, another version of the dance, most likely evolved as a cross between the Lindy Hop, Collegiate Shag, and Charleston dancing. The St. Louis basic step is an eight-count pattern, which makes it easy to dance in conjunction with the eight-count Lindy Hop, and it has long been popular with West Coast Swing dancers, too. The closed position basic consists of triple steps and kick steps, however, stomps and taps are also generally thrown into the mix, creating a flurry of footwork within the eight-count foundation of the dance.

St. Louis Shag began as a regional Missouri style. But when dancers from other areas of the country were exposed to it (mainly during dance competitions), its popularity spread. Being the least historically documented of the three styles of Shag, it is difficult to guess exactly when it originated. However, there are a number of variations fundamental to the style, including one-handed, high-speed crossing steps and Charleston kick patterns, reflective of popular movement from the late twenties and early thirties. Both the Collegiate style and the St. Louis Shag can be danced to extremely fast swing music.

The "official state dance" of South Carolina, the Carolina Shag emerged in the 1930s on the boardwalks of beachfront towns in the Carolinas and Virginia. Its precise point of origin is generally pinpointed as north Myrtle Beach, SC, and while its historical origin is unclear, it may have been an evolutionary blend of the Collegiate Shag, the St. Louis Shuffle, and the Lindy Hop—created as a slower-paced, smoothed out version of those dances in response to the music of rhythm and blues. In the segregated South of the 1940s, when white teenagers were denied access to black music on mainstream radio stations, they headed for black-owned sections of beach. Jukeboxes (in black-owned businesses) provided the sounds they were longing for. There, along the strands, they learned the dances of their black contemporaries. One of those dances was called "Shag." By the 1950s, Shag dance contests were cropping up throughout the South; by the late 1960s into the early 1960s, Carolina Shag reached its peak of popularity. "Beach music" was the name given to the sounds of "Shag-danceable tunes" recorded by black musical artists in those years, with some of the most popular songs being The Dominoes' "Sixty Minute Man," Gene Chandler's "Duke of Earl," and Fats Domino's "Ain't That a Shame."

Carolina Shag mixes six and eight-count rhythms and moves in a straight-line slotted style resembling West Coast Swing. However, the basic feel of the dance is more relaxed, with less arm tension than its West Coast cousin. Because this style developed on beachfront land, dancers had to keep it "toned-down" so as not to kick sand in their partners' faces. Gliding on the balls of their feet, dancers move as if on ball-bearing skates. There are turns, however, which often highlight the leaders ability to crank out solo spins, and while St. Louis Shag is based on patterns that are led and followed, there are occasional choreographed sequences worked out between partners (more often than in other styles of Swing). Al Munn's film documentary, *Shaggin' on the Strand* (1985), and the Hollywood film *Shag, The Movie* (1989, Hemdale Film Corp.), both give glimpses into the importance of beach music and Shag dancing in the culture of the Carolinas. Like West

Coast Swing, Carolina Shag continued to evolve throughout the years. Southern social clubs and nightclubs offering Shag lessons and dances grew in popularity in the eighties and nineties. The Society of Stranders (SOS) was formed in 1980, encouraging Shag celebrations and competitions; clubs such as Fat Harold's and Duke's Beach Club at North Myrtle Beach continued to draw dancers to the Carolina beaches into the twenty-first century.

In the decades of the thirties and forties, the "family tree" of Swing constantly sprouted new branches. Although some of the dance styles covered in this chapter evolved in later years, they have all had significant impact on the genre of Swing. Boogie Woogie, Jive, the New Yorker, Blues, Rockabilly, Jamaica Swing, Rock and Roll, and Ceroc are some of the other (too numerous to mention) styles that have identities of their own and became important to groups of dancers in various regions around the country.

# 8

# The Decline

Throughout the years of America's involvement in World War II, as men either enlisted or were drafted, women lost their social dancing partners. Dance troupes like Whitey's Lindy Hoppers broke up, and the professional Swing dancing women often found themselves "flying solo." Renowned Lindy Hopper Norma Miller managed to reinvent her performance career, but most of the "ladies of Swing" left show business altogether. Many of the big swing orchestras were forced to disband, as the war left them short on players and bandleaders. The swingin' big bands that did survive in those years faced a variety of difficult circumstances. First, wartime gasoline rationing prohibited bands from cross-country touring. As patrons cut back on driving to dance venues, ballroom owners found their crowds and profits decreasing, making it difficult to hire the expensive larger bands. Material shortages caused a scale-down in the production of records, and a 1942 musicians' union strike, which banned its members from working with record companies, devastated the music industry in general. Interestingly, the ban applied to bandleaders and all big band musicians but not to vocalists, as singers were not recognized as "musicians" by the union. The strike lasted over two years; when it ended, solo vocalists had gained a foothold on the music scene and it was their songs that were climbing the charts. Another giant blow to the big bands came in 1944 when a federal fee, a "cabaret tax," was imposed on dance music venues. While some of the smaller nightclubs reformatted themselves as restaurants, bars, or "music listening" venues, many of the ballrooms were forced to close. Midnight curfews, called "brown-outs," further discouraged dancers from stepping out for an evening on the town.

When World War II ended, and servicemen re-entered civilian life forever changed by their time and experiences abroad, they searched for stability. After the anxieties and uncertainties of war, many longed to settle down and start families. Big bandleader Les Brown asserted that it was difficult to organize any touring band because the musicians were all choosing marriage and easier work, as Brown puts it, "comfortable berths in movie and radio studios," over life on the road (*Time*, "Music: Band Businessman," Feb. 25, 1952).

These were some of the various causes leading to the demise of the big bands and the subsequent decline of Swing dancing. Another factor, however, was the changing nature of pop culture. Trends change—it's a simple fact. And a country's involvement in a war is bound to affect that country's consciousness and influence its popular trends. By the mid-forties, the big swing bands were fading out and crooners like Frank Sinatra, Kay Starr, and Nat King Cole, with their sweet and often sorrowful sentimental ballads, had become more popular. However, it was the combined talents of two charismatic bandleaders that took jazz in a completely new direction with their postwar creation: a new type of music called "bebop."

## Postwar Trends and Bebop

Dizzy Gillespie and Charlie "Bird" Parker innovated the musical style known as "bebop." It emerged in 1945 as the hot new sound, paving the way for "modern" jazz and influencing musical artists into the twenty-first century. In Ken Burns' *Jazz: The Story of America's Music*, Geoffrey C. Ward explains bebop as:

> . . . the kind of jazz musicians had always played to entertain themselves after the squares had gone home. (Five-CD boxed set booklet, 2000, 37)

Bebop discarded the standard conventions of big band swing. Instead of large ensembles, bebop bands were generally five-piece combos, and instead of cashing in on catchy tunes, bebop melodies were harmonically complex with chord changes going in every direction. The style emphasized experimental phrasings, fast tempos, and percussive rhythm changes along with complex improvised solos—all of which highlighted the remarkable talents of the musicians. Bebop was a style of music that jazz aficionados could appreciate listening to, but it wasn't generally danceable. So, suddenly, as a direct result of bebop's popularity, social dancing fell out of vogue.

Most of the bebop musicians of that time had previously played with swingin' big bands, so there were some swing–bebop fusions. Bandleader Lionel Hampton, for instance, recorded "Hey Bop A Re Bop" in 1945 when the bebop craze was new; the song has a wonderful Swing dancing rhythm. Swingin' jazz vocalist Ella Fitzgerald married bebop bassist Ray Brown in 1948, and although their marriage collapsed a few years later, her scat renditions of tunes like: "How High the Moon" and "Lady Be Good" became huge crossover hits. Bebop was so popular in the late forties, that even the "King of Swing," Benny Goodman, had his own bebop orchestra. But for the most part, bebop was considered "musical art" meant to be watched and heard rather than "musical entertainment" for audiences to dance to.

This 1947 photograph shows Dizzy Gillespie explaining some of the nuances of bebop on the chalkboard of a New York City classroom. The bebop sound was distinct in its use of musical ninths and flatted fifths, along with experimental harmonies and complex, generally "undanceable" rhythms. (AP Photo.)

Charlie Parker, known as "Yardbird" or simply "Bird," is credited (along with Dizzy Gillespie) with creating the musical style of "bebop." Parker's understanding of musical harmonics, along with his technical skills on sax led to his becoming a legendary jazz giant. In this 1949 photo, Parker (on the left) sits beside musician Russell "Big Chief" Moore, in a performance for the International Jazz Festival in Paris. (AP Photo/Jean-Jacques Levy.)

World-renowned Lindy Hopper Frankie Manning was forthright in admitting he never felt comfortable dancing to bebop. He does note in his autobiography, however, that the dancers who adapted to the new sound developed a style of Bebop dancing called "Boppin'." According to Manning, Boppin' was a mix of Lindy steps and "jerky" Charleston-ish moves (203).

Dizzy Gillespie himself admitted that bebop was "difficult to dance to," and he expressed concern that, because of it, the style could not garner mass appreciation. He is quoted in *DownBeat* magazine as saying:

> We'll never get bop across to a wide audience until they can dance to it. They're not particular if you're playing a flatted fifth or a ruptured 129th, as long as they can dance. ("Bird Wrong-Bop Must Get a Beat," October 7, 1949, np)

One year after that quote, in 1950, the bebop fad collapsed (Scott Yanow, 2000, 43).

There were documented complaints from both the public as well as from music industry insiders, on the "un-danceability" of bebop music, and the musical trends that followed bebop were all about "the steady beat." Yet, it is hard to guess what actual role the "un-danceability" factor played in bebop's short-lived popularity. The genre did, however, mark the beginning of a new era catering to the musical "audience" rather than the "dancing participant"; television was just emerging in the bebop years and was quickly becoming an important source of home entertainment for American "audiences."

By 1950, television had taken the country by storm: as viewers sat in the comforts of their own living rooms, crowds dwindled at the bebop cabarets and nightspots. Many of the large ballrooms either closed at this time, or reinvented themselves as banquet halls or exhibition centers. Lon Gault's well-researched book *Ballroom Echoes* notes that, occasionally, a well-known band at a publicized event could still draw a crowd. For instance, the Ray Anthony Band brought over 7,000 patrons to the Hollywood Palladium in 1952, and Perez Prado brought in an equally sizable crowd in 1956. But, for the most part, dance crowds in the fifties declined to an extent that even some of the most famous venues—the Trianon in Chicago, the Glen Island Casino in New Rochelle, New York, and Detroit's Graystone Ballroom—shut their doors. Even "The Home of Happy Feet," the world famous Savoy Ballroom in Harlem, saw the last of its glory days in 1958, when the ballroom was forced to auction off $25,000 of its furnishings. The auction included a piano that had been played by swing royalty—the likes of Count Basie and Duke Ellington—which sold for $450. The Savoy was eventually torn down and replaced by middle-income housing (Gault, 1989, 77, 243).

Ruth "Sugar" Sullivan was a dancing regular at the Savoy Ballroom in New York City from the time she was old enough to get in (1948)—until the ballroom closed down. She remembers that Whitey's Lindy Hoppers would sometimes show up at the Savoy when they were between jobs. Those were "exciting nights" when she could watch the professionals dancing there. But she recalls that by the early 1950s, the Savoy was trying other dance styles besides Swing to bring in customers: "There were a lot of different themes, Latin nights, and even Square dance nights!" (Telephone Interview with Sullivan) Although, it didn't matter too much to Sullivan what was going on there. She explains that whatever kind of music was being played, she still went and danced the Lindy Hop. Eventually Sullivan became a professional dancer herself. In 1955, she was crowned Swing champion of the Harvest Moon Ball, along with her husband and dancing partner, George Sullivan. Recalling the prizes she received for her first-place win, she explains: "I won a gold medal, a bouquet of roses, a nice contract for stage and television, and," with noted enthusiasm she exclaims, "a check!"

Eventually Sullivan teamed up with the 1958 Harvest Moon Ball winner, Sonny Allen, joining his all-girl touring revue called, "Sonny Allen and the Rockets." The group toured throughout the United States and Canada, performing "various styles of dance—African, Latin, Modern Jazz, and Tap." But Allen and Sullivan always finished the show with a full-out fast Lindy Hop number (Telephone interview).

This 1980s photograph shows Savoy Ballroom regulars Al Minns (a member of Whitey's Lindy Hoppers) and Ruth "Sugar" Sullivan. Both were winners (separately, and on separate occasions) of the Harvest Moon Ball Lindy Hop competition in New York City. This photo is from the archives of the Sandra Cameron Dance Center in New York, where Minns instructed and inspired a new generation of Swing dancers in the early 1980s. (Courtesy of Larry Schulz, Sandra Cameron Dance Center.)

## Rockin' and Rollin' in the Fifties

For a number of years after World War II, teenagers didn't do much dancing. They swayed to the popular sentimental ballads and listened to bebop. But by the early fifties, they were ready to "participate" again, and a key ingredient in the success of a newly recorded song was its good, danceable beat. As bebop faded from popularity, Cleveland radio disc jockey Alan Freed felt the restless pulse of a new group of listeners: American teenagers who were tuning in to up-tempo party music recorded by black musical artists. The recordings by these artists were labeled "race records" and at the time only received airplay from black DJs on black-owned radio stations. They were listed on the segregated music charts under the category of R&B ("rhythm and blues")—a musical style that mixed swingin' jazz, boogie woogie, gospel, and soulful blues. But many of the songs began to cross over the color line. Louis Jordan and his Tympany Five is a good example of one of the first swingin', R&B "jump bands" whose music began to resonate with white teen audiences. Their recordings of "Caledonia" and "Ain't Nobody Here But Us Chickens," for example, were in the top 10 on both the R&B and the pop music charts, and Louis Jordan's 1946 recording of "Choo Choo Ch'Boogie" sold over two million copies (Starr and Waterman, 2003, 171).

Rebelling against segregation and ignoring music industry taboos, Alan Freed promoted the African American musicians, and used his radio show to play their songs. In 1951, when Freed launched his *Moondog Rock and Roll Party* on the air, offering an entire program of "race record" music, most of his listeners were black. But a steady stream of white listeners started to tune in, and would outnumber his original audience within a few years (Stearns and Stearns, 1994, 2).

Alan Freed's term "rock n' roll" struck a chord with listeners, just as white audiences were finding the beat they were looking for in black musical traditions and the sounds of rhythm and blues. It was a swingin', danceable beat. And as white musicians added their own swing nuances and country and western flavors to the beat, the integration produced something that seemed nostalgic, yet "new." Teenagers across the country began to embrace the new sound and the new label for it, and the era of rock and roll got underway.

By the early 1950s, teenagers in America were setting the trends in popular culture. With good jobs in a prosperous economy, they became a powerful consumer force. They bought records like never before, and they wanted to dance. A number of regional dance programs catering to the teenage market sprang up on television. These shows featured nonprofessional teen dancers doing the latest steps. Suddenly, social dancing was "in" again. Slow dancing was popular throughout the decade, and teens danced Cha-Cha and Mambo to Latin sounds. But when the dancers "cut loose" to the rhythms of rock and roll, they danced Swing. They used the Swing steps they'd seen in Hollywood films, or that their parents had showed them, or that they'd learned from dance classes at school or from Arthur Murray. Murray's own weekly television dance show debuted in 1950, and attendance at Arthur Murray Studios climbed during that decade (Giordano, 160).

The most popular of the teen dance shows was Philadelphia's WFIL television program, *Bandstand*. The show went national in 1957 and was renamed *American Bandstand*. With "on-air host" Dick Clark spinning the latest pop records, *American Bandstand* aired for an hour and a half every day and became a colossal network hit. Dick Clark became a television celebrity, eventually of mega proportions. In a 1958 article in *The Billboard* magazine, Bob Rolontz reported that Dick Clark was very adamant about the music and dancing on his show. All the songs had to have a musical beat, and the dances had to be well-known to the teens on the show, like "the Stroll" and "the Bop" ("From Radio Jock to Nat'l Name—How Clark Does It" March 24, 4, 9).

The Stroll is a line dance in which dancers face each other in two straight lines. They take turns, two individuals at a time, solo dancing down the middle of the line; from crazy to cool, funky to smooth, anything goes!

While the Stroll is a clearly defined line dance, the partnered Swing dance called Bop is more elusive. The word "bop," in the 1950s, was refashioned as part of the rock and roll craze, and it began turning up everywhere. Gene Vincent's "Be-Bop-A-Lula" and "Dance to the Bop," along with Ricky Nelson's "Be-Bop Baby" are just of few of the chart-topping songs of that decade that included the word "bop" in their titles. The dance Bop was definitely a Swing style popular among teenage "rock and rollers" of the 1950s.

## Bop and Rock and Roll Dancing

In 1957, recording artist Ray Coniff released an album for Columbia Records titled "Dance the Bop." Each album included an eight-page instructional manual, *How to Dance the Bop*, written by dance instructor Art Silva. Surprisingly, Silva was convinced that there was no relation between bebop music of the prior decade and Bop dancing. He asserts that youngsters of the fifties chose the name "Bop" for their new dance simply because they liked the word (Coniff album liner notes; Silva, 1). However, in hindsight, there are two connections between bebop and Bop. First, it seems reasonable that a progressive link exists from the word "bebop," to the dance words "Boppin'" and then "Bop." When Lindy Hop legend Frankie Manning returned to the Savoy Ballroom in 1946, after having spent three years in the Army, dancers were trying to "adapt the Lindy to bebop, trying to mix the two." He explains: "We actually called that kind of dancing Bebop or Boppin'" (Manning and Millman, 203). This would suggest that there was at least some public use of the word "boppin'" in reference to a particular Swing dance style of that time. Bop dancing appeared in the fifties, as rock and roll was helping dancers define a steady beat and a more tangible dance style. There are also definite musical connections between bebop and the particular rock and roll rhythms that inspired the dance Bop. Those connections are worth further examination for an understanding of the Swing trends of the fifties.

   In the golden age of the big bands—the mid-thirties through the early forties—swing rhythms were fluid and smooth. The swingin' pulse stayed steady and flowing, perfect for Lindy Hopping. Bebop music was generally rhythmically unsteady and difficult for dancers to make sense of. However, bebop tunes were often a blend of swing and Latin instrumentations, and in fact both Latin records and swing records were often referred to as bop. One example is *The Billboard* magazine's "Record Reviews," on September 24, 1949, which describes particular "hot jazz" and "Latin" recordings as "bop tunes" (114–115). Dizzy Gillespie was long fascinated by Afro-Cuban music, and he recorded with a number of musicians who helped create his bebop-Latin sound, including Mario Bauza, Chano Puzo, and Frank Grillo (known as "Machito"). These Latin sounds and percussive elements continued to be popular into the fifties.

Music of the Caribbean Islands, especially everything "Jamaican," moved into the mainstream spotlight alongside rock and roll. In 1956, *The Billboard* lists Harry Belafonte's *Calypso* album, which included his top-of-the-chart hit, "Banana Boat Song," as the nation's "Best Selling Pop Album" (September 29, 40). By the following year, the same year Ray Coniff's *Dance the Bop* album was released, the calypso craze was in full gear. Art Silva suggests that Bop dancing, with its traveling steps and tapping, is actually a close relative of the Calypso. Three calypso-themed motion pictures were released in 1957: *Calypso Joe* (Allied Artists), *Bop Girl Goes Calypso* (United Artists), and *Calypso Heat Wave* (Columbia). The promotional trailer for *Calypso Heat Wave* touts that the film is "from the same producers of the 1956 film, *Rock Around the Clock*." (Bill Haley and the Comet's 1955 version of "Rock Around the Clock" is generally acknowledged as the first rock and roll record to reach the number one spot at the top of the pop charts.) Calypso was often linked with, or compared to, the music of rock and roll. In fact, the two styles were often pitted against each other over the question: In a competition of calypso versus rock and roll, which style will win out? (Silva, 1; the trailer is viewable on YouTube.com).

Calypso music, as it turned out, was a short-lived fad. But for dancers in the fifties, a song like Harry Belafonte's "Banana Boat Song" and rock and roll shared a strong two-beat pulse—a heavy downbeat followed by a fat high hat (backbeat), best described by the words, "boom-chick." Somewhere in the years between Boppin' and Bop, popular music had settled into this strong, two-beat rhythm. And teenagers Swingin' on the dance floor weren't about to ignore it.

Art Silva's manual, *How to Dance the Bop*, advises students to say the words "BOOM CHICK" out loud. To start dancing the Bop, Silva instructs: " . . . simply bend your knees on BOOM and straighten up on CHICK." There is a step, then a tap with the other foot, creating a two-beat double rhythm. Dance instructor Sonny Watson's well-researched website, *StreetSwing.com*, describes the original version of Bop as "a hip-twisting, body-swaying double-rhythm style." Bop's double rhythm is also noted by Cay Cannon, managing editor of *Dance Action* magazine. She explains that Bop is Swing done in "double rhythm (holding beat 'one' and stepping on beat 'two')." Cay Cannon asserts that Bop was popularly danced "on the East Coast from 1950 to 1952." Using Cannon's timeline and Frankie Manning's recollection, Bop most likely appeared within a five-year period after Boppin' (Silva, 1; Cannon, "Action Briefs," March, 1988, 30).

*American Bandstand* host Dick Clark asserts that Bop developed in Southern California. He claims that it started in direct response to Gene Vincent's 1957 rockabilly recording of the song, "Be-Bop-A-Lula." The "boom-chick" pulse of rock and roll was also found in the recordings of certain country western bands of the mid-1950s, and their music (often called "rockabilly") may have actually given birth to Bop dancing. Another note of interest is that, as 'Fessa John Hook points out in his historical dance book *Shagging in the Carolinas,* in the eastern areas of North Carolina, "Bop was the word for Shag" (Shore and Clark, 1985, quoted in Giordano, Vol. 2, 2007, 152; Hook, 2005, 57).

There are various descriptions of what Bop dancing actually looked like. Dick Clark commented that Bop dancers "jumped up and down in place, grinding their heels back and forth each time they landed" (From Shore and Clark, quoted in Giordano, 2007, 152). Author Robert Pruter suggests that black youth in Chicago created numerous, subtlety varied versions of Bop, "each with its own footwork and sense of timing to fit the music of a particular record." Bob Rolontz, in his 1958 article in *The Billboard* magazine, may have gotten it exactly right when he notes that teenagers do the Bop, "in various versions, everywhere," which suggests there is no consensus as to a standard basic step for the dance (Pruter, 1992, 207; Rolontz, "From Radio Jock to Nat'l Name," March 24, 9). Wherever it came from, and however short-lived its popularity may have been, the dance Bop retained a lasting image tied to poodle skirts, blue jeans, bobby sox, and Swing dancing in the fifties.

Social dancing in the 1950s was well represented on television. As the Hollywood film industry focused on the lucrative teen market, numerous lower-budget movies were released that spotlighted rock and roll bands and often included scenes of Swing dancers. It should be pointed out that although R&B artists were increasingly listened to and celebrated by white audiences, America was still very segregated. The television dance shows of the fifties did feature African American performers who had hit records at the time. But because interracial dancing was strictly prohibited everywhere in the country (even solo style), most of the shows banned African American dancers. In Hollywood, there were a number of white Lindy dancers (many of whom had danced in movies of the forties), who managed to secure

In this 1958 photograph taken on the Philadelphia set of American Bandstand, 28-year-old host Dick Clark spins the records from his podium (upper left). The all-white dancing teens are Swingin', Rockin' and Rollin', and Boppin' to the latest hits. (AP Photo.)

employment in the fifties rock and roll films. The fact that these Swing dancers were white made them marketable across the country. With their remarkable dancing skills (in both social and performance-styles), they became the onscreen representatives of rock and roll Swing dancing. Their Swing styles were emulated by the "dancing regulars" on the television teen dance shows and by teen audiences across the country. One of those Lindy dancers was Freda Angela Wyckoff. Her first film appearance was in the 1954 comedy, *Living It Up* (Paramount Pictures), which features Hollywood comedic stars Dean Martin and Jerry Lewis. In the movie, Martin and Lewis take part in a lavish Swing dance production number. In real life, Jerry Lewis was a friend of Swing dancer and promoter Dean Collins (Lewis was a longtime acquaintance of the entire Collins family). When Swing dance extras were needed for a scene in the movie, Lewis called upon Dean Collins to provide them—and Freda Angela Wyckoff was one of the dancers hired. Wyckoff was good friends with Dean Collins and had been a dancing "regular" at the Hollywood Palladium in the 1940s. She danced in many subsequent movies of that decade. Reminiscing about the style of dancing she was doing back then, Wyckoff says, "We just adapted our Lindy to whatever style of music we were dancing to at the time. It didn't matter what the movie was, or what the song was, we danced the Lindy." Another one of the many Swing dancers hired in *Living It Up* was Jack Carey, who concurs: "We just adapted our dancing to the music." Carey admits that while he did dance the Lindy, he always preferred his "own style of Swing," which was, in his words, "a Bal type," referring to Balboa. He and his wife, Lorraine Edwards, won the Los Angeles Harvest Moon Dance Festival Swing championship of 1949 (Hal and Betty Takier had won it the previous year). Carey and Edwards danced together in *Living It Up*, and can be seen doing a mix of six-count and eight-count Lindy moves, plus Balboa and lots of aerials.

In regards to her work in the 1957 film *Calypso Heat Wave*, Freda Angela Wyckoff explains that she and the other dancers didn't actually do *any* Calypso dancing. They danced eight-count and "bouncy" six-count Swing (adapted to suit the film's calypso rhythms). Wykoff confirms, once again, that she and her co-performers were "Lindy dancers." She comments, "We danced the same Lindy in *Calypso Heat Wave* that we always danced. And we never did the Bop."

Wyckoff partnered Hollywood Lindy dancer Lenny Smith in the Swing scenes of the movie *Rock Around the Clock* (1956). She recalls that another Hollywood Lindy dancer, Lou Southern, acted as an assistant to the choreographer on that film. (Jack Carey was also asked to dance in the film, but he explains that he had "a real job" at the time and couldn't leave work for the filming.) There is an on-screen moment in *Rock Around the Clock*, in which a Swing dancer is asked what type of dance she and her partner are doing. The emphatic reply is: "It's Rock 'n' Roll, Brother! And we're rockin' tonight!" Wyckoff confirms that in general, "Swing dancing was labeled 'Rock and Roll' at that time. Although," she adds, "everyone knew what you meant if you said 'Jitterbug'" (Telephone interviews with Wyckoff and with Carey).

Arthur Murray's 1959 edition of *How to Become a Good Dancer* includes an instructional section on Rock 'n' Roll dancing, which is described in the book as the "newest variation of Swing" (207–214). Similar to Bop, Murray's Rock 'n' Roll used a "tap-step," double rhythm version of the East Coast Swing. This "newest variation," however, at least as showcased by professional Lindy dancers in Hollywood films, was nothing more than a slightly modified version of the original style of Swing, the Lindy Hop.

Other films from the fifties which include Swing dancing are *Rock Rock Rock* (1956), *Untamed Youth* (1957), *Don't Knock the Rock* (1957), and *Juke Box Rhythm* (1959), to name just a few. Along with the teen dance television shows of the time, these movies give a historical look at the specific characteristics of Swing in that decade. A double-rhythm (both a tap-step, and a step-tap), perhaps made popular by Bop, was used in abundance. A "kick-ball-change" frequently replaced a "rock-step," and followers occasionally left off the rock-step entirely and instead walked straight forward on counts 1–2. Both eight-count and six-count patterns continued to be juxtaposed, but there was a trend toward "one-handed" six-count basics (the leader's left hand generally held the follower's right hand). Some of the early variations of the Lindy Hop (moves such as "Shorty George," the "Skate," and "Slow Boogie," etc.) continued to be incorporated into social styles and performance routines, as did a variety of aerials.

## Going "Solo"

Television in the fifties not only showcased social dance styles, but also introduced a variety of dance fads. These fads, like the Bunny Hop and the Conga for example, were mostly line dance routines made up of "learned" steps. Most of the steps were uniform; that is, everyone did the same moves at the same time (although, there were some exceptions, like the Stroll). But the fads, along with the solo gyrations of performers like Elvis, encouraged individual movement, and they fueled a virtual tidal wave of dance crazes into the sixties. The Twist, the Pony, the Monkey, the Watusi, the Mashed Potato, and the Jerk, were just a few of best-known fads. As legendary Lindy Hopper Frankie Manning explained, "a new song would come out and it would last a week. And there was a dance to each one of those songs. And *they'd* last a week!" (PBDA video archives, 1993).

Frankie Manning's son, Chazz Young, recalls that the Twist was a "huge fad." Chubby Checker introduced the dance on Dick Clark's *American Bandstand* in 1960. During that year, Young was touring and performing with Norma Miller and Her Jazzmen, but on free nights he would also dance socially at nightclubs. He comments that when the Twist came out, "It didn't matter where you were at that time or what band you were dancing to, you danced the Twist. *Everybody* danced the Twist." Chazz Young started his career with Norma Miller and Her Jazzmen at the age of 17 in 1949, and danced with her troupe until it disbanded in 1968. Young always specialized in Tap dancing, but he performed a little of everything with Miller's troupes, including Swing and Jazz. He reports that when swing music went out of popularity, it became harder to find performance work. One of the most difficult jobs, he recalls, was in the late fifties, when he and the rest of Norma Miller's group performed their Swing and Jazz show—"to the accompaniment of a rock and roll band." Young explains, "The band tried to play swing music for us. But it was a tough job. There were electric guitar wires running all over the stage!" In the mid-sixties, Young taught Tap dance in New York and he drove a cab for a while. Then, like his father, he worked for the U.S. Postal Service (from 1972 to 1994). Young, a wonderful dancer with natural grace and style, continues to maintain a full schedule of performance and teaching jobs (Telephone interview).

While the fifties, with its "new suburban communities," emphasized teamwork and conformity, the sixties were marked by a counterculture of rebellion (political and social unrest over civil rights concerns and the Vietnam War) that led from the unison dance crazes to a new found freedom of solo movement and individual expression. Suddenly, everyone in America began "doing their own thing" on the dance floor. There were occasional Swing dance performances and swing band concerts, but Swing dancing was hard to come by, as partnered dancing in general had become scarce. A number of ballrooms across the country that had previously held big Swing dancing events began hosting Latin parties at this time.

Latin musicians in the early sixties created their own new sound. They combined Latin instrumentations and percussions with rhythm and blues and rock and roll music and named the blend "boogaloo." The Boogaloo dance was a cross between Mambo and Swing. It was a partnered dance, although it involved a lot a breakaway solo "shine moves," and was danced to tunes like Joe Cuba's iconic boogaloo song, "Bang Bang." But the quick footwork of Boogaloo, the partnered kick-steps, and St. Louis–style Shag variations, strikingly resembled East Coast triple-step Swing dancing! The music of boogaloo swept the nation, and pushed Latin bands into national prominence.

Suddenly, there were lots of places to go out Latin dancing. For instance, Salsa dancer Tony Perez remembers dancing at The Hollywood Palladium in Los Angeles every Sunday night in 1962. He describes the "old big band ballroom with white table covers on all the tables" as being a "very classy place," with beautiful chandeliers, a huge circular floor with a large stage, and a balcony that wrapped all the way around the floor. "You could go up into the balcony and look down at all the people dancing. The place was always packed!" At 15, Tony Perez met his future wife, Nydia, at the Palladium, when they were both there socially dancing one night. He explains, "You had to be 18 to get in, but I went around to the back and helped the musicians unload and carry in their instruments." Perez adds enthusiastically, "Sometimes there'd be five big Latin bands all playing The Palladium on the same night!" (Personal interview).

Mainstream pop culture, however, was focused on another new genre of music that emerged in the sixties: "rock." The concept of the "listening" audience that had developed during the bebop fad of the late forties was now a basic element in popular culture, and rock festivals (such as Woodstock's 1969 "Three Days of Peace and Music") soon morphed into sit-down live music concerts. In the seventies, these "rock concerts" were often staged in giant arenas, attracted mass audiences, and opened whole new windows of profitability for the music industry. Latin music in the seventies consolidated under the term "salsa" while pop music featured a new term called "disco," which came from the word "discotheque"—the name for the nightclubs of the sixties that offered uninterrupted recorded music. In an overview of social dancing, what's remarkable about the 1970s is that once again, whether for Latin dancing or Disco dancing, people began dressing up and going out to glamorous dance clubs. And they were walking into these clubs *expecting to dance*. While Swing dancing was rarely seen during the sixties and seventies, as each generation takes something from what came before it, builds upon it, and makes it their own, these decades were important in the eventual resurgence of Swing dance in the 1980s.

# 9

# The Road to Resurgence

With the decline of the big bands and swing music in the 1950s and 1960s, the lives of the professional Lindy Hoppers were all greatly affected. After his service in the Army, legendary Lindy Hopper Frankie Manning, for example, started his own Swing troupe, "the Congaroo Dancers," in 1947 (originally named "the Four Congaroos," and later called "the Congaroos"). But as the Swing scene faded in the fifties, he disbanded the group (in 1955) and went to work for the U.S. Postal Service. Iconic Lindy Hop dancer Norma Miller toured both nationally and internationally with her jazz performance troupes in the fifties and early sixties but disbanded her team in 1968. Drawing on her varied personal talents, she toured as a solo act singer-dancer comedian throughout the seventies (Manning in PBDA video archives, 1993, Miller and Jensen, 222).

In Southern California, dance aficionados like Dean Collins and Ray Fox (originally from Chicago) created social clubs and networks that helped keep Swing dance alive in the Los Angeles area in the fifties and sixties. Their clubs included the Los Angeles Swing Club, the Southern California Swing Club, and the L. A. Swing Dance Club. Later, there was also the West Coast Dancers' Club and The West Coast Swing Dance Club. Purported arguments over what styles of music were most "Swingable" led to schisms within the various organizations—clubs split and often reformed under different names. Nonetheless, the dancing continued. In the 1940s, Dean Collins had established himself as a professional Swing instructor. Throughout the fifties and sixties, the celebrities who took private lessons with him included Shirley Temple, Cesar Romero, Abbott and Costello, Joan Crawford, and even Arthur Murray. Collins taught in a basement studio at the home he shared with his wife Mary in Glendale, California. The studio had a large wooden floor, which Mary explains they "won at an auction." An entire building was being sold off (a convent), and the couple drove to it and pulled up the floorboards. Mary Collins remembers, "It was beautiful oak, and we installed it in our home." Alycia Keys, a niece of Dean and Mary Collins, adds: "It was a huge floor! And there were always dance students going in and out of Uncle Dino's house." Dean and Mary were introduced to each other by Hollywood Lindy dancer Freda Wyckoff at the Tailspin nightclub in Hollywood in 1960. Although Wyckoff's final movie appearance was in *Juke Box Rhythm* in 1959, she continued to stay involved in the social Swing dance scene in Los Angeles into the twenty-first century (Telephone interviews with Mary Collins and Alycia Keys).

Hollywood Lindy dancer Jean Phelps Veloz traded in her swingy skirts for elegant ballroom gowns in the late 1940s, thanks to her introduction to Ballroom dance extraordinaire, Frank Veloz. He was one-half of the renowned Ballroom duo of Veloz and Yolanda, whose photo was once featured on the cover of *Life* magazine with the caption: "Greatest Dancing Couple" (October 30, 1939). Married couple Frank Veloz and Yolanda Casazza had become the Ballroom dance darlings of stage shows, movies, and supper-clubs across the country. Jean Phelps went through the Veloz training curriculum, learning all styles of Ballroom to further her dance career. When Yolanda retired from performing, Jean began partnering Frank in his stage and television performances. Frank and Yolanda Veloz subsequently divorced and, eventually, Frank married Jean. Jean Phelps Veloz was rediscovered during the Swing dance revival of the 1990s and continued enjoying celebrity status into the twenty-first century (Personal interview).

Former Hollywood Lindy dancer Irene Thomas pursued a successful career in Ballet and Tap dancing in the forties. She was hired for a lengthy run at New York's Copacabana, and then toured throughout Canada and the United States. While she continued dancing throughout the 1950s, she was never interested in returning to professional Swing dancing. However, Thomas left a lasting mark on the genre (as did Jean Veloz) by creating some of the signature moves of the Hollywood Swing style, which were later emulated and celebrated during the swing revival of the nineties. Dancer Chuck Saggau made his last film performance in 1944 in the 20th-Century Fox motion picture *Home in Indiana*, starring Jeanne Crain. He was drafted into World War II later that year. While he never returned to dancing professionally after the war, he met his wife Sally Saggau en route to a dance at the Casino Ballroom on Catalina Island in 1950. They were both traveling aboard the Big White Steamship to the island. Sally recalls, "Chuck was doing a lot of dancing to the live band on the boat." She adds, "He was quite a dancer, and a crowd had gathered around him to watch." Chuck passed Sally a note through the crowd, which read: "Call me." She did, and they were married seven months later! (Telephone and personal interviews with Jean Veloz, July 8–23, 2009; Telephone interview with Irene Thomas, Aug. 6, 2009; Telephone interviews with Chuck and Sally Saggau, July 31, Aug. 20, 2009.)

The Casino Ballroom continued to hire dance orchestras into the 1960s. From the mid-sixties throughout the seventies, however, swing bands played there only "intermittently." Count Basie, for example, headlined there for one special night of dancing in 1971 (Telephone interview with Jeannine Pedersen, Curator of the Catalina Museum).

After his service in World War II, early Hollywood Lindy dancer Ray Phelps frequented the small nightclubs that still offered swing music in the Los Angeles area. But he was disappointed that "there were no more Swing dance contests." Hollywood Swing dancer Jack Carey was also disappointed that, in the postwar years, there were no Swing contests in Los Angeles. So, in 1949 or 1950, Carey began hosting his own Swing parties at nightclubs, and he organized and MC'd contests at these clubs. He noticed that certain couples (the talented Gil and Nikki Brady, for instance) were "winning all the time," so he devised a way of getting a more diverse group of dancers to join in. He created the "Jack and Jill" (sometimes written "Jack & Jill, or Jack 'n' Jill"), which in his original version entailed pulling names out of a hat. Dancers competed with the dancer whose name they pulled—it was the luck of the draw what partners were chosen to dance together. Eventually, there were other versions of the "Jack and Jill," but Carey created the original concept and first tried it in 1955 at Hank and Stan's nightclub in Downey, California.

Along with his longtime partner, Annie Hirsch, Carey continued to dance into the twenty-first century, with a full schedule of teaching, and competition judging. Hirsch and Carey have long been devoted

Jack Carey and his partner (on the dance floor and in life), Annie Hirsch are shown here performing West Coast Swing together in the early 1980s. Carey is credited with creating the "Jack and Jill" Swing competition; Hirsch co-created the World Swing Dance Council, among other achievements. They have continually worked for the preservation and resurgence of Swing dance. (Courtesy of Ann M. Hirsch.)

to "promoting" Swing, helping to "keep it alive" nationally and internationally (Telephone interviews with Ray Phelps and Jack Carey).

## The 1970s and the Return of "Touch Dancing"

The 1970s offered a mixed bag of musical styles. Country and western music (called simply "country" during the decade), along with reggae, hard rock, soft rock, punk rock, disco, soul, and many others, were popular genres with their own loyal followers. "Partnered" dancing was mainly found at private parties, or at occasional public big band events, in retirement communities, and onboard cruise ships. And although social dance classes were sometimes offered in college curriculums and community classes, solo dancing was still, overall, the most popular trend. However, the decade of the seventies introduced two key elements that influenced the return of Swing dancing. First, the political and social unrest of the 1960s had led to a nationwide nostalgia for "the way things used to be," and the "simpler days of old." Many Americans began to look back at the 1950s as the carefree, innocent "golden years." When the theatrical stage production *Grease* debuted in 1972, with its youthful cast and a plot about high school kids in 1959, the show scored a record-setting run on Broadway and sparked a fifties fad. This led to the first airplay of "oldies" music (a term referring to popular tunes of the 1950s and early 1960s), on New York's radio station WCBS-FM (Giordano, 2007, Vol. 2, 247). The new "oldies" fad continued with the release of Universal's motion picture *American Graffiti* in 1973. The movie's slogan asks, "Where were you in '62?"; the film's trailer opens on a gymnasium sock hop with teenagers dancing to Danny and the Junior's 1957 hit, "At the Hop." Interestingly, dancers in that trailer are mostly doing the Twist, but there are also Swing dancers in the crowd, with one couple, camera-center, performing a standard, iconic Lindy Hop aerial.

Television scored a big hit in 1974 with the *Happy Days* series; the show featured fifties rock and roll music, sock hops, the Twist, and even a "Harvest Moon" dance contest. Dean Collins and Skippy Blair were among the many onscreen dancers in the made-for-television movie, *Queen of the Stardust Ballroom* (1975), which depicted the glamorous "days gone by" of elegant dance halls and Ballroom dancing (*Happy Days* episodes, and scenes from *Queen of the Stardust Ballroom* are viewable on YouTube.com).

The seventies nostalgia that had people thinking about partnered dancing again also sparked an appreciation for live music (after the prior decade's emphasis on DJ'd music), and a number of musicians either formed or reformed big bands. Duke Ellington and Count Basie both continued leading their iconic big bands, and were still admired and sought after for special event gigs. Bandleader Woody Herman, who continued working in the seventies, added a corps of young musicians to his orchestra, giving his music a more contemporary sound. New York's Harlem Blues and Jazz Band, on the other hand, was created in 1973 made up entirely of "veteran greats" from the classic years who had played with the likes of Count Basie, Duke Ellington, Glenn Miller, Artie Shaw, and Louis Jordan (promotional band bio, personal archives).

Erin Stevens, renowned Swing dancer and instructor from Pasadena, CA, recalls that she and Steven Mitchell, her dance partner from 1977 into the 1990s, followed their favorite swing bands all over the Los Angeles area in the late seventies and early eighties. She explains:

> We were lucky in that we had a lot of exposure to big band music in those years. Top bands played the Hollywood Bowl, and both Disneyland and The Hollywood Palladium were great dance venues that hired the top "name" big bands too. But Steven and I also danced to local bands that were performing in smaller clubs and hotel ballrooms. There were bandleaders such as: Tracey Wells, Memo Bernabei, brothers Bill and Gary Tole, and Bob Keane. They held a lot of promotional contests at that time: We won a lot of money dancing in those years! (Personal interview)

Erin Stevens and Steven Mitchell took first place in so many of Bob Keane's dance competitions that he finally hired them to perform with his band at numerous Los Angeles gigs. Music promoter George Patton also produced large-scale Ballroom dance events in the Los Angeles area in the late seventies, and he hired Stevens and Mitchell (along with Erin's sister, Tami, and her various partners) on a regular basis as well. Both couples performed mostly Ballroom and Cha-Cha numbers at that time. Patton hired top-notch swing orchestras and, with a huge mailing list of older generation dancers, was able to pack venues like The Hollywood Palladium.

The widespread popularity of Latin dancing continued in the seventies, and the various Latin dances were unified under one name: "Salsa," which meant a "mix," as in a mix of spicy sauces—or spicy dances! Salsa emerged as a new, long-lasting craze that sizzled with romance and glamour, and helped bring partnered dancing back to ballrooms around the country. But by the late 1970s, "swing" music was definitely resurfacing. Erin Stevens remembers competing with Steven Mitchell in a Cha-Cha contest, circa 1979; when they arrived, they discovered it was a Swing competition instead. The pair knew only the basics in six-count Swing at that time; however, Steven ran and jumped over Erin's head landing in a perfect splits on the floor, she twisted around him, and they incorporated a number of their Cha-Cha aerials. They managed to win the first-place cash prize. From that point forward, they focused not only on learning to Swing, but on the historical roots of the dance. By the early eighties, "Swing was their thing," and most of Stevens and Mitchell's professional performances were as Swing dancers. At that time, there was an older generation of Americans who were nostalgic for swing music and dance, and they were especially appreciative of and encouraging toward young Swing dancers like Stevens and Mitchell (Personal Interview with Erin Stevens).

The second key element that led the nation back to Swing dancing was a seventies phenomenon known as "disco fever." The deejay'd music played in American discotheques developed a unique sound— synthesized melodies and repetitive lyrics accompanied by a metronomic beat. This new "disco" music inspired the Hustle, the decade's hottest dance craze. Van McCoy's 1975 song "The Hustle" is often credited as having sparked the craze, and there was a specific line dance created at that time named "the Hustle." But it was the "partnered" style of Hustle that a 1975 *New York Times* article referred to when it announced, "The 'Hustle' Restores Old Touch to Dancing." The article explains that in doing the Hustle, dancers were touching each other again. After so many years, "touch dancing" was finally replacing "solo dancing" as the new trend. The partnered Hustle spread rapidly throughout the country (Dena Kleiman, July 12, 1975, 56).

In 1977, John Travolta's onscreen dance numbers in the motion picture *Saturday Night Fever* (Paramount Pictures) further popularized the Hustle. In discotheques across the country, with strobe lights flashing and loud music pulsating, people were "touch dancing" again. The Hustle became the biggest craze since the Twist. However, there were marked differences between the two crazes: the Twist was mainly a solo dance, while the Hustle was a social partnered dance that relied on leading and following. The Twist was an easy dance to imitate, and most people learned it by watching someone else. The Hustle, however, was more complex and generally required that dancers take lessons to "get the basics down."

Dancers who knew Swing in those years had a distinct advantage in learning Hustle because of the similarities between the two dances. The basic step of the Hustle is a "flowing" six-count pattern that, in many ways, resembles Swing, especially the smooth style of West Coast Swing. And the numerous spins and arm patterns of Hustle can be, and were at that time, easily converted to Swing dancing variations.

When the disco craze ended, many dancers continued their "touch dancing" with the slotted style of Swing. Randy Albers, a Southern California dancer, goes so far as to assert that, "the Hustle morphed

From the 1977 Paramount Pictures film, *Saturday Night Fever*, John Travolta and Karen Gorney dance in a nightclub, under "mirror-ball lighting," to the popular music of the time: disco. (AP Photo/HO.)

into Swing!" Albers was born in 1935 and began Swing dancing in the early fifties. By his own admission, he "didn't dance at all in the sixties," but he started dancing the Hustle in the disco era of the seventies. When "disco died," he avidly took up Swing dancing again. For as far back as Albers can remember, he has called his style "West Coast Swing" (Telephone interview). But the Hustle also exposed a whole new group of "first-time dancers" to partnered social dancing. And when they sought out other partnered dances, many moved from Disco to Swing. Dance instructors were suddenly important again, as Hustle dancers looked for teachers who could show them more steps and other styles. It was this pursuit of dance knowledge, and this desire to "learn" dances—rather than simply freestyling creative solo moves, that helped reawaken an interest in Swing dancing.

In the late 1970s, dancer Cliff Gewecke wanted to learn the Hustle. He worried that a large chain studio "might be a ripoff," but he saw a "Dance" sign in a studio window in Downey, CA, along with another sign with "dashes and dots" (this will be explained later in this chapter). This dance school seemed quaint and inviting, so he walked inside. Gewecke was told that the school was actually a "teacher's training school." Undeterred, he decided that he would get more in-depth information if he trained as an instructor. However, the school "didn't actually offer Hustle per se, but specialized in West Coast Swing." So, Gewecke signed up for a training course in Swing. The school was run by celebrated California dance instructor, Skippy Blair. Gewecke explains that he was able to supplement his income over many years by teaching dance (Telephone interview).

## Movers and Shakers in California

It is again important to point out that in California, the style of slot dancing known as Lindy, Sophisticated Swing, Western Swing, or West Coast Swing (these distinct labels for the same dance were used at various times, in various circles), was preserved and propagated from the days of its birth, right on into the twenty-first century by a group of avid dancers and dance teachers. Dance instructor Skippy Blair agrees that it was the "underground clubs" that helped keep it going in the fifties and sixties. Blair played an important role in its survival as well.

In 1958, Blair opened her first dance studio in Downey, CA, with the sole purpose of training teachers in the art of West Coast Swing. At the time, she called the dance "Western Swing" which she acknowledges (along with "Sophisticated Swing") was an Arthur Murray term. But, working originally as an Arthur Murray instructor herself, Blair challenged how the dance was being "counted" under the Murray program. She explains that she longed to teach it, and count it, in its "correct musical form."

Born in 1924, Blair got her start as a Tap dancer, and won virtually every amateur contest she entered as a youngster. However, as she puts it:

> I was no Shirley Temple. I was a skinny kid with knobby knees. But I always won the contests. And I think the reason for that was because I understood musicality.

Blair established the Golden State Dance Teachers Association (GSDTA), which standardized the "walk-walk" step in West Coast Swing as being counted as 1–2 (rather than as the 5–6 of the dance). She developed a unique system of dashes and dots, called the "Universal Units System," to help her students understand the basic rhythms and musical elements of dance.

In the mid-sixties, while designing an ad for her Western Swing classes to run in the local Downey newspaper, the paper's copy editor warned Blair that "no one would attend classes billed as 'Western.'" Country and western was, apparently, not a popular trend (at least not in Downey) at that time. But Blair corrected him, explaining that in this case, "western" meant "west coast." He suggested that she use the term "West Coast Swing" in her ad; and she began using and popularizing that label. Blair is often credited for naming the dance, but she doesn't accept full credit. She notes the existence of an old printed booklet written by Lauré Haile, who was Arthur Murray's national dance director in the mid-1940s and co-owner of five Murray franchises. In the booklet, Haile had suggested the name "West Coast Swing" for the slotted California style. Blair contends that, whoever coined the term first, the name of the dance officially became "West Coast Swing" in the mid-1960s. This seems to be the general consensus among dancers from that time period.

Blair ran dance schools from 1958 into 2010, offering instruction in West Coast Swing and her Universal Units System. Her former student-turned-teacher, Cliff Gewecke, explains: "The dashes and dots are two-beat units that we'd put together like words. You keep adding more units until you make a complete sentence, an entire dance pattern." Over the years, Blair has seen the dance change and evolve— and witnessed its many phases, as it was affected by "disco music in the seventies, by country-western music in the eighties, and a Hustle resurgence in the nineties." But she is resolute that "Swing is a dance that is here to stay!" (Telephone interview with Cliff Gewecke; Telephone interview with Skippy Blair, Ph.D.). One of the factors in West Coast Swing's longevity is its compatibility with so many diverse musical rhythms, tempos, and moods. This remarkable dance can be attacked with vigor and strength, or caressed with "soft as butter" pliability. It can be silly or sensuous; danced with playful bounce or the smoothest fluid lines. Adjusting to such a wide variety of musical styles, some form of West Coast Swing is bound to stay "contemporary"!

California Swing dance instructor Sonny Watson has specialized in the West Coast style since 1982. He explains that it was "the music" that drew him to the dance in the early 1980s, and he's been hooked ever since. He also agrees that the dance is remarkably adaptable to "very diverse" musical sounds. In Watson's words:

From big band swing sounds, to blues, rock and roll, country and western, pop tunes, techno music, sixties beach music, disco, and even

Latin sounds—West Coast Swing can be danced to practically anything!
(Telephone interview)

Fascinated by the historical aspects of dance, Swing research became a
hobby for Watson, and he amassed a collection of books and research
materials on the subject. He created a website in 1988 called Sonny
Watson's StreetSwing.com. The site is a monumental effort, devoted
to giving swing aficionados some background in all the various styles.
By Watson's own admission, this is a lifelong work in progress, and
requires continual updates as he uncovers new historic information
and source materials (Telephone interview).

Into the 1980s, popular California West Coast Swing instructors
included Sonny Watson, Phil Adams, Martin Parker, and the Stevens
sisters of the Pasadena Ballroom Dance, to name just a few. Buddy
Schwimmer, an award winning dancer and highly respected instructor, was one of Skippy Blair's early students. Schwimmer was making
his own mark on the genre of West Coast Swing in the 1980s, training
children and young adults. (He opened his 5678 dance studio in the
mid-1990's in Redlands, CA, where he has continued to encourage
youth and contribute to the preservation of Swing.) Tom Mattox,
another of Skippy Blair's early students, incorporated country and
western music and moves into his style; and Jaime and Gail
Arias beautifully paired Hustle and West Coast Swing. All of these
instructors continued to push contemporary musical trends into their
teachings.

In 1983, Jack Bridges produced a Swing competition in the grand
ballroom of the Disneyland Hotel in Anaheim, California. Aware of
the various Swing dance clubs around the country (he himself had
been the president of the San Diego Swing Dance Club), Bridges' aim
was to bring the nation's Swing dancers together for one large
competition (Interview on *Eye on LA* television production, 1984). To
make the event happen, Bridges enlisted the help of his wife Mary
Ann and many of his friends, including Deejay and MC Kenny Wetzel
who, in the early sixties, had started weekly Swing contests at The
Ivanhoe nightclub in Temple City, CA, and had gone on to host
numerous various Swing events in Orange County; Annie Hirsch, who
became the competition's head judge; and Jack Carey, in an advisory
position. Bridges also involved a number of dance instructors (including
Bridges' personal friend, Dean Collins), who encouraged their students

to participate. Bridges' U.S. Open Swing Dance Championships were "open" to all styles of Swing. However, the early competitors and judges were, in general, West Coast Swing slotted style dancers.

Mary Ann Nuñez, along with her dance partner for the competition, Lance Shermoen, won the showcase division of the first U.S. Open Swing Dance Championships in 1983. Friends of Dean Collins, the pair of young dancers had asked him to choreograph their competition routine. Nuñez explains: "He [Dean Collins] did about half of our dance routine then he had to go out of town for awhile, so Lance and I finished the other half." Collins was in the audience at the competition and got to see them win first place. Mary Ann Nuñez and Lance Shermoen were repeat first place winners in 1984.

A tiny, perky, remarkably talented dancer, Mary Ann Nuñez could follow even the most creative of leads with grace and ease. Into the twenty-first century she has continued to be tough to beat in Jack and Jill competitions as she developed the ability to catch on to a variety of leaders' moves at lightening quick speed. Coming to her West Coast

Two of the most recognized and celebrated dancers in the West Coast Swing community (left to right), Mary Ann Nuñez and Lance Shermoen won the first U.S. Open Swing Dance Championships in 1983. They went on to dominate competitions throughout the 1980s. Note that Jack Bridges, producer of the U.S. Open, can be seen sitting at the table (upper left of photo). (Courtesy of Mary Ann Nuñez.)

Swing via Country Two-Stepping in the early eighties, Nuñez originally caught sight of Swing dancing (the West Coast style) at a country western dance club. She was intrigued, wanted to see more of it, and attended her first Swing club, the Tahitian Village, in 1983. Although she recalls being the youngest person in the club, Nuñez says that she instantly "felt at home." She began hanging out at other Swing spots, such as Lion D'or and Kings Table (which later became The Press Box). She met Dean Collins at a once-a-month Swing event at Bobby McGee's in Orange County. While she never took formal lessons from him, Nuñez says, "He would just take me on the dance floor and lead me, and I would follow. [I] enjoyed every minute of it." That same year, 1983, Dean Collins was hired to choreograph a Swing dance routine for a Steve Allen television special called *In the Swing*. He invited Nuñez to be one of the dancers on the program, and introduced her to Lance Shermoen, her partner for the program's performance. With naturally artistic dance lines and the muscular strength to easily lift, flip, or throw a partner up in the air, Shermoen honed his competition and performance abilities and became one of the most recognized and best-regarded leaders of the West Coast Swing community. Five-time showcase division winner of the U.S. Open Swing Dance Championships, Shermoen may have inherited his dance talent from his parents, Lawrence "Laurie" and Ronnie Shermoen, who were both part of Dean Collin's group of Swing dancers in the 1940s. Shermoen notes that his father always pushed him to "work out, so he could throw his dance partners even higher" (E-mail interview with Nuñez; Shermoen's online obituary to his father, "Passing of My Dad Laurie Shermoen").

The dance performance of *In the Swing* is a great example of how the slotted style of Swing lends itself to formation performance routines. Dean Collins choreographed his dancers in a straight line, five couples across. They perform a sequence of moves in unison (there are also spotlighted solos), with television cameras recording from a variety of angles including from an overhead, aerial perspective. The dancers featured on *In The Swing* include Dean and Mary Collins, Lance Shermoen and Mary Ann Nuñez, Bart Bartolo and Kathy Lovelady, Tom Boots and Shirley Fietsam, and Bobby Hefner and Natalie Esparza.

Sylvia Sykes and Jonathan Bixby of Santa Barbara, CA, took private lessons from Dean Collins from 1981 to 1984. The first year of the U.S.

Open Swing Dance Championships, they signed up to compete together. But, as Bixby explains:

> We weren't *encouraged* to enter the contest—we were *forced* to enter! With Dean, there was no getting around it. (Telephone interview)

Bixby and Sykes both describe the slotted style of Swing they dance as "Smooth Style Lindy." And although they were "standouts" in the competition, Bixby recalls that at the U.S. Open Swing Dance Championships, everyone was dancing West Coast Swing. "Everyone except us," he comments. However, it didn't really come as a surprise because, as Bixby continues:

> When we entered the U.S. Open, we already knew we were "different." We'd been hanging out at various clubs in Orange County and we knew that most people in that area were dancing West Coast Swing.

Prior to entering the competition, Bixby and Sykes had already been dancing together for some 20 years. They met and first danced together when she was 14 and he was 15 years old. In the mid-1960s, they were guest regulars on the KTLA dance show, *Shebang*. Sykes confirms that they watched "old-timers," like Maxi Dorf, kick up their heels at places like Lion D'or, and Bobby McGee's in Orange County. It was Dean Collins who suggested that they study Balboa with Dorf. They took lessons from Dorf from 1984 to 1987, becoming beautifully adept at mixing their Balboa into their Smooth Lindy style (Telephone interviews with Sykes and Bixby).

In 1978, Erin Stevens and Steven Mitchell were teaching New York Hustle during noon-hour dance classes at Pasadena City College. Sylvia Sykes and Jonathan Bixby also taught Hustle in the years of disco music's popularity. Erin Stevens went on to attend the University of Irvine and graduated with a degree in choreography and the teaching of dance. As the disco craze faded, Stevens and Mitchell both learned six-count Jitterbug/East Coast Swing. Erin explains, "We picked up some West Coast Swing, but that was being done more in Orange County." Stevens and Mitchell loved dancing to the song "Sing, Sing, Sing," which the local Los Angeles bands were all playing. Erin recalls, "It was fast and flying and we went crazy with our six-count moves. But we knew there was something more, and it wasn't what any of the West Coast Swing dancers were doing. Steven kept saying, 'I feel something

Internationally acclaimed Swing dancers and instructors Sylvia Sykes and Jonathan Bixby (shown here dancing together in the 1980s), studied with such dance masters as Dean Collins and Maxi Dorf. Experts in Balboa, and in a style they refer to as "Smooth Lindy," Sykes and Bixby were at the forefront of the Swing dance revival of the late 1990s. (Courtesy of Sylvia Sykes.)

in my soul that I'm not seeing anyone at any of the clubs doing.'" Two things then happened that changed the course of both of Stevens's and Mitchell's lives. First, Erin's sister Tami brought home a video of the Marx Brothers movie *A Day at the Races* (with a Whitey's Lindy Hoppers' dance scene). Videotape was a fairly new technology in 1980, and Erin reports:

> We were blown away! We could tell that the dancers in that movie were feeling so much more than we'd ever seen. So, we started learning their moves backwards and forwards. I think it was very motivating for Steven to see black dancers moving with that fast energetic freedom. They motivated me too, and we both said, "That's what we want to do!"

Shortly thereafter, the Stevens sisters' father brought home a copy of the August 23, 1943, *Life* magazine with the Lindy Hop on the cover. It was late 1983, and it was the first time Stevens and Mitchell had ever seen the term "Lindy Hop." They had no knowledge of what Lindy Hop was, but the article included the words "Broadway" and "Harlem," and they recognized Leon James as one of the dancers from *A Day at the Races*. So, in early 1984, on a mission to find the roots of Swing, they boarded a plane for New York City.

## New York, New York

A renewed interest in Swing, which had started to formulate in the late 1970s and early 1980s, led directly to a rediscovery of a lost treasure— the Lindy Hop, the original style of Swing. This treasure was hidden in New York City. Knowledge of the Lindy Hop was restlessly waiting to be reawakened there—and the early 1980s brought the awakening.

In a Greenwich Village phone booth, in the pouring rain, Erin Stevens called every Leon James listed in the phone book. When no one she spoke with had a clue who they were talking about (Steven Mitchell stood there with Stevens), they decided to call a dance studio. It was 1984, and Sandra Cameron's Dance Center had the largest ad in the yellow pages under "dance studios." Stevens asked someone at the dance studio if they knew of any original Lindy Hoppers who were still dancing. She was told that Leon James was no longer alive but was given the home phone number of Al Minns, an innovative, early dancer at the Savoy Ballroom in the 1930s and winner of the Harvest Moon Ball in 1938. Minns was teaching a small group of students at the Sandra Cameron Dance Center at that time. He had also recently worked with a trio of Swedish dancers—two founding members of the Rhythm Hotshots, Anders Lind and Lennart Westerlund, and the Swedish Swing Society secretary, Henning Sorenson (Manning and Millman, 272). Minns met with Erin Stevens and Steven Mitchell for a series of private lessons. He taught them some wonderful tricks and aerials, then took them to Harlem by taxi and showed them where the Savoy Ballroom had once stood. He also took them to the New York Library of the Performing Arts, and sat with them in a little viewing booth to watch old Lindy Hop footage. "That's when," Stevens says, "we went from thinking about Al as a great old dancer, to understanding we were studying with a national treasure!" They studied with Minns for that whole week. When they left New York, they felt their lives had changed. They were on a mission: to bring back the Lindy Hop.

Steven Mitchell and Erin Stevens (left to right) studied Lindy Hop in the 1980s, first with Al Minns, and then with Frankie Manning. Manning credited them as being his first students, launching his "second era of Swing" career. In this 1986 photo taken in Pasadena, CA (at the PBDA), note the Harlem Blues & Jazz Band onstage behind the dancers. The band included such veteran musical greats as trombonist Eddie Durham and vocalist Laurel Watson. Band founder Dr. Al Vollmer can be seen on soprano sax (center stage). (Photographer: Ed Kriegel, PBDA photo archives.)

Erin Stevens and Steven Mitchell competed in the U.S. Open Swing Dance Championships in 1984, the second year of the Anaheim event. They had taken a number of private lessons from Al Minns and had incorporated Lindy Hop moves into their dancing by then. They were also performing Swing with a variety of Los Angeles area bands. But they were dancing an entirely different style of Swing from everyone else in the U.S. Open competition. Stevens comments, "We were dancing East Coast Swing combined with Lindy Hop moves, like Back Charleston. The judges didn't know what to make of us." They placed sixth in the competition that year, with one of their judge's comment cards reading, "Does not know the basic step" (Personal interview with Erin Stevens).

The Sandra Cameron Dance Center in New York City played a vital part in the rediscovery of the Lindy Hop style of Swing and its subsequent resurgence. Three-time U.S. Ballroom champion Sandra Cameron, along with her studio business manager and husband, Larry Schulz, deserve tremendous credit for coaxing Al Minns into the teaching arena in 1981. It came about through an event they attended that year, an annual dance competition run by Mama Lou Parks. Schultz explains that there was social dancing in between the competitive rounds. He noticed an older gentleman, a standout in the crowd, whose dancing was remarkable. Schulz was working for WNBC television at the time, and he did a lot of newsworthy stories on fads and crazes. He'd seen a lot of Swing dancing before this particular event, but this older gentleman had a natural grace and a "connection to the music" like no one Schulz had seen before. The dancer was Al Minns. Schulz spoke to Minns at the event, and arranged a private lesson between Minns and Sandra Cameron. Minns was very reluctant to teach at first, as Schulz recalls, saying something like, "I wouldn't know how to teach this, and besides, no one cares about this kind of dancing anymore. It's over." But Larry Schulz was persistent. He remembers adamantly telling Minns, "No. *This must not die.*" Their meeting, and the private lesson in which Sandra Cameron saw the Lindy Hop for the first time, ultimately led to Minns teaching classes at the Dance Center. Cameron helped him work out how to "count" what he was dancing, and she hired him to teach both weekly, one-hour group classes and private lessons at her school. Minns soon developed an enthusiastic group of students (some of whom later formed the New York Swing Dance Society).

The Sandra Cameron Dance Center is unique in its focus on competitive International Ballroom dance styles along with a dedicated commitment to Social dance. In 1987, Frankie Manning joined the school's teaching staff, and he remained with the school—instructing there between his frequent traveling gigs—until his passing (Telephone interview with Schulz).

The fact that it was a "Mama Lou" (also written Mama "Lu") event that brought Al Minns to the attention of Larry Schulz and Sandra Cameron—and, thus, to teaching—is only one instance of Mama Lou Parks' influence in "bringing back Swing." Parks was a tireless crusader for the preservation of the Lindy Hop from the mid-fifties until her death in 1990. Dance Historian Terry Monaghan points out that the original spelling of Parks' name was "Mama Lou" until a press agent in the seventies changed it to "Lu." (On that basis, Monaghan hopes to standardize the spelling to "Lou.") Originally a hatcheck girl at Harlem's Savoy Ballroom, Parks became "a significant dancer there in her own right," with a list of formidable accomplishments. She developed an intensive training program for Harlem youngsters interested in learning the Lindy Hop, and she established the Mama Lou Parks' Jazz Dancers, a troupe that specialized in choreographed flashy Lindy Hop routines and performed across the U.S. and internationally. But it was also "Mama Lou" who kept the Harvest Moon Ball afloat after the Savoy Ballroom closed in 1958. The Savoy had traditionally hosted the preliminary rounds of the Lindy Hop competition, and when the ballroom closed, Parks took over the running of the prelims (at an alternate venue) herself. Then, when the organizers of the official Harvest Moon Ball cancelled the Lindy Hop division of their event altogether, Mama Lou Parks linked her prelims with Germany's World Federation of Rock 'n' Roll Swing competition, and called her annual contest an "International Ball." Finalists in her event were flown to Germany to compete (Monaghan, "'Mama Lu' Parks: Crashing Cars & Keeping the Savoy's Memory Alive," savoyballroom.com website; Telephone interview with Terry Monaghan, March 28, 2010).

The enthusiasm and hard work of "Mama Lou" Parks created a spinoff of interest in various individuals that kept Lindy Hop alive in the sixties and seventies, and led to a widespread resurgence of interest in the eighties and nineties. For example, when Parks' troupe toured the UK in 1983, Terry Monaghan and Warren Heyes attended her dance workshops. The following year, these two dancers, inspired by Parks, teamed up to create the professional dance company, the Jiving Lindy Hoppers. And Cynthia Millman, co-author of Frankie Manning's autobiography, notes that it was "a performance by the Mama Lu Parks' Dancers at the Brooklyn Academy of Music in 1983" that first inspired her to learn the Lindy Hop (Telephone interview with Terry Monaghan; Millman in Manning and Millman, 2007, 15).

As Al Minns' classes grew and evolved at the Sandra Cameron Dance Center, a group of his students began "hanging out together" after class. Eleven of those "diehard" students founded the nonprofit New York Swing Dance Society. Original board member Margaret Batiuchok notes that many of the early NYSDS "contributors" were regulars at a weekly swing night at a country western nightclub called City Limits. When the club closed down in 1984, some in the group began driving to Small's Paradise in Harlem, which held Swing dances on Monday nights. Frankie Manning and Norma Miller attended several of those evenings, although Manning often noted that because he was working for the post office at the time, he didn't go as often as he would have liked to. Batiuchok suggests that it was the fact that City Limits closed, coupled with the long drive up to Harlem, that actually prompted the founding of the NYSDS. The group was looking for a place to dance downtown, with a sizeable floor that could open up swing dancing to a large general population. Another board member, Jerry Goralnick, found just the place: The Cat Club, a wonderful venue in an old roller-skating rink on East 13th Street. It had a large dance floor where the group could gather for meetings and hold dances. The New York Swing Dance Society was founded on March 6, 1985, devoted to "the revival, preservation and development of swing dancing." Two months later, the group held its first dance at The Cat Club. By the following year, dances were being held there every other Sunday night with bands like the Loren Schoenberg Big Band, Al Cobb's C & J Band, and the Harlem Blues and Jazz Band; over 300 dancers attended every evening (E-mail interview with Batiuchok; Goralnick, "Swing Dancing Makes a Comeback at The Cat Club," *Footnotes*, 1986, 1; Amy D'Auita, "The Swing Dance Society: A Brief History," *Footnotes*, 1986, 1).

The New York Swing Dance Society (NYSDS) has made, and continues to make, enormous contributions to the national Swing scene. When Gabrielle Winkel joined the 11 "original" board members of the NYSDS, she became editor of the organization's quarterly newsletter, *Footnotes*, working with editorial board members Robert Crease, Amy D'Aiuta, Jerry Goralnick, Duncan Maginnis, and Cynthia Millman (co-author of Frankie Manning's autobiography). Robert Crease did a series of published interviews with original Savoy dancers specifically for the newsletter, which were called "Profiles of Original Lindy Hoppers." The first interview of the series debuted in the April–June edition of 1986 and spotlighted Norma Miller. In subsequent editions, Crease's series covered dancers such as Frankie Manning, Elnora Dyson, Billy Ricker, Mildred Cruse, Sandra Gibson, George Lloyd, and many others. These profiles provide a treasure trove of biographical information on many of the original Savoy dancers.

After Al Minns passed away in 1985, Erin Stevens and Steven Mitchell continued to pursue their historical studies of the Lindy Hop. It was Robert Crease who made them aware of the name "Frankie Manning." This time, Erin went to the Pasadena Library looking for a New York phone book. She recalls that, "There were three Manning's listed." Stevens asked the first Frank Manning who picked up the phone, "Are you Frank Manning the dancer?" He answered, "No, I'm Frank Manning the postal worker." But then, after a short pause, he added, "But I used to be a dancer." Stevens had found the Manning she was searching for.

# 10

# The Second Era of Swing, and Beyond

Writing about the resurgence of Swing dancing gets tricky—there are many different interpretations of which driving forces were most responsible for making it happen, and how and why it became so popular again—but the early and mid-years of the 1980s lit sparks of interest in a few individuals who started the ball rolling. Soon, from major cities to the smallest of towns in the United States and abroad, there were dance teachers, performance groups, and historians diligently working to reignite an interest in Swing dancing. The rediscovery of the original style, the Lindy Hop, along with the involvement of surviving original masters of the dance, such as Frankie Manning and Norma Miller, drove Swing's popularity forward. Then, as the national mainstream media began to spotlight Swing dancing in movies and on television, the Lindy Hop was introduced to a whole new generation of dancers. Bolstered by a general "retro" trend in popular culture, Swing dancing raced toward the peak years of its revival. The years 1998–2000 were at the heart of what can legitimately be called "the second era of swing."

Dancers in Sweden, surprisingly, were among those at the forefront in the effort to preserve and promote the Lindy Hop. In a wonderful 1986 article in *The Atlantic Monthly*, Robert P. Crease explains that of all the European countries, the Lindy Hop was originally "met with the greatest enthusiasm" in Sweden. Like the Lindy, the Swedish folk dance, the Hambo, is fast-paced and improvisational in nature. In fact, the Lindy Hop became known as the "American Hambo" and was popular with Swedish youth in the 1930s. In the late 1970s, dance instructor Lasse Kühler (whom Crease describes as the "Bob Fosse of Sweden"), began teaching classes in the American Lindy Hop. Some of his students eventually formed the Swedish Swing Society and organized and hosted a three-day dancing event outside of Stockholm, in the village of Herräng. Their "Herräng Dance Camp" debuted in 1982 with 25 registered attendees, and grew to become the largest and most international Swing camp in the world. In 1985, Lennart Westerlund, a member of the Swedish Swing Society (and who funded Al Minns' teaching sojourn to Sweden in 1984), formed the Rhythm Hot Shots, a professional Swing dance performance company renowned for their precise recreations of Lindy Hop routines from early American films. The troupe's astounding dance abilities, both on the ground and in the air, wowed audiences wherever and whenever they performed. The Rhythm Hot Shots can be credited with exposing multitudes of new audiences to the Lindy Hop and other American vernacular dances (Crease, "Swing Story," 77–82; herrang.com).

Meanwhile, in the United States, the Sandra Cameron Dance Center in New York, which had originally hired Al Minns as an instructor in 1981, forged ahead in the mid-1980s in promoting Lindy Hop through teachers like Paul Grecki, and a variety of mediums. For example, Cameron's husband, Larry Schulz, worked in conjunction with Norma Miller in producing a jazz show at the Village Gate in 1984 called "A Night at the Savoy: A Salute to Swing," which featured the Norma Miller Jazz Dancers, with Miller herself serving as master of ceremonies. The show ran for subsequent performances and served as a reunion hub for many of the "old-timers" of Swing, including Billy Ricker, Al Minns, Frankie Manning, and others, helping respark their enthusiasm for the Lindy Hop. But when the New York Swing Dance Society began hosting its own Monday night dances at The Cat Club, in 1985, the flame was truly reignited. The popularity of the dances—the energy and the joy of those evenings—led Frankie Manning to finally decide, "Okay, it's coming back." The second era of swing was building up steam (Manning and Millman, 2007, 225, 226).

In 1986, when Erin Stevens first asked Frankie Manning for Swing lessons, his answer was "No," because he was "not" an instructor, and he was a "*retired* Lindy Hopper." But Steven Mitchell recalls, "He did agree to meet with us if we were ever in New York again." That's all Stevens and Mitchell needed to hear: once again, they headed to New York City to rendezvous with Manning at a nightclub. After meeting them and watching them socially dance together, he agreed to teach them after all. As he put it, they had "soul" and "wonderful rhythm," and he wanted to help them improve their skills. In fact, he picked them up at their hotel the next morning and drove them to his apartment in Queens for their first of many private lessons. According to Manning's autobiography, that was his "first real teaching experience" (Deborah Huisken, "We'd Like to See the Whole World Swinging," *Hoppin'*, Autumn, 1993, 4–5; Manning and Millman, 227–228).

Rolling back his living room rug, Manning told the young dancers, "Show me what you can do." Stevens describes the moment:

> We put our cassette tape into his machine. The song was our favorite, "Sing, Sing, Sing," and we took off showing him our tricks and our aerials. But Frankie walked over and stopped the tape deck. He put in a different cassette, Count Basie's version of "Shiny Stockings." We had no idea how to dance to that rhythm and tempo! We thought we already knew how to Swing dance, but Frankie had to show us what to do, and what to feel. We started right there from scratch. (Interview)

In that first lesson, although he couldn't break down the steps, or count what he was dancing, Manning helped them understand the essence of Swing dancing. He led Stevens in various moves so that Mitchell could see them, and Stevens could feel them. He worked on their rhythmic bounce, getting them to feel the "groove" of the basics under their feet. Stevens has consistently said, "Al Minns gave us the tricks and flashy moves, but Frankie Manning gave us the heart and the soul of the Lindy Hop." Footage from one of their early lessons in Manning's apartment is included in the made-for-television documentary, *Frankie Manning: Never Stop Swinging* (Cohen, 2009). Stevens laughs and says, "Those are our baby movies!"

On their second trip to New York City to take private lessons from Frankie Manning, they joined him for a Swing dance evening at The Cat Club. The evening was organized by the Jiving Lindy Hoppers' manager Terry Monaghan (the UK-based troupe was in New York at the time), in conjunction with Robert Crease of the New York Swing Dance Society. Erin Stevens refers to that evening at The Cat Club as the "close encounters" event. It was March 23, 1986, and there was an international contingency of dancers in the club that night, all sharing a common purpose. Stevens explains, "If you asked people that night, 'Why are you here?' one after another, it seemed, they all answered the question the same way, 'We're here in search of the roots of Swing.'" Her eyes widen and she adds, "It was surreal!" (Interview).

## Close Encounters of the "Swing Kind"

The Pasadena Ballroom Dance Association (PBDA) was started in 1983, offering group classes in American Social Ballroom and Swing. Co-founded by sisters Erin and Tami Stevens, the school was unique at the time in that it was based entirely on "Social" dance, as opposed to "International" style Ballroom, and offered progressive six-week series of classes without contracts. In the pre-revival years of Swing, the PBDA had large East Coast and West Coast Swing classes. In late 1984, Lindy Hop was added to the schedule. However, as "the American public was not familiar with the term 'Lindy Hop,'" Erin Stevens notes, "We started writing 'Jitterbug/East Coast Swing/Lindy Hop' to get students in the door. Then we'd sneak the Lindy Hop in on them." By the mid-1980s, the PBDA was working hard to make people aware of the Lindy Hop. "But," Stevens adds, "There was this one amazing evening at The Cat Club, in 1986, when we met a roomful of people who were working to do the same thing!" (Personal Interview; Jeff Nicoll, "A Talk with Erin Stevens," *L. A. SWINGINFO NEWS*, April 2004, 4).

The Cat Club evening in New York City, which featured the Harlem Blues and Jazz Band, social dancing, and a variety of dance performances, has come to be viewed, in the words of Robert Crease, as a "now legendary" episode in the history of Swing ("Jitterbug Revue Swings in the Rockies," *Footnotes*, 1987, 3). Along with Erin Stevens, Steven Mitchell, Frankie Manning, and Norma Miller, two of the other American dancers at The Cat Club that night were Sylvia Sykes and Jonathan Bixby, from Santa Barbara, California. Like Stevens and Mitchell, they had also studied old footage from the early movies, and were in New York hoping to study with some of the "old timers" of Swing. By the following year, 1987, Sykes and Bixby were themselves producing monthly Swing dances in Santa Barbara, featuring a variety of live bands. The pair traveled extensively as Lindy and Balboa instructors, and continued to be recognized and celebrated for their pioneering work in "bringing back Swing."

This photograph was taken on March 23, 1986, at The Cat Club in New York City, at a now "historic" gathering of international Swing dancers. Back row (left to right): Bob Crease, Claudia Gintersdorfer, Warren Heyes, Angie Selby, Frankie Manning, Norma Miller, Laurel Watson (vocalist on stage), Jeanefer Jean-Charles, Yvonne Washington, Pepsi Bethel, Ryan Francois. Front row (left to right): Jonathan Bixby, Sylvia Sykes, Steven Mitchell, Erin Stevens. (Courtesy of Paul Armstrong.)

The London-based professional dance troupe the Jiving Lindy Hoppers were also at The Cat Club that historic evening in 1986. They had flown to New York for three weeks to work with early Savoy Ballroom Lindy Hopper, Pepsi Bethel. One of the most renowned Lindy Hoppers of the nineties Swing revival, Ryan Francois, was dancing on the Jiving Lindy Hoppers team at that time. By the following year, Francois was touring and performing with his own dance company, Zoots and Spangles Authentic Jazz Dance Company. There was also a group from Boulder, Colorado, at The Cat Club, led by dancer Joe Maslan, known as "Jitterbug Joe." His Colorado group danced six-count Swing, but they had read about the eight-count Lindy Hop in Bob Crease's *Atlantic Monthly* article, "The Swing Story." Curious about the original style, they flew to New York City to connect with the New York Swing Society, and were particularly thrilled to meet Norma Miller. They had watched her in the Marx Bros. movie, *A Day at the Races*, rewinding the video over and over to try to learn the eight-count moves.

Not knowing the names for the particular steps, they made up their own. One of Norma Miller's swing-outs became their "Miller" step. They worked out an easier version of it, and called it the "Miller Lite." Jitterbug Joe's group returned to Colorado after their evening at The Cat Club, and founded a performance team called "Jitterbug Revue," dedicated to preserving the Lindy Hop (Crease, "Jitterbug Revue Swings in the Rockies," *Footnotes*, 1987, 3).

## Instigating a Rebirth: The Late 1980s

Other individuals and groups in the United States involved in bringing back the Lindy Hop in the 1980s included the multitalented dancer, choreographer, bandleader, and stand-up comic Chester Whitmore, from Los Angeles, California. Whitmore had organized a team of dancers that performed all forms of early American vernacular jazz. The Santa Barbara Swing Dance Club, in California (co-founded by Sylvia Sykes and Jonathan Bixby), inspired numerous noteworthy dancers, including Jann Olsen, Melinda Comeau (whose Jitterbug Jam was a favorite event in the Swing revival years), and Rob Van Haaren, who went on to teach internationally and produce his own international Swing events. Anne Townsend began social Swing dances in the Washington, D.C., area and founded the Washington Swing Dance Committee, which continues to produce and host Swing events into 2011. Bill Borgida brought "Lindy awareness" to the community of Ithaca, New York. Involved in establishing the Ithaca Swing Dance Network, Borgida also helped steer the dancing careers of teenagers, most notably, the Lindy Hopping troupe of youngsters known as "Minnie's Moochers." Some of these young performers went on to become the brightest dancing stars of the revival and postrevival periods.

In 1987, Monica Coe and Pat McLaughlin formed an official dance company of the New York Swing Dance Society called the Big Apple Lindy Hoppers. They worked with Frankie Manning in learning aerials and choreographing routines (he coached them and often performed with them), and their troupe was among the first to showcase the performance side of the Lindy Hop. Alan and Lisa Rocoff, Rebecca Reitz, and John Wise and Gabrielle Winkel with the New York Swing Dance Society organized Boogie in the Berkshires, a Swing weekend in Kent, Connecticut, in 1989, which drew 225 attendees. The event featured classes with Frankie Manning, John Lucchese, and Margaret Batiuchok among others, along with a Jack and Jill dance contest. In Seattle, Washington, Walter and Nancy Anna Dill started another of the earliest Lindy Hop–based workshop events, called Wild Week, at Fort Worden in Port Townsend. They also founded Living Traditions in 1990, a company that produced CDs and video tapes, including the definitive Savoy Lindy Hop instructional series with Frankie Manning and Erin Stevens (Crease, "On Stage with the Big Apple Lindy Hoppers, *Footnotes*, Nov.–Dec., 1988, 5; Kerry B. Stevens, "A Letter Home . . . " *Footnotes*, Nov.–Dec., 1989, 5).

Craig "Hutch" Hutchinson wrote a syllabus of moves for West Coast Swing dancers (his own codified system of putting Swing moves on paper) in the 1970s, and established the Potomac Swing Dance Club in the 1980s, which explored a variety of Swing styles. His Virginia State Open Swing Dance Championships was one of the first to "add on" a Lindy Hop category (in 1992) for its competitors. Hutchinson's dedication led to broader appreciation of the interconnection between all varieties of Swing, and to the founding of the Jam Cellar in Washington, DC, a weekly venue of workshops and dances with a roster of top-notch instructors.

From its opening day, Disneyland in Anaheim, California, always featured swing music in the park. Stan Freese, talent casting and booking director for Disney, comments that "it has arguably been the longest running big band venue in the world." He recalls that during the 1970s and '80s, such bands as "Count Basie, Cab Calloway, Duke Ellington, Stan Kenton, Buddy Rich, Tommy Dorsey, Lionel Hampton, and Louis Prima" (his list is lengthy!), all performed for Disneyland's park visitors. Many "old-timers of Swing," original Swing and Balboa dancers of the 1930s, frequented the park in the 1980s. Balboa phenomenon Hal Takier is just one example of the "early greats" who danced there three to four times a week. Disneyland served as an inspirational hub in those years for a younger generation of dancers who watched the "old-timers," learned from them, and helped bring Swing back into mainstream popularity (Telephone interview with Freese, John Devorick, "We Had a Hell of a Good Time," *Dance Action*, October, 1988, 9).

By the late 1980s, early American vernacular dance was being researched and celebrated in the visual and performing arts. Frankie Manning and Norma Miller co-choreographed a Lindy Hop number for the Alvin Ailey American Dance Theater in 1988. ABC television profiled Frankie Manning on *20/20* in 1989, and, he won the Tony Award that same year (along with Cholly Atkins, Henry LeTang, and Fayard Nicholas) for best choreography for the Broadway musical *Black and Blue*. The show's theatrical dancers were highly trained in Ballet and Modern Jazz, but these particular choreographers were hired to instill in them, "authentic vernacular movement." Theater audiences were exposed to authentic Jazz dancing then, and *Black and Blue* played a part in bringing both Tap and Swing back into mainstream pop consciousness. Also, in 1989, artist Richard Yarde was celebrated for his outstanding work in the creation of a mural for the Joseph P. Addabbo Federal Building in Jamaica, New York, depicting early Lindy Hoppers from the Savoy Ballroom. But 1989 should also be noted for an event in Sweden that profoundly affected the revival of Swing dancing in the United States. The Rhythm Hot Shots performance team became actively involved in producing the Herrang Dance Camp and hired Frankie Manning to "headline" the event. Manning had been to Sweden previously to work one-on-one with the troupe, but as the official Herrang instructor, he taught all camp attendees. With Manning as an annual draw, Herrang grew into an annual month-long event of enormous proportions. By the late 1990s, the camp was billing itself as the world's most "spectacular Afro-American dance camp," and was hiring upwards of 40 international teachers annually. It remained the largest of the camps throughout, and after, the peak revival years of Swing. Herrang was the original prototype for the multitudes of subsequent global Lindy Hop camps; yet, with its sideshow attractions, cabarets, and self-described "semi-surrealistic reality" (herrang.com) it was a creative original, impossible to copy! All those who attended Herrang brought home better dancing skills, a dose of Swedish creativity at its best (lots and lots of mosquito bites!), and memories of an unforgettable, truly spectacular experience.

## Neo-Swing in the Early 1990s

In the early 1990s, a number of bands began combining rock and roll, rockabilly, and jump blues with the sounds of classic swing, and a new musical offering emerged called "neo-swing." When the Los Angeles–based band, Royal Crown Revue, released its "Kings of Gangster Bop" CD in 1991, the word "gangster" prompted most record stores to file the CD in their "rap" music section. But it wasn't "gangsta" with an "a." As lead singer and band founder, Eddie Nichols has often pointed out his band's use of the word "gangster" was meant to conjure up sounds and images of the 1940s. Their swingin' retro sounds, infused with a nineties modern feel, inspired a new generation of youth to appreciate the music of their parents and grandparents, the genre of swing. In the early 1980s, "Rock This Town" was a rockabilly hit record for Brian Setzer and his popular band, the Stray Cats. In the following decade, Setzer debuted his Brian Setzer Orchestra, a band devoted to the new sounds of the retro swing renaissance. In 1989, in Northern California, LaVay Smith and Her Red Hot Skillet Lickers began performing in San Francisco's rock and roll clubs. The band gathered steam in the early 1990s with Smith's strong vocals and their retro swingin' sounds. Cherry Poppin' Daddies was perfecting their irreverent outlandish style of neo-swing in the early 1990s, in Eugene, Oregon, while Big Bad Voodoo Daddy was touring in California. Originally recording on their own label, "Big Bad Records," Big Bad Voodoo Daddy's fame and popularity swelled during the swing revival. They secured a contract with Capital Records, provided songs for the cult film, *Swingers*, and were hired to perform during the half-time show for Super Bowl XXXIII.

A few of the other early neo-swing bands of the 1990s were Lee Press On and the Nails, Flattop Tom & His Jump Cats, the Blue Room Boys, Rick Joswick's The Jumpin' Joz Band, Steve Lucky & the Rhumba Bums, James Intveld's "Jimmy & the Gigolos," The New Morty Show, Red & the Red Hots, Big Time Operator, The Senders (with the velvety voice of Charmin Michelle, who developed her own solo career as a jazz singer), and the J Street Jumpers. The widely popular group Indigo Swing, formed in 1993, produced some of the most extraordinary "sweet swing" recordings of the revival era.

In 1999, swing dancers throughout the country lamented the demise of Indigo Swing, when the musicians disbanded. Swing dancer and swing music aficionado Gene Hashiguchi was one of Indigo Swing's many avid fans. Hashiguchi notes that it was the "combination" of talented players, a magical musical blend of vocalist Johnny Boyd, pianist William Beatty, and Baron Shul on saxophones and flute that made the band special. In Hashiguchi's words, "It was a classic example of the whole being greater than the sum of its parts." He notes that long after Indigo Swing's disbanding, their music continued to be played at

Royal Crown Revue, shown here, was generally considered the first of the 1990s revival bands that helped launch the "second era" of swing. (Courtesy of Royal Crown Revue and Right Brain Entertainment.)

Swing dances everywhere. For example, in 2009, on the ABC network's "reality television" hit *Dancing with the Stars*, Kym Johnson and Donny Osmond danced to Indigo Swing's version of "Choo Choo Ch' Boogie," and went on to win the show's season 9 competition (E-mail Interview with Hashiguchi, April 19, 2010).

The Bill Elliott Swing Orchestra sprung onto the music scene, in 1993, with a sound virtually indistinguishable from the swing styles of the late 1930s and early 1940s. Casey MacGill and The Spirits of Rhythm created their own unique sound in MacGill's ability to make the ukulele swing, and the high-profile Squirrel Nut Zippers served up a hot vintage sound and gained a loyal following of fans. The

Swing Session, a popular jump blues band from San Francisco (later called Stompy Jones), retained their popularity with Swing audiences well past the peak revival years of the late 1990s. David Rose, string bass player with the band, originally played with Indigo Swing. He debuted The Swing Session band at the HiBall Lounge in San Francisco, which, along with other nightspots such as Club Deluxe, Bimbo's 365 Club, and Café Du Nord, was at the forefront of the neo-swing scene. Bandleader George Gee formed his Make Believe Ballroom Orchestra in the 1980s. Gee, who plays the string bass (but does not play an instrument with his band, conducting his orchestra instead) created an offshoot band of 10 musicians in 1998 and named it "The Jump Jive and Wailers" in response to the extreme popularity of swing.

## Media Attention

When the national media began to spotlight the emerging swing renaissance in the 1990s, it set in motion a whirlwind of interest. Popular culture went "retro" in all things from clothing styles to musical sounds, and Swing dancing became trendy. Spike Lee's film, *Malcolm X*, released in 1992 (Warner Bros. Pictures), featured energized Lindy Hopping, with Frankie Manning serving as dance consultant to Otis Sallid's choreography. Norma Miller worked as an assistant to Manning. The following year, the film *Swing Kids* (Hollywood Pictures) hit the big screen, portraying a group of German youths dancing American Swing against the backdrop of Nazi Germany. Otis Sallid also choreographed this film; Lindy Hopper extraordinaire Ryan Francois served as assistant choreographer. The dance sequences in *Swing Kids* influenced a broad segment of society and pushed the Swing revival forward. Countless numbers of teenagers responded to the movie's themes of rebellion and angst and began listening to swing music. Suddenly there was a new generation of youngsters thinking about the clothing styles and the hairdos of "the swing kids," and about the retro dance called "Swing."

Stan Freese, talent director at Disneyland in CA, remembers watching the movie *Swing Kids*. "That's when I first recognized the resurgence of swing!" he exclaims. "Disneyland had the big bands, but we'd never punched it up to get the young kids involved at the park." Freese immediately presented a proposal to his superiors, and he was soon hiring many of the top local swing bands. He hired the

The 1993 Hollywood Pictures film *Swing Kids* pushed the swing revival forward and inspired a broad segment of society to seek out Swing dance lessons. Shown here (from left) are Robert Sean Leonard and Tushka Bergen dancing Hand-to-Hand (cross-hold) Charleston Kicks to Benny Goodman's classic swing tune, "Sing Sing Sing." Choreographer Otis Sallid hired Internationally acclaimed Lindy Hopper Ryan Francois as his assistant on the film. Photograph by Frank Connor, courtesy of Photofest. (Buena Vista Pictures/Photofest.)

Pasadena Ballroom Dance Association to teach basic Swing dancing to tourists in the park, as well as to choreograph and perform weekly Swing routines. The PBDA also brought in various local and international Swing performance teams, and Carnation Gardens became the "Jump Jive Boogie Swing Party" on Friday nights (Telephone interview with Freese, February 16, 2010).

In 1994, the movie *The Mask* (New Line Cinema) pushed not only swing music but also retro "zoot suit fashion," into the limelight. Royal Crown Revue's appearance in the film helped the group emerge as the most widely recognized band of the neo-swing era. In 1996, the lower-budget, cult-swing movie *Swingers* (Miramax) portrayed the "cocktail culture" lives of a group of unemployed Hollywood actors. Much of the film's action took place at The Derby, a Los Angeles 1940s style supper/dance club. That helped promote the concept of the Swing dance venue as being "cool" and "trendy."

The Derby on Los Feliz in Hollywood, CA, was ground zero for the swing scene in Los Angeles. Originally opened as a restaurant in the 1920s by Cecil B. DeMille, the building was reopened in 1993 with all of its old Hollywood glamour restored. In an article in the *Los Angeles Times Magazine*, Tammi Gower, who co-owned The Derby (along with her husband Tony Gower), noted that the club became a "tourist attraction" during the swing revival, with many of her patrons showing their passports, instead of their drivers' licenses, to get in ("That Swing Thing," October 31, 1999, np). Most of the top neo-swing bands played The Derby during the revival years of swing, and both Royal Crown Revue and Big Bad Voodoo Daddy had regular gigs at the club. In the peak years of the revival, swing music and dancing was offered at The Derby seven nights a week.

Los Angeles dancer Minn Vo was already an advanced Hip Hop dancer when he visited The Derby for the first time, circa 1996. He was thoroughly inspired to learn more Swing dancing, and he became a "regular" at the club. One of the best things about The Derby, in Minn Vo's opinion, was that everyone who went there truly wanted to dance. In his words:

> At the hip hop clubs, girls would often give you the cold shoulder because they thought you were trying to pick up on them. But at The Derby, the girls really wanted to dance. Everyone was there to Swing! (Telephone interview, April 24, 2010)

Minn Vo recalls that the first formal Swing event he attended was Swing Camp Catalina, in 1997; by the following year, he was teaching Swing in several of the local clubs. He partnered with the wonderfully talented Corina Acosta, and together they won numerous competitive events. Into 2011, Vo continued to teach at workshops and Swing camps around the globe.

By the late 1990s, Swing was getting a lot of media attention, and major newspapers and magazines published articles regarding its revived popularity. An article by Zan Dubin in the *Los Angeles Times* in 1999, notes that "The swing-dancing craze shows no sign of slowing." That same year, the *Smithsonian* magazine's March cover featured a Swing dancing couple along with the words "The Return of the Jitterbugs." *People* magazine ran a story on Frankie Manning called "Swing Man: The dance style that went around comes around again for Frankie Manning," alluding to the fact that the Lindy Hop was back in full force (Dubin, "The Joints Keep Jumpin'," January 7, 6; *Smithsonian* (cover); *People*, Patrick Rogers, Longley and Heyn, July 12, 1999, 150–152).

Scores of smaller regional swing magazines and newsletters also emerged in the 1990s. *Strutter's Quarterly*, a newsletter covering the Minneapolis/Saint Paul area, was founded by Cindy Geiger in 1991. Geiger began teaching Swing in the 1970s and later joined forces with Terry Gardner. Together, offering classes and hosting guest instructors, they kept the Twin Cities Lindy Hop scene jumping. In 1993, Deborah Huisken created a quarterly newsletter, *Hoppin'*; although the newsletter was published in the UK, *Hoppin'* was directed toward the global Lindy Hop community and was internationally popular.

Other 1990s swing publications printed in the United States included *Swivel Magazine*, *Swing Time Magazine*, *Atomic Magazine*, and *5678*, which focused on all styles of Swing, plus Country, Hustle and Ballroom. A few of the smaller regional newsletters included the Savoy Swing Club's *Savoy Swingline* from Seattle, Washington; *Steppin' Out*, serving Swing dancers of the Washington, DC area; and *West Coast Swing America*, focusing on the Atlanta, Georgia, area. All of these magazines and newsletters focused on such diverse topics as neo-swing bands, 1940s hairstyles and "Swing-wear," historical articles, and reviews of the contemporary clubs.

While motion pictures and print media were focusing attention on Swing dancing in the 1990s, it was actually a television commercial, an advertisement for khaki pants, which thoroughly ignited the swing frenzy of the peak revival years. The year was 1998, when four couples were featured Swing dancing to Louis Prima's classic jump swing song "Jump Jive and Wail," on a Gap commercial. With swing-themed movies still in the public's recent memory, and with "retro" being totally in style, the Swing choreography struck a chord with

By the late 1990s, Frankie Manning was an international Swing celebrity. He is seen here performing with Erin Stevens, and surrounded by a tight crowd of onlookers, in Germany at an event organized by the Boogie-Barens Whitsun Swing Dance Camp. Note that one of the event organizers, internationally acclaimed dancer Marcus Koch, is visible in the crowd (center of photo). (Courtesy of Karl Hirt.)

young audiences mesmerized by the speed of the song and the air steps of the dancers. Swing was suddenly all the rage, and people of all ages began taking dance lessons, wanting to "Swing it" like the Gap commercial dancers. Swing dancer/instructor Steve Bailey was hired by the Ballroom Club at the University of Maryland to teach a Swing class, that same year of the Gap commercial. Bailey recalls, "Christi Etcher and I agreed to teach the class, and we were expecting maybe 15 or 20 students. But 300 to 400 people showed up at the door! We squeezed 100 people into the classroom somehow, but there were hundreds more dancing out in the hallway—it was crazy!" (Gap commercial viewable on YouTube.com; personal interview with Bailey).

By 1998, the year of the Gap commercial, most Swing dancers already knew the name "Frankie Manning," as he was traveling and teaching around the world then, and "Lindy Hop" was becoming a familiar term to the general American public. That same year, Manning's first students Erin Stevens and Steven Mitchell were invited to the White

House to perform the Lindy Hop for President Bill Clinton and First Lady Hilary Clinton. The performance was televised nationally on PBS television's *In Performance at the White House*. Steven Mitchell, who became one of the best-known and most admired instructors on both national and international levels, also emerged as a remarkable singer/songwriter in 1998. Classic swing and neo-swing recordings were both solid markets at the time, and Mitchell released a CD of original tunes titled "Just Wanna Swing." The CD included a song that became immensely popular among dancers, "The Jitterbug Stroll" (based on the line-dance of the same name, created by Ryan Francois, circa 1992). Versed in all styles of Swing, Jazz dance, Ballroom, African dance, and Hip Hop, Mitchell made his mark on the second era of swing as an all-around talent. Later, Mitchell teamed with Virginie Jensen and continued his traveling and teaching well into the twenty-first century.

## The "Line Dances" of Swing (the Shim Sham, the Big Apple, the Madison, and the Jitterbug Stroll)

Legendary Lindy Hopper Frankie Manning is credited with keeping a Swing dance version of the Shim Sham Shimmy alive by continuing to teach it into the twenty-first century. Leonard Reed and Willie Bryant actually created the dance, however, as a Tap routine, in the 1920s. Tap dancer Joe Jones also claimed to have been involved in its creation (and it's impossible to verify or deny his claim), and the dance was reportedly popularized at Connie's Inn, in Harlem in 1931, while Jones' troupe (the "Three Little Words") was performing there. Eventually, as the Shim Sham caught on with a wider audience, it was learned not only by Tap dancers, but also by chorus dancers, Jazz dancers, Broadway show dancers and Swing dancers alike. Manning always explained that after-hours at nightclubs, when professional dancers (sometimes even singers and musicians) were all brought up front for recognition and applause, they generally knew the Shim Sham and could all dance it together. It became the standard line dance known to professionals in all the dancing genres. Swing dancers at the Savoy Ballroom in New York danced it as a group activity in the 1930s, while Dean Collins created a popular, slightly altered, version of the dance on the West Coast. Manning always maintained, however, that the Shim Sham didn't gain its mass popularity as a "Swing" line dance until many years later, thanks to the efforts of organizers of various Swing clubs and classes the world over. Especially noteworthy in this regard was the New York Swing Dance Society and Margaret Batiuchok, who made sure it was included in the weekly dances at The Cat Club in the 1980s. Frankie Manning's version is normally danced to Jimmie Lunceford's recording of "T'aint What You Do," or Erskine Hawkin's version of "Tuxedo Junction," and ends with participants "grabbing a partner" and dancing through the end of song. Into the twenty-first century the Shim Sham as a Swing dance tradition had been well preserved.

The Big Apple burst onto the scene, in the summer of 1937. There are numerous magazine and newspaper articles, circa that year, referring to the dance's popularity. As an article in the *New York Times* put it:

> It's the Big Apple ("yeah man!") and everybody's doing it—in the night clubs, in the roadhouses, and in the home. (Bosley Crowther, "From the Turkey Trot to The Big Apple," 1937, np)

When an abandoned synagogue in Columbia, South Carolina, was sold to Elliott Wright (nicknamed Fat Sam), it was re-opened as Fat Sam's Big Apple Night Club, "a juke-joint for African Americans," which meant: "music was played there on a juke box" (and, in the segregated South, also generally meant "no whites allowed"). Black dancers there combined popular Swing steps and improvisational moves in circle formation, possibly in the Afro-American tradition of the "Ring Shout" (see Chapter 1). Betty Wood was one of the white Big Apple dancers recognized for popularizing the dance nationwide in the 1930s and again in the 1990s. Wood credited her friend Billy Spivey for re-creating the Swing steps he had seen at the club, then adding others they were "already familiar with," and choreographing a dance that became popular 'immediately'" (Personal interview with Wood). *Life* magazine noted, in 1937, that dance instructor Arthur Murray jumped on the bandwagon right away, organizing teams of dancers to perform the Big Apple at nightclubs, hotels, and holiday parties ("1937 Closes with Big Apple," Dec. 20, 29).

Dance historian Lance Benishek adds that Billy Spivey originally visited The Big Apple Nightclub in 1936, along with two other white youngsters, Donald Davis and Harold Wiles, and were charged admission of 25 cents a piece to observe, from the balcony, the original black dancers doing the Big Apple. Benishek also notes that it was "the white kids who actually named the dance, 'Big Apple,' after the club."

To do the Big Apple, dancers gather in circle formation and a caller "initiates" (Benishek prefers the word "conducts") the moves. Steps including Truckin, Suzy Q, Charleston Swing, Peckin' and Posin', and Organ Grinder's Swing, were original moves, which were all popular Swing steps of the time. In addition, Benishek has documented over 400 "called" moves, which were incorporated into the dance—coming from regional parts of the country. Frankie Manning choreographed a number of Big Apple routines over the years, and his routine for the movie *Keep Punching* (M. C. Pictures, 1939) is a memorable iconic version of it. However, dance historian Judy Pritchett aptly points out that the Big Apple was never meant to be a choreographed dance. Although it was "called" and everyone participating generally knew the moves, it was still a "Social dance" meant to be danced on the social ballroom floor (Telephone interviews with Benishek and Pritchett). In 2009, Judy Pritchett narrated her own documentary film on the history of the Big Apple, *Dancing The Big Apple 1937: African-American's Inspire a National Craze*, which provides a fascinating look back at the roots of the dance.

In 1960, *Time* magazine commented that a "new dance" known as "the Madison" was becoming "the biggest dance craze since the Big Apple." The article asserts that the origins of the dance were hazy but that it "probably" emerged in either Baltimore, Detroit, or Cleveland. In that same year, of 1960, *The Billboard* magazine states that the dance was born in Baltimore, while an article in *Ebony* magazine asserts it was "imported to Baltimore" from Chicago. Into the twenty-first century the origins of the dance are still hazy. One thing, however, is clear: when the dance debuted on *The Buddy Deane Show*, a television dance program for teens broadcasting live from Baltimore, Maryland, it ignited a nationwide craze.

Al Brown's Tunetoppers recorded the original song, "The Madison," in early 1960, with a set of "called steps" instructing dancers on how to move to it. Later that same year, over the airwaves on his *WEBB* Baltimore radio show, disc jockey Eddie Morrison began calling out moves of his own invention that reflected the pop culture of the era, such as the Rifleman, Jackie Gleason, The Wilt Chamberlain Hook, and Birdland—and his young listeners responded enthusiastically. Columbia Records hired Morrison to record his new "called" version of the dance, along with the Ray Bryant Trio. That song (with music by Bryant and lyrics by Morrison) was called "The Madison Time" and was also released in 1960. Columbia sent out teams of teenage dancers to advertise the dance and plug the record, and disc jockeys around the country were hounded with play requests for the song. In its first two weeks of release, the single sold 200,000 copies (*Time*, "THE JUKEBOX: The Newest Shuffle," April 4, 1960, np; *Ebony*, "The Madison," July, 1960, 71–74).

Swing dancers doing the Madison today generally use the Ray Bryant version. This was also the version chosen by writer-director John Waters for use in his 1988 movie *Hairspray* (New Line Cinemas), a film that reignited the Madison as a craze within the Swing dance community. Swing dancer Paolo Lanna, who has studied the Madison's history and produced an instructional DVD on how to dance it, asserts that the original dancers featured on *The Buddy Deane Show* of the 1960s deserve credit for the dance's rise to fame. Known as "the Committee," the show's dancers developed a large following of youngsters who copied their style and all their moves. When "the Committee" showcased the Madison, that's when the dance burst into popularity and received attention nationwide. As black youngsters were not allowed participation on *The Buddy Deane Show*, and as the dance most likely originated within the black community of one of the cities previously noted, the Madison is often exampled as one of the "Negro dances taken over by white enthusiasts" (E-mail interview with Lanna; *Ebony*, "The Madison," July 1960, 71–74).

In the early 1990s, internationally acclaimed Lindy Hopper Ryan Francois created a line dance based on early Jazz dance steps. He called his new dance the Jitterbug Stroll, and introduced it to the tune "Woodchopper's Ball." Based on a twelve-bar blues chorus, the Jitterbug Stroll consists of steps like the Shorty George, Tick-Tock, and the Suzy Q, to name a few, which are included in four separate repeated patterns. Dancers "quarter turn" to start each of the four patterns at a new angle on the floor. Swing dancer Steven Mitchell's "Jitterbug Stroll" was an original song, written and recorded specifically to accompany Ryan Francois' choreography. In the song, Mitchell calls out the various moves of the dance. Francois's choreography and Mitchell's song became inexorably linked, and around the globe Swing dancers began shouting out, "Ayo-de-yo-de" and rushing out to the dance floor to join in the Jitterbug Stroll.

## Camps, Events, and Exchanges of the 1990s

Dance camps such as Herrang, with international attendees, propagated themselves ("Let's bring those instructors to our town!"), and
fueled the development of thriving Swing dance communities around
the globe. The Pasadena Dance Association produced Swing Camp
Catalina, which debuted in 1994 in Avalon, California, on Catalina
Island, a one-hour boat trip from the Los Angeles harbor. The camp
ran annually through 2004, with Frankie Manning as the teaching
headliner. A few of the many other instructors hired at Swing Camp
Catalina included Chazz Young, Steven Mitchell, Virginie Jensen,
Lennart Westerlund, David Dalmo, Eddie Jansson and Eva Lagerqvist
(along with the entire Rhythm Hot Shots troupe), Paul Overton and
Sharon Ashe, Ryan and Jenny Francois, Marcus Koch and Bärbel
Kaufer, Sing Lim, Fern Soh, Julie Oram, Louise Thwaite, Simon
Selmon, and Kenneth and Helena Norbelie (with their "Shout and Feel
It" Swedish dance team). With classes and nightly dances held in the
magnificent historic Casino Ballroom at water's edge, offering
spectacular views of the ocean and the twinkling lights of Avalon
Harbor, Swing Camp Catalina was a remarkable event in a truly
magical setting.

Tom Koerner and Debra Sternberg teamed as dance partners and
founded their Gottaswing productions in the Washington, DC, area.
They taught classes and hosted various Swing events throughout
the 1990s and beyond, having a tremendous impact on the Swing
community there. Their Groovie Movie Weekend, featuring many of
the original Swing dancers from the *Groovie Movie* film, started in
1996; a number of young dancers involved in their Swing scene went
on to become well-respected instructors themselves, including such
notables as Steve Bailey and Carla Heiney. Bailey credits Koerner and
Sternberg for teaching "literally hundreds and hundreds of people to
Swing dance," helping make the DC area an epicenter of the Swing
revival movement (Telephone interview with Bailey, May 28, 2010).

The year 1996 saw the debut of such notable and diverse events as
the Great Southwest Lindyfest, in Texas, produced by the Houston
Swing Dance Society, and Lindy in the Park—the popular outdoor
dance gathering founded by Chad Kubo and Ken Watanabe and held
every Sunday in San Francisco's Golden Gate Park. Beantown Lindy
Hop Summer Camp, in Massachusetts, began in 1997, and Monsters

of Swing, produced by sisters Tammy and Terri Finocchiaro, in Ventura, CA, started that same year, offering "Club-Style Swing." Big Bad Voodoo Daddy was the camp's featured band, giving many dancers their first-time exposure to neo-swing music. The following year, Los Angeles area dancer Hilary Alexander began her Camp Hollywood, featuring Swing dance instruction and nightly open dances in tandem with the National Jitterbug Championships. Hilary Alexander proved to be not only an excellent promoter and organizer, but also a wonderful singer with a continued career as a swing band vocalist. Into 2011, both Camp Hollywood and Beantown continued as important international Swing dance events.

Organizers of established West Coast Swing competitions across the country began to add "Lindy Hop" as a separate category for their contestants during the 1990s. But in 1998, Paulette Brockington created and directed the first annual American Lindy Hop Championships, billed as an event "by Lindy Hoppers for Lindy Hoppers." Brockington, a professional actress, dancer, and choreographer, had studied intensively with Frankie Manning and was eager to bring about increased awareness to the Lindy Hop style of Swing. Her event was popular well into the twenty-first century (*Strutters Quarterly*, "1st Annual American Lindy Hop Championships," 1998, 3).

A few of the other early camps and notable Swing events of the 1990s included the Augusta Swing Camp in West Virginia, Flyin' Home in the Washington, DC, area, Camp Swing in the Mendocino Woodlands, as well as the Boston Tea Party, Swing Out New Hampshire, and Melinda Comeau's Jitterbug Jam in California. Denise Steele was hosting Frankie Manning workshops in Oregon; the Land o' Loons Lindy Hoppers had organized in Minneapolis; the Triangle Swing Dance Society was going strong in North Carolina, and in Seattle, Washington, the Savoy Swing Club was holding ongoing classes, weekend workshops, and dances. Hi De Ho, another independent Seattle-based organization, was also dedicated to the preservation of the Lindy Hop, while the Illinois Swing Dance Club kept things hoppin' in Peoria. Cindy Geiger and Terry Gardner started their camp Sving du Nord, in 1999, which was also the year in which they married—with a reported 710 guests attending their Swing dance/wedding event! (*Strutter's Quarterly*, "P.S. from Cindy & Terry," Fall 99, 3).

In the late 1990s, while Swing camps continued in popularity, "Lindy Exchanges" also came into vogue worldwide. The Exchanges were an alternative way for Swing dancers from various cities to mingle and exchange ideas, music, and new moves. Originally, small groups of dancers from one city were "hosted" by event organizers from another. The hosts would arrange airport pickups, and provide housing accommodations for their dancing guests. Unlike organized camps, which generally reserved blocks of hotel rooms for participants, Exchanges encouraged sleeping bags and lower-budget housing options. The Exchanges started out small (with often no more than a handful of dancers traveling together), but in some cities they grew into large-scale "convention like" events, with bands hired, club events organized, promotional tee shirts printed, and throngs of dancers attending. While the Exchanges may not have introduced many new people to the genre of Swing, they provided an inexpensive alternative to the camps for dancers already Lindy Hopping. Another unique creation of the swingin' 1990s was an event called the "Lindy bomb," in which dancers would descend upon an unsuspecting music venue, with an organized plan to basically "take over the place," as in "Let's Lindy bomb them!" Instantly, then, that particular venue was turned into a Lindy Hop "happening," generally to the delight of all.

## Swing Frenzy

In 1999, Swing dancing was "in full swing." Some 1,800 admirers, including new pupil Bette Midler, showed up to celebrate Manning's 85th birthday at New York City's Roseland Ballroom (*People*, "Swing Man: The dance style that went around comes around again for Frankie Manning," 1999, 152). That same year, at the Pasadena Ballroom Dance Association, in California, the Stevens sisters' classes were attracting as many as 300 students per class, and the school was averaging 1,400 students per week. Their Swing Camp Catalina, which debuted with 90 dancers in 1994, was a complete "sellout" in 1999. It was the camp's peak year: 1,850 dancers purchased full camp passports (and could attend any and all of the classes and dances), and an additional 432 dancers purchased tickets to attend only the Saturday night dance at the Casino Ballroom. Beantown Camp, in Massachusetts, was split into two separate weeks in 1999 to accommodate its large number of attendees. Also that year, Brian Setzer's Swing Orchestra was the first neo-swing group to be nominated for the best pop album Grammy Award. Big Bad Voodoo Daddy performed for the televised Super Bowl half-time show, and Broadway celebrated the new swing craze with a musical revue titled, simply, *Swing!* Publicity releases advertised the show as an all-singing, all-dancing musical celebration featuring a hot swing band, world-class Swing dancers, and "over 30 dance numbers." Lindy Hoppers Ryan Francois and Jenny Thomas, and West Coast Swing and Country Swing dancers Robert Royston and Laureen Baldovi were just a few of the top-name Swing dancers hired as performers, swing musician Casey MacGill had a featured role (as a bandleader) in the production as well (Dave Muzii and Charlie Moore, "Swing!," *5678*, Dec. 1997, 9).

By the time *Swing!* opened on Broadway, in December of 1999, the Lindy Hop was once again the hottest dance craze in both the United States and Europe. A new generation of Swing dancers, the "hepcats" and "hepkittens," decked themselves in zoot suits, fedoras, and wing-tip shoes (often combing vintage clothing stores for threads of the 1930s and 1940s). For followers, twirling skirts and two-tone shoes were the essential attire. Songs like "Zoot Suit Riot" recorded by Cherry Poppin' Daddies, and "Mr. Zoot Suit," recorded by the Flying Neutrinos, inspired the wearing of the full zoot suit for well-dressed Swing dancing leaders. In Fullerton, California, El Pachuco Zoot Suits, a small family-run business that rented and sold zoot suits with all the trappings and trimmings, became a magnet for Lindy Hoppers. Their wide brimmed hats and ultra baggie pants with suspenders were absolute "musts" for the zoot-suited Swing dancer. In the 1990s, Swing dancers from all around the globe were visiting El Pachuco Zoot Suits. Kenneth and Helena Norbelie, of Sweden, for example, purchased El Pachuco zoot suits for their entire Shout and Feel It dance troupe. Other retails shops such as Aardvark's Odd Ark clothing store, in Los Angeles, California, and Heart's Desire in Springfield, Virginia, are just two of the numerous shops specializing in vintage Swing-wear. "ReVamp" created new clothing (limited editions) based on vintage fashion designs, and Bleyer's, a German shoe company, sold two-tone flat shoes for both women and men throughout the United States with a special rubber sole—a German commodity (purportedly unavailable in the United States), that became all the rage for Swing dancers, especially Lindy Hoppers, during the height of the swing revival.

## The Internet Swings!

As the Internet developed in the 1990s, message boards and online dis-cussion groups were flooded with news and conversations regarding Swing dancing. One of the earliest websites on swing was The US Swing Dancer Server, started by Aswin van den Berg, Ph.D., in 1994, at Cornell University; the site eventually became Swingcraze.com. Soon there were multitudes of online sites offering event calendars, links to other regional swing websites, and a general plethora of information for the avid Swing dancer. As Swing groups emerged in various cities across the nation, and as the Internet evolved, dance communities became better linked together, and the "all-swing" websites became more sophisticated. Yehoodi, started in 1998 by Manu Smith and Frank Dellario, became one of the largest and most comprehensive of these Internet websites. Taking its name from the Cab Calloway song "Who's Yehoodi?" and billing itself as a site "for the hardcore lindyhopper [sic] with the intent of fostering the community online and off," the website set out to cover both national and international swing news. Yehoodi continued in popularity, sponsoring dance events of its own, hosting a calendar of Swing events, a discussion board, a biweekly talk show, and a 24/7 Internet radio show.

Numerous websites also emerged in the 1990s, which focused specifically on the history of the Lindy Hop (with one of the most in-depth sites being kclindyhop.com, the Internet home of the Kansas City Lindy Hop Society). As the swing revival gained momentum, online stores selling swing merchandise emerged. Judy Pritchett started her online store, SavoyStyle Swing Dance Shop, in 1995, offering an assortment of items such as instructional videos, books, artwork, cloth-ing, CDs, and more. Pritchett met Frankie Manning in 1986, when she attended one of his dance classes organized by Margaret Batiuchok. She eventually became Manning's long-term companion (until his passing in 2009) and collaborated with him in documenting the history of the Lindy Hop. Pritchett's shop (swingdanceshop.com) evolved from her "Archives of Early Lindy Hop" (savoystyle.com) historical pages featuring a wealth of information, including biographies of many original Lindy Hoppers. Her online store continued to remain popular with Swing dancers well into the twenty-first century (Personal interview, Nov. 10, 2008).

Dancestore.com was started by Swing dancers in the Washington DC area in 1997 offering a wonderful array of clothing, accessories, and shoes for all styles of Swing. TC Swingin' Hepcats (from the St. Paul/Minneapolis area) gave free Swing bumper stickers with their online merchandise orders; Daddy-O's offered Swing-wear fashions with the online motto, "Where the coolest get their coolness."

## Swing Gangs

Coinciding with the exploding popularity of swing, and the rise and development of the Internet, Swing dance "factions" developed, which surprisingly began to turn against each other. West Coast Swing continued to thrive in many areas during the 1990s, but acclaimed dancer Mary Ann Nuñez sums it up with the comment, "the swing revival of the 90s didn't really help or encourage West Coast Swing." Lindy Hop was the newest "retro" term, and a new generation of Swing kids wanted to learn it. Even Michael A. Harvey, editor of *West Coast Swing America*, a magazine devoted to West Coast Swing enthusiasts, noted that "Swing Kids," dancing East Coast Swing and Lindy Hop, were taking over at the clubs—relegating West Coast dancers into smaller back rooms. He cheerily notes, however, that, "It's incredibly refreshing to see people enjoying dancing while breaking almost every West Coast Swing rule in existence" ("'Swing Kids' Takeover," July/August 1998, 1).

It's difficult to guess why the swing renaissance began to suffer a "negativity factor," but for a short while it was pervasive. Within many Lindy Hop groups, the word "Westie" referenced a West Coast Swing dancer and took on a negative connotation. While West Coast Swing had been immensely popular in California in the 1980s, its sophisticated air and its slinky "bump and grind" moves that had been so admired after the disco era now seemed in direct opposition to the whimsical, wacky, innocence of the Lindy Hop. A rift developed between the two styles. In California, Swing was further divided by what was perceived to be two separate schools of style: the Frankie Manning circular style, labeled "Savoy Style," and the Dean Collins slotted style of Lindy, which became known as "Hollywood Style" at that time. A war of words was waged over the Internet, and groups of angry dancers, certain that their style was "the only way to Swing it" made their voices heard. The winds of change eventually, however, calmed the divisive voices. Interestingly, in the Los Angeles area where the voices originally resonated the loudest, dancers of both schools finally blended their styles together to the point that complete purists (those who only danced either "Savoy Style" or "Hollywood Style") became almost extinct. And as the peak years of the revival subsided, so too did the divisiveness. By the year 2010, in most Swing dance communities around the globe, an acceptance of all styles was finally attained. A renewed interest in West Coast Swing emerged in 2010, as the ultra-fast music that had so inspired the younger generation of dancers, began giving way to slower, "blues-ier" tunes. The cycle of popular culture was spinning again.

# Conclusion

Throughout the global dance community, Swing dancing is now fully recognized and celebrated as an American art form, born of Afro-American roots and developed by dancers at New York's Savoy Ballroom in Harlem. Its various styles are connected to each other—like branches on the same tree, all owing their existence to the original style, the Lindy Hop, along with all the multiethnic vernacular movements that influenced its creation.

The years 1998 through 2000 are generally referred to as the peak years of the "second era of swing," and although there was a decline of interest in Swing dancing throughout the broader population immediately following those years, dancers who were "hooked on Swing" continued to enjoy it and to bring in new recruits. Social partnered dancing, into the year 2011, continued on as a popular American pastime. And while none of the established schools or venues experienced the massive numbers of dancers they had seen during the peak revival years, The New York Swing Society continued hosting events and classes; the Pasadena Ballroom Dance Association still produced dances and went on holding large group classes in all styles of Swing; and camps like Beantown Lindy Hop Summer Camp, and Camp Hollywood still attracted crowds. Cleveland's All Balboa Weekend, Houston's Lindyfest, and the USA Grand Nationals were still going strong. The International Lindy Hop Championships (ILHC) began in 2008, in Washington D.C., and attracted a growing number of international attendees in 2011.

Chazz Young, seen here performing with his legendary father, Frankie Manning (left to right), is a renowned Tap dancer and celebrated Lindy Hopper in his own right. A highlight of Swing dance events was to watch this father/son duo perform together. (Courtesy of Chazz Young.)

The Sandra Cameron Dance Center, in N.Y., continued its Swing program, and world-renowned instructors, such as Ryan and Jenny Francois, Steven Mitchell and Virginie Jensen, Dawn Hampton, Carla Heiney, Jeremy Otth and Laura Keat, Sylvia Sykes, Nick Williams, Peter Strom, Skye Humphries, Nina Gilkenson, and Ramona Staffeld (to name just a few), continued to travel and inspire dancers around the globe. Swing bands such as: Pete Jacob's Wartime Radio Revue and Dean Mora's Modern Rhythmists made themselves more versatile, offering Swingtet ensembles and a broader range of Swingable tunes. Into 2011, they, along with an assortment of other bands (The Boilermaker Jazz Band, Jonathan Stout and his Campus Five, the Solomon Douglas Swingtet, The Eric Ekstrand Ensemble, Lil' Mo and the Dynaflos, and the Harlem Renaissance Orchestra, to name just a few), continued to play for dancers at Swing events and festivals.

It took the efforts and contributions of many dedicated dancers and Swing preservationists to "bring back swing" for its second era (along with media interest, music trends, and the right social climate in art, fashion, and movies), but there is general consensus amongst dancers and preservations that swing will be a cyclical thing, and that a "third" era is in our future. In 2010, Camp Hollywood producer Hilary Alexander commented that she would love to see "a return of interest in the California 'Smooth slotted style' of Swing like that of dancers Dean Collins and Jean Veloz" (noting that many of their original moves, "like the quick stop that once got cheers in the jam circles of the 1990s," had become relatively unknown among dancers by 2010). But then she confidently asserted that it "will come back," because "everything cycles around." Alexander also echoes another general consensus in the Swing community: that dancers are getting "better" all the time, continuing to raise the bar, "taking Swing to a whole new level" (E-mail interview, 2010). Along with the second era of Swing pioneers, a number of youthful dancers (who were first exposed to Swing during the 1990s as teenagers) have carried the torch forward. Members of the stellar Lindy Hop performance troupe, the Silver Shadows, as one example, have continued to compete in events and continued to teach both nationally and internationally. Innovative Balboa competitors such as Mickey Fortanasce and Kelly Arsenault are driving that dance forward. The West Coast Swing circuit, with a network of teachers, dance studios, and competitions all recruiting young competitors, has also continued to produce top-notch dancers. Swing dancer and long-time competition judge, Annie Hirsch, co-founded the World Swing Dance Council (in 1993) with Skippy Blair, and by 2011, many of the top competitive dancers were accumulating points under their *WSDC*'s system. And while Lindy Hop performers push for higher aerials and faster speed, West Coast Swing dancers show their prowess in slinky sophisticated dips and tricks, remarkable flexibility, and a rhythmic complexity in their footwork—often synced precisely with the music, down to the minutest of detail. With numerous awards and championship titles, Jordan Frisbee and Tatiana Mollman are two of the twenty-first century's top West Coast Swing dancers. Competing and teaching across the United States and internationally, they continue to innovate new moves and push the dance in new directions. Renown West Coast Swing instructor, Buddy Schwimmer has continued to train children and young adults, helping to keep Swing alive. His offspring, Benji and Lacey, who were both West Coast Swing competition winners as children, have become national dance celebrities. Their television coverage and movie roles, continue to bring "Swing awareness" to a broader audience. All of these talented dancers, and future dancers inspired by them, will move the genre forward—as every new generation that embraces a dance improves upon it. The previous generation provides the inspiration and the building blocks, and the next generation grabs hold of the old and builds upon it.

Over the past decade, the Internet made accessible a treasure trove of historical dance clips, and the free sharing of that material (as well as contemporary clips) on YouTube has exposed the entire world to Swing dancing and its development throughout the years. A general trend of the twenty-first century has been diversification among dancers, as the second era of swing brought exposure to, and education in, all the various styles of Swing—creating a universal respect for all the styles.

Only the future will tell what the next music or dance craze will be, and how Swing dancing will "fit in" to American pop culture in the years ahead is anyone's guess. Popular music styles will invariably change, and Swing dancing is likely to evolve right with them. Some may rally for a return to the classics, noting the inextricable connection between Swing dancing and the music from which it came. Others prefer to push the envelope with nontraditional music and movement. But as long as there are dancers who feel the inner joy of a swingin' beat, who are unafraid to move to the rhythms that inspire them— Swing dancing will continue.

Over the Memorial Holiday weekend, 2010, there was a gathering at the gravesite of legendary Lindy Hopper, Frankie Manning, for the unveiling of an artisan-crafted headstone. The gravesite is at the top of a small hillside in the cemetery's "jazz section," where Manning is in good company, surrounded by the graves of such luminaries as Duke Ellington, Illinois Jacquet, and Lionel Hampton (whose headstone reads two simple words so familiar to his fans, "Flyin' Home"). With loving words, live swingin' music (and, yes, even dancing at graveside), the gathering was a final fitting tribute to this ambassador of Swing and remarkable man. But it was also a moment to reflect on the many lives touched by Frankie Manning, and on the resolution that "they'll teach their children to Swing, and those children will teach their children," so that this American treasure—this joyous dance—will be kept alive.

With an infectious smile that radiated an inner joy when he danced, Frankie Manning, "Ambassador" of the Lindy Hop, touched many lives. He helped ensure that the Social dance tradition of Swing (whether to the sounds of live bands or DJ'd music) will forever be preserved. (Courtesy of Tamara Stevens.)

Cynthia Millman, co-author of *Frankie Manning: Ambassador of Lindy Hop*, has graciously contributed, here, her thoughts and desires regarding the future of the Lindy Hop:

> While I can't predict the Lindy's future, I do have aspirations for it. First, I hope that there will always be people who, with great affection and respect, are dedicated to preserving the original swing dance as a living form. At the same time, because the Lindy is such a vital and lively dance, it's inevitable that it will evolve. So my second hope is that modern-day Lindy hoppers will continue to find appropriate ways to build on the foundation, extending the dance in directions that sustain the soul of the original moves and music. Finally, I would be delighted if Frankie's joy of dancing and tolerant spirit is trumpeted through the ages from ballroom and dance studio to stages and arts festivals by Lindy hoppers everywhere. Life will be richer for us all. (E-mail)

It is difficult to imagine that many social dancers, once they've learned the art of leading or following a partner, would ever wish to trade it all in for "solo" dancing again. Time has shown, however, that new trends have the capacity to erase all remnants of the previous ones. For this reason, Swing dancing will need to be continually celebrated and preserved. The immortal words of Frankie Manning may serve as a battle cry of the future: "A one, a two, you know what to do!" (Keep Swingin'!).

# Bibliography

## Books

Aloff, Mindy. *Dance Anecdotes*. Oxford: Oxford University Press, 2006.

Bean, Annemarie. "Blackface Minstrelsy and Double Inversion, Circa 1890." In Elam, Harry J. Jr., and David Krasner. *African American Performance and Theater History: A Critical Reader*. Oxford: Oxford University Press, 2001, p. 189.

Beauregard, Nettie H. *Lindbergh's Decorations and Trophies*. St. Louis: Missouri Historical Society, 1935.

Begho, Felix. "Traditional African Dance in Context." In Asante, Kariamu Welsh, ed. *African Dance: An Artistic, Historical and Philosophical Inquiry*. Trenton, NJ: Africa World Press, 1998, p. 170.

Britt, Stan. *Dexter Gordon: A Musical Biography*. New York: Da Capo Press, 1989.

Bushell, Garvin, and Mark Tucker. *Jazz from the Beginning*. New York, NY: Da Capo Press, 1998.

Castle, Vernon, Mr. and Mrs. *Modern Dancing*. New York: The World Syndicate Co., 1914.

Chaucer. *Romaunt of the Rose: Troilus and Creseide and the Minor Poems (with Life of the Poet by Sir Harris Nicholas)*, Volume 1. London: William Pickering, 1846.

Chilton, John. *Let the Good Times Roll: The Story of Louis Jordan and His Music*. Michigan: The University of Michigan Press, 1997.

Clayton, Buck, and Nancy Miller Elliott. *Buck Clayton's Jazz World*. Oxford: Bayou Press Ltd., 1989.

Cohen, Ronald D. "Music Goes to War: California, 1940–45." In Lotchin, Roger W., ed. *The Way We Really Were: The Golden State in the Second Great War*. Illinois: Board of Trustees of the University of Illinois, 2000.

Cory, Charles Barney. *Hunting & Fishing in Florida*. Princeton University: Estes & Lauriat, 1896.

Dahl, Linda. *Stormy Weather: The Music and Lives of a Century of Jazzwomen*. New York: Limelight Editions, 1984.

DeVeaux, Scott Knowles. *The Birth of Bebop: A Social and Musical History*. California: University of California Press, 1999.

Dickens, Charles. *American Notes for General Circulation*, Volume 1868, Part 1. New York: D. Appleton and Company, 1868.

Dunaway, Wilma A. *Slavery in the American Mountain South*. New York: Cambridge University Press, 2003.

Dunham, Katherine. "The Negro Dance." In Brown, Sterling, A., Arthur P. Davis, and Ulysses Lee. *The Negro Caravan*. New York: Dryden Press, 1941, p. 999.

Ellington, Duke. *Music Is My Mistress: Memoirs by Duke Ellington*. New York: Da Capo Press, 1976.

Emery, Lynne Fauley. *Black Dance: From 1619 to Today*. Hightstown, NJ: Princeton Book Company, 1988.

Erickson, Hal. *"From Beautiful Downtown Burbank": A Critical History of Rowan and Martin's Laugh-In, 1968–1973*. Jefferson, NC: McFarland & Company, Inc., 2000.

Falconbridge, Alexander. *An Account of the Slave Trade on the Coast of Africa*. London: James Phillips, George Yard, Lombard Street, 1788.

Farrand, Livingston, A. M., M.D. *Basis of American History 1500–1900*. New York: Harper & Brothers, 1906.

Federal Writers' Project. Slave Narratives, 1936–1938. (See "Slave Narratives").

Ferrero, Edward. *The Art of Dancing Historically Illustrated*. New York: Edward Ferrero 1859.

Firestone, Ross. *Swing Swing Swing: The Life and Times of Benny Goodman*. New York: W. W. Norton & Company, Inc, 1993.

Fordham, John. *Jazz*, New York: Dorling Kindersley, 1993.

Frank, Rusty E. *Tap!: The Greatest Tap Dance Stars and Their Stories 1900–1955*. New York: Da Capo Press, 1994.

Frazier, Ian. *Great Plains*. New York, NY: Picador, 1989.

Friedrich, Otto. *City of Nets: A Portrait of Hollywood in the 1940s*. Berkeley, CA: University of California Press, 1997.

Gault, Lon A. *Ballroom Echoes*. N.P.: Andrew Corbet Press, 1989.

Gerald Jonas. *Dancing: The Power of Dance Around the World*. Woodlands, London: BBC Books, 1992.

Gioia, Ted. *The History of Jazz*. Oxford: Oxford University Press, 1998.

Giordano, Ralph G. *Social Dancing in America: Fair Terpsichore to the Ghost Dance 1607–1900*, Vol. 1. Westport, CT: Greenwood, 2006.

Giordano, Ralph G. *Social Dancing in America: Lindy Hop to Hip Hop 1901 to 2000*, Vol. 2. Westport, CT: Greenwood, 2006.

Glass, Barbara S. *African American Dance: An Illustrated History*. Jefferson, North Carolina, and London: McFarland & Company, 2007.

Golden, Eve. *Vernon and Irene Castle's Ragtime Revolution*. Lexington, Kentucky: University Press of Kentucky, 2007.

Gottschild, Brenda Dixon. *Waltzing in the Dark: African American Vaudeville and Race Politics in the Swing Era*. New York: St. Martin's Press, 2002.

Gourley, Catherine. *Gibson Girls and Suffragists: Perceptions of Women from 1900 to 1918*. Minneapolis, MN: Twenty-First Century Books, 2007.

Greene, Meg. *Billie Holiday: A Biography*. Westport, CT: Greenwood Press, 2007.

Gregory, Jack, and Rennard Strickland. *Sam Houston with the Cherokees: 1829–1833*. Oklahoma: University of Oklahoma Press, 1996.

Grove, Lilly, Mrs., F. R. G. S., and other writers. *Dancing: with Musical Examples*. London: Longmans, Green & Co., 1907.

Herskovits, Melville J. *The Myth of the Negro Past*. New York: Harper and Brothers, 1958.

Hook, 'Fessa John. *Shagging in the Carolinas*. Charleston, SC: Arcadia Publishing, 2005.

Huggins, Nathan Irwin. *Harlem Renaissance*. New York: Oxford University Press, 1971.

Kellner, Bruce, ed. *The Harlem Renaissance: A Historical Dictionary for the Era*. New York: Methuen, Inc., 1987.

Kmen, Henry A. *Music in New Orleans: The Formative Years: 1791–1841*. Baton Rouge, LA.: Louisiana State University Press, 1977.

Knowles, Mark. *Tap Roots: The Early History of Tap Dancing*. Jefferson, North Carolina, and London: McFarland & Company, 2002.

Koestler-Grack, Rachel A. *Osceola* 1804–1838. Mankato, Minnesota: Capstone Press, 2002.

Kolchin, Peter. *American Slavery 1619–1877*. New York: Hill and Wang, 1993.

Levin, Floyd. *Classic Jazz: A Personal View of the Music and the Musicians*. Berkeley, CA: University of California Press, 2000.

Levinson, Peter J. *Tommy Dorsey: Livin' in a Great Big Way, a Biography*. New York: Da Capo Press, 2006.

Lott, Eric. *Love & Theft: Blackface Minstrelsy and the American Working Class*. New York: Oxford University Press, 1993.

Manning, Frankie, and Cynthia Millman. *Frankie Manning: Ambassador of Lindy Hop*. Philadelphia: Temple University Press, 2007.

McDougal, Dennis. *The Last Mogul: Lew Wasserman, MCA, and the Hidden History of Hollywood*. New York: Da Capo Press, 2001.

McGill, Donald D., and Richard S. Demory. *Introduction to Jazz History*. Englewood Cliffs, New Jersey: Prentice Hall, 1989.

Miller, Norma, and Evette Jensen. *Swingin' at the Savoy: The Memoir of a Jazz Dancer*. Philadelphia: Temple University Press, 1996.

Murray, Arthur. *How to Become a Good Dancer*. New York: Simon and Schuster, 1959.

Nevell, Richard. *A Time to Dance: American Country Dancing from Hornpipes to Hot Hash*, New York: St. Martin's Press, 1977.

New York Public Library. *The New York Public Library African American Desk Reference*. The Stonesong Press, Inc. and the New York Public Library, 1999.

O'Meally, Robert G., ed. The *Jazz Cadence of American Culture*. New York: Columbia University Press, 1998.

Pruter, Robert. *Chicago Soul*. Champaign, IL: University of Illinois Press, 1992.

Remini, Robert V. *A Short History of the United States*. New York: HarperCollins, 2008.

Rice, Edward Le Roy. *Monarchs of Minstrelsy, from "Daddy" Rice to Date*. New York, NY: Kenny Publishing Company, 1911.

Rosenbaum, Art, and Johann S. Buis. *Shout Because You're Free: The African American Ring Shout Tradition in Coastal Georgia*. Athens, GA: University of Georgia Press, 1998.

Saxton, Alexander. "Blackface Minstrelsy." In Bean, Annemarie, James Vernon Hatch, and Brooks McNamara. *Inside the Minstrel Mask: Readings in Nineteenth-Century Blackface Minstrelsy*. Hanover, NH: Wesleyan University Press, 1996. pp. 70–71.

Schuller, Gunther. *Early Jazz: Its Roots and Musical Development*. Oxford: Oxford University Press (paperback), 1986.

Spiller, John, Tim Clancey, Stephen Young, Simon Mosely. *The United States, 1763–2001*. New York: Routledge, 2005.

Starr, Kevin. *California: A History*. New York: Modern Library, 2007.

Starr, Larry, and Christopher Waterman. *American Popular Music: From Minstrelsy to MTV*. Oxford: Oxford University Press, 2003.

Stearns, Marshall, and Jean Stearns. *Jazz Dance: The Story of American Vernacular Dance*. New York: Da Capo Press, 1994.

Straw, Richard Alan, and Tyler Blethan, ed. *High Mountain Rising: Appalachia in Time and Place*. Illinois: University of Illinois, 2004.

Stuckey, P. Sterling, "Christian Conversion and the Challenge of Dance." In *Dancing Many Drums: Excavations in African American Dance*. Thomas F. DeFranz, ed. Madison, WI: The University of Wisconsin Press, 2002, pp. 39–58.

Suskin, Steven. *Second Act Trouble: Behind the Scenes at Broadway's Big Musical Bombs*. New York: Applause Theatre & Cinema Books, 2006.

Thorpe, Edward. *Black Dance*. Woodstock, New York: The Overlook Press, 1990.

Toll, Robert C. *Blacking Up: The Minstrel Show in the Nineteenth Century*. New York: Oxford University Press, 1974.

Van Vechten, Carl. *Parties: A Novel of Contemporary New York Life*. New York: A. A. Knopf, 1930.

Wadleigh, Frances E. "*Pattin' Juba*." In Garrett, Phineas, ed. *The Speaker's Garland Literary Bouquet: Comprising 100 Choice Selections*, Vol. VIII, xxx. Philadelphia: Penn Publishing, 1900, p. 85.

Walker, Stanley. *The Night Club Era*. New York: Frederick A. Stokes Company, 1933.

Walser, Robert, ed. *Keeping Time Readings in Jazz History*. New York: Oxford University Press, 1999.

Waters, Ethel, and Charles Samuels. *His Eye Is on the Sparrow: An Autobiography*. New York: Da Capo Press, 1989.

Wedgwood, Hensleigh. *A Dictionary of English Etymology*. London: Trubner & Co, 1878.

Wheaton, Jack. *All That Jazz*. New York: Ardsley House, 1994.

White, William Sanford, and Steven Kern Tice. *Santa Catalina Island: Its Magic, People and History*. Glendora, CA: White Limited Editions, 2000.

Williams, Gregory Paul. *The Story of Hollywood: An Illustrated History*. United States: BL Press LLC, 2005.

Willoughby, David. *The World of Music: Fourth Edition*. Boston: McGraw-Hill College, 1999.

Winter, Marian Hannah. "Juba and American Minstrelsy." In Magriel, Paul, ed. *Chronicles of the American Dance: From the Shakers to Martha Graham*. New York: Henry Holt and Company, 1948, p. 50.

Yanow, Scott. *Bebop*. San Francisco, CA: Miller Freeman Books, 2000.

## Periodicals

4 STAR Records Advertisement, *Google Books: The Billboard*, April 13, 1946, p. 23, http://books.google.com/books?id=8RkEAAAAMBAJ&pg=PA1942&dq =billboard+april+13,+1946&hl=en&ei=Le5PTJSDK5OisQOE5NijBw& sa=X

&oi=book_result&ct=result&resnum=2&ved=0CC0Q6AEwAQ#v=onepage&q =barbarians&f=false (accessed April 10, 2009).

"14 Couples Survive Eleven Days' Dance: Pecora Deems Derby Illegal, but Cannot Act Unless a Complaint Is Filed," *New York Times*, June 21, 1928, p. 27.

"1937 Closes with Big Apple: New version of old square dance dominates holiday parties," *Life*, Vol. 3, No. 25, December 20, 1937, p. 29.

*Africans in America: America's Journey through Slavery*, Episode Three, Brotherly Love, Part 3: 1791–1831 (aired October 1998), pbs.org, http://www.pbs.org/ wgbh/aia/part3/3narr6.html (accessed October 12, 2008).

Allen, Zita, "From Minstrel Show to Center Stage," *Free to Dance*, pbs.org, http:// pbs.org/wnet/freetodance/behind/behind_minstrel.html (accessed October, 13, 2008).

"Amusements: King of Swing Shift," *Time.com*, August 23, 1943, np, http:// www.time.com/time/magazine/article/0,9171,885073,00.html (accessed August 25, 2009).

"Bar Collegiate Dancing: Masters at Toronto Convention Oppose New Trend," *New York Times*, August 16, 1932, p. 20.

Barnett, Lincoln, "Fred Astaire: He Is the No. 1 Exponent of America's Only Native and Original Dance Form," *Life*, Vol. 11, No. 8, August 25, 1941, pp. 74, 76.

Bernstein, Adam, "Dancer-Choreographer Popularized Lindy Hop," *Los Angeles Times*, Obituaries, Tuesday, April 28, 2009, p. A20.

"Best Selling Pop Albums," *Google Books: The Billboard*, September 29, 1956, Vol. 68, No. 39, p. 40, http://books.google.com/books?id=hwoEAAAAMBAJ&pg= PA58&dq=billboard++sept+29,+1956&hl=en&ei=FCtRTK7DHJO6sQO1sM2 mAQ&sa=X&oi =book_result&ct=result&resnum=1&ved=0CCUQ6AE wAA#v=onepage&q =billboard%20%20sept%2029%2C%201956&f=false (accessed November 11, 2009).

*The Billboard 1944 Music Year Book*, (Sixth Annual Edition,) p. 367.

Brockington, Paulette, "1st Annual American Lindy Hop Championships," *Strutters Quarterly*, Vol. 8, Issue 4, Autumn, 1998, p. 3.

Burns, Ken, *Jazz: The Story of America's Music*, five-CD set booklet, written by Geoffrey C. Ward, Sony Music Entertainment, 2000.

Burns, Ken, "Norma Miller and Frankie Manning," *Jazz A Film by Ken Burns*, transcripts, June 26, 1997, p. 15, http://www.pbs.org/jazz/about/pdfs/Miller_ Manning.pdf (accessed October 13, 2009).

"C. Barnet's Sepia Circuit," *Google Books: The Billboard*, December 5, 1942, Vol. 54, No. 49, p. 20, http://books.google.com/books?id=OQwEAAAAMBAJ &pg=PT69&dq=billboard+magazine+dec+5+1942&hl=en&ei=wX1PTMXjN I76sAOIgIngBw&sa=X&oi=book_result&ct=result&resnum=3&ved =0CDQQ6AEwAg#v=onepage&q&f=false (accessed May 15, 2009).

"Cab Calloway: Words of the Week," *Jet*, Vol. XIII, No. 4, November 28, 1957, p. 30, http://books.google.com/books?id=-bcDAAAAMBAJ&printsec =frontcover&dq=jet+magazine+november+1957&hl=en&ei=PuFQTP S8KoKosQPjmMzlCw&sa=X&oi=book_result&ct=result&resnum=7&ved =0CE8Q6AEwBg#v=onepage&q=cab%20calloway&f=false (accessed October 13, 2009).

Cannon, Cay, "Action Briefs," *Dance Action*, Vol. 1, No. 2, March 1988, p. 30.

"Captain Charles A. Lindbergh in Fox News Reel" at the Bridge Theater, *The Record-Post*, July 7, 1927, 4. North New York Library Network, http://news2.nnyln.net/essex-county/search/html (accessed July 20, 2010).

"Carranza Secretive on Washington Hop: Mexico's leading flier, Captain Emilio Carranza, becomes more like Colonel Charles A Lindbergh in his everyday methods," *New York Times*, June 11, 1928, p. 21.

Contratto, Jimmy, "From a Night Club to a Ballroom," *Google Books: The Billboard*, Vol. 54, No. 2, January 10, 1942, p. 11, http://books.google.com/books?id=NwwEAAAAMBAJ&pg=PP1&dq=billboard+january+10+1942&hl=en&ei=JPZPTJqzAo6gsQOo6emiBw&sa=X&oi=book_result&ct=result& resnum=1& ved=0CCgQ6AEwAA#v=onepage&q=trianon&f=false (accessed April 16, 2009).

Crease, Robert P., "Birthday Salute to Norma Miller," *Footnotes*, Vol. 5, No. 1, Spring 1990, p. 1.

Crease, Robert, "Jitterbug Revue Swings in the Rockies," *Footnotes*, Vol. 2, No. 3, July–September 1987, p. 3.

Crease, Robert P., "On Stage with the Big Apple Lindy Hoppers," *Footnotes*, Vol. 3, No. 3, November–December 1988, p. 5.

Crease, Robert, "Profiles of Original Lindy Hoppers: Eunice Callen," *Footnotes*, Vol. 4, No. 3, November–December 1989, p. 1.

Crease, Robert P., "Profiles of Original Lindy Hoppers: Wilda Crawford," *Footnotes*, Vol. 3, No. 3, November–December 1988, p.1.

Crease, Robert, "Profiles of Original Lindy Hoppers: Mildred Cruse," *Footnotes*, Vol. 3, No. 1, January–March 1988, p. 1.

Crease, Robert P., "Profiles of Original Lindy Hoppers: Elnora Dyson," *Footnotes*, Vol. 4, No. 1, January–March 1989, p. 1.

Crease, Robert P., "Profiles of Original Lindy Hoppers: Sandra Gibson," *Footnotes*, Vol. 2, No. 2, April–June 1987, p. 1.

Crease, Robert, P., "Profiles of Original Lindy Hoppers: Willie Jones," *Footnotes*, Vol. 5, No. 1, Spring 190, p. 5.

Crease, Robert, "Profiles of Original Lindy Hoppers: Al Leagins," *Footnotes*, Vol. 1, No. 4, October–December 1986, p. 3.

Crease, Robert, "Profiles of Original Lindy Hoppers: George Lloyd," *Footnotes*, Vol. 1, No. 3, July–September 1986, p. 1.

Crease, Robert, "Profiles of Original Lindy Hoppers: Frankie Manning," *Footnotes*, Vol. 2, No. 1, January–March 1987, p. 1.

Crease, Robert, "Profiles of Original Lindy Hoppers: Norma Miller," *Footnotes*, Vol. 1, No. 2, April–June 1986, p. 1.

Crease, Robert, "Profiles of Original Lindy Hoppers: Billy Ricker," *Footnotes*, Vol. 2, No. 3, July–September 1987, p. 1.

Crease, Robert P., "Remembering Killer Joe Piro," *Footnotes*, Vol. 4, No. 1, January–March 1989, p. 5.

Crease, Robert P., "The Savoy Ballroom Remembered," *Footnotes*, Vol. 5, No. 2, Fall 1990, pp. 1–4.

Crease, Robert P., "Swing Story," *The Atlantic*, February 1986, pp. 77–82.

Crowther, Bosley, "From the Turkey Trot to The Big Apple," *New York Times*, November 7, 1937, np, http://select.nytimes.com/gst/abstract.html?res=F50F1EF8385A157A93C5A9178AD95F438385F9&scp=1&sq=bosley+crowther+turkey+trot+big+apple&st=p.

"Dance," *Time.com*, July 9, 1928, np, http://www.time.com/time/magazine/article/0,9171,723478-1,00.html (accessed March 5, 2009).

"Dance To License Bureau: Couple in Harlem Contest to Be Married While Shuffling," *New York Times*, June 29, 1928, p. 27.

D'Auita, Amy, "The Swing Dance Society: A Brief History," *Footnotes*, Vol. 1, No. 1, January–March 1986, p. 1.

Deitch, Mark, "Pepsi Bethel-Master of Jazz Dance," *New York Times*, August 6, 1978, pp. D12, 16.

Devorick, John, "We Had a Hell of a Good Time," *Dance Action*, Vol. 1, No. 2, October 1988, p. 9.

Dubin, Zan, "The Joints Keep Jumpin'," *Los Angeles Times*, January 7, 1999. p. 6.

Duncan, Donald, "Irene Castle in 1956," *Dance Magazine*, Ballroom USA, October 1956, p. 87.

Emerson, Ken, American Experience, "Stephen Foster," Blackface Minstrelsy, pbs.org, http://www.pbs.org/wgbh/amex/foster/sfeature/sf_minstrelsy_1.html (accessed October 13, 2008).

"Fannie Brice Enlivens New Bill At Palace: Duncan Sisters, With Improved Act, Are Also Favorites in Entertaining Program," *New York Times*, November 22, 1927, p. 33.

Gardner, Cindy and Terry, "P.S. from Cindy and Terry," *Strutters Quarterly*, Vol. 9, Issue 4, Fall 1999, p. 3.

Gilbert, Gama, "Higher Soars the Swing Fever the Business of Jam Jive and Jitterbug Seems to Suit the Temper of the Times," *New York Times*, August 14, 1938, p. 6.

Goldberg, Jane, "The Shim Sham Shimmy: Tap's National Anthem," *Footnotes*, Vol. 4, No. 3, November–December 1989, p. 1.

Goralnick, Jerry, "Swing Dancing Makes a Comeback at The Cat Club," *Footnotes*, Vol. 1, No. 1, January–March 1986, p. 1.

"Greatest Dancing Couple," *Life*, Vol. 7, No. 18, October 30, 1939, cover.

"Harlem Blues and Jazz Band," promotional band biography pages, Robert M. Gewald Management, INC., PBDA print archives.

"Harlem Dancers Dwindle: Only Four Couples Left in Derby on Sixteenth Day," *New York Times*, July 3, 1928, p. 11.

"Harlem Dancers Get Cash: No Move Made to Halt Marathon as It Enters 14th Day," *New York Times*, July 1, 1928, p. 8.

"Harlem Dance Derby Prize Divided," *New York Times*, July 7, 1928, p. 11.

"Harlem's New "Congeroo" Gives Girls a Workout," *Life*, Vol. 10, No. 24, June 16, 1941, pp. 49–50.

Harvey, Michael A. ed., "Swing Kids' Takeover," *West Coast Swing America*, Vol. 3, No. 4, July/August 1998, p. 1.

Heckman, Don, "50 Years Later, Goodman Recalls Birth of Swing," *Los Angeles Times*, Part VI, August 21, 1985, p. 2.

Heimann, Jim, "Those Hollywood Nights," *Los Angeles Times*, 125 Years / Hollywood—Commemorative Edition, May 21, 2006, p. S18.

Huisken, Deborah, "We'd Like to See the Whole World Swinging," *Hoppin'*, Issue 1, Vol. 1, Autumn 1993, pp. 4–5.

Jackson, Delilah, "Remembering the Spirit of Mura Dehn," *Footnotes*, Vol. 2, No. 2, April–June 1987, p. 3.

"Juba at Vauxhall," *Illustrated London News*, August 1848, p. 77.

"The Jukebox: The Newest Shuffle," *Time.com*, April 04, 1960, np, http://www.time.com/time/magazine/article/0,9171,869454,00.html (accessed July 20, 2010).

Kelvin, Alice J. "Cheek to Cheek is double chic, the second time around: In nightclubs and dance schools, the young and the young at heart rediscover the elegant, romantic pleasures of ballroom dancing," *Smithsonian*, March 1989, Vol. 19, No. 12, pp. 84–95.

Kleiman, Dena, "The 'Hustle' Restores Old Touch to Dancing," *New York Times*, July 12, 1975, p. 56.

"Life Goes to a Swing Shift Dance: These California kids work until midnight and then step out for fun," *Life*, Vol. 12, No. 3, January 19, 1942, pp. 86–89.

"Lindbergh at Beach Party, Spends the Fourth as Guest of F. Trubee Davisons," *New York Times*, July 5, 1928, p. 7.

"Lindbergh Starts East For Paris Hop; Young Pilot Flies from San Diego for St. Louis to Take Transatlantic Plane," *New York Times*, May 11, 1927, p. 3.

"Lindbergh Tests Junkers, Flies New Craft at Curtiss Field," *New York Times*, July 3, 1928, p. 7.

"The Lindy Hop: A True National Folk Dance Has Been Born in U.S.A." *Life*, Vol. 15, No. 8, August 23, 1943, pp. 95–103.

"Lindy Onscreen Friday–Saturday," *Catskill Mountain News*, Vol. 65, No. 4, March 23, 1928, p. 1.

Livingston, D. D., "Taps for Bill Robinson," *Dance Magazine*, January 1950. np.

"Loads of Dough for Orks, Halls in 'Swing Shift Hops,' and War Workers on West Coast Love 'Em," *Google Books: The Billboard*, July 11, 1942, Vol. 54, No. 28, p. 21, http://books.google.com/books?id=DwwEAAAAMBAJ&pg=PT63&dq=billboard+july+11,+1942&hl=en&ei=KvJPTOiDBpGWsgO74pDZBw&sa=X &oi=book_result&ct=result&resnum=3&ved=0CDMQ6AEwAg#v=onepage &q&f=false (accessed April 10,2009).

Loggins, Peter, "The History of Collegiate Shag," http://collegiateshag.com/history.html (accessed July 29, 2010).

Mackrell, Judith, "Jumping Jive Revived," *The Independent*, April 22, 1988, np.

"The Madison," *Ebony*, Vol. XV, No. 9, July 1960, pp. 71–74, http://books.google.com/books?id=8mJeQDZHc5oC&pg=PA4&dq=ebony+magazine+july+1960+madison&hl=en&ei=aGNRTNeDOZCcsQPf18yEAQ &sa=X&oi =book_result&ct=result&resnum=3&ved=0CD0Q6AEwAg#v=onepage&q&f =false (accessed July 20, 2010).

"Medicine: Family Dance," *Time.com*, October 28, 1940, np, http://www.time.com/time/magazine/article/0,9171,764889,00.html (accessed March 3, 2009).

Monaghan, Terry, "George Snowden," *Savoyballroom.com* (accessed January 22, 2009).

Monaghan, Terry, "'Mama Lu' Parks Crashing Cars & Keeping the Savoy's Memory Alive," *Savoyballroom.com* (accessed March 22, 2010).

"Music: Artie Shaw on Tour," *Time.com*, September 22, 1941, np, http://www.time.com/time/magazine/article/0,9171,795518,00.html (accessed March 2009).

"Music: B and Businessman," *Time.com*, February 25, 1952, np, http://www.time.com/time/magazine/article/0,9171,816048,00.html (accessed August 20, 2009).

Muzii, Dave, and Charlie Moore, "Swing!: Behind the Scenes of Broadway's Hottest New Musical," *5687*, December, 1999, No. 7, p. 9.

"New York Beat," *Jet*, Vol. XVI, No. 3, May 14, 1959, p. 63, http://books.google.com /books?id=EUIDAAAAMBAJ&pg=PA66&dq=Jet+magazine,+May+14, +1959&hl=en&ei=FeNQTIDqB42osQPzxrX3Bw&sa=X&oi=book_result &ct=result&resnum=2&ved=0CDYQ6AEwAQ#v=onepage&q=new%20york %20beat&f=false (accessed October 13, 2009).

Nicoll, Jeff, "A Talk with Erin Stevens," *L.A.SwingInfo News: A Dancer's Guide to Los Angeles*, April 2004, pp. 1–4.

"Parade of Dances Present at Fair: Irene Castle, Guest of Honor, Is Applauded by 6,000 in the 'Castle Walk,'" *New York Times*, July 30, 1939, p. 28.

Pritchett, Judy, "Archives of Early Lindy Hop," *Savoystyle.com*, http:// www.savoystyle.com/whiteys_lindy_hoppers.html (accessed January 22, 2009).

Pritchett, Judy, "Savoy Style" swingdanceshop.com, http://www.swingdance shop.com/.

"Record Reviews," *Google Books: The Billboard*, September 24, 1949, Vol. 61, No. 39, pp. 114–115, http://books.google.com/books?id=MvYDAAAAMBAJ&pg =PA94&dq=billboard++sept+24,+1949&hl=en&ei=LihRTIT1F4-ksQP848l -&sa=X&oi=book_result&ct=result&resnum=4&ved=0CDYQ6AEwAw# (accessed January 22, 2009).

Rogers, Patrick, Jennifer Longley, and Eve Heyn, "Swing Man: The dance style that went around comes around again for Frankie Manning," *People*, July 12, 1999, pp. 150–152.

Rolontz, Bob, "From Radio Jock to Nat'l Name—How Clark Does It," *Google Books: The Billboard*, March 24, 1958, Vol. 70, No. illegible, pp. 4, 9, http:// books.google.com/books?id=SiEEAAAAMBAJ&pg=PA5&dq=billboard+ +march+24,+1958&hl=en&ei=DSRRTO6jLoicsQPR4fAM&sa=X&oi=book _result&ct=result&resnum=1&ved=0CCUQ6AEwAA#v=onepage&q=bill- board%20%20march%2024%2C%201958&f=false (accessed November 27, 2009).

Savoy Staff, "Context Original Descriptions All About the Savoy," *Savoyballroom.com* (accessed October 1, 2009).

"Science: Lost Found," *Time.com*, March 28, 1927, http://www.time.com/time/ magazine/article/0,9171,730259,00.html (accessed June 3,2009).

Shermoen, Lance, "Passing of My Dad Laurie Shermoen," *Google groups*, February 6, 2008, http://groups.google.com/group/rec.arts.dance/msg/ad3c97c75 8514a34 (accessed March 4, 2010).

Silva, Art, "How to Dance the Bop," *Dance the Bop*, Columbia Records, 1957. Eight- page instructional manual, p. 1, http://www.rayconniff.info/discography/ original/albums/HowToDanceTheBop.pdf (accessed 2009).

"Slave Narratives: Federal Writers' Project, 1936–1938," *Library of Congress*, http:// memory.loc.gov/ammem/snhtml/ (accessed, October 2008-January 2009).

Smith, Ernie, "Recollections and Reflections of a Jazz Dance Film Collector," *Dance Research Journal Congress on Research in Dance*, Popular Dance in Black America, Spring 1983, Vol. 15, No. 2, pp. 46–48.

Stevens, Kerry B., "A Letter Home from Boogie in the Berkshires." *Footnotes*, Vol. 4, No. 3, November–December, 1989, p. 5.

Stewart, Dean, "Dean Collins, Remembering Swing Dancer's King," *Los Angeles Times*, August 5, 1984, reprinted in *Dance Action*, March 1988, Vol. 1, No. 2, pp. 12–13.

Stewart, Doug, "This Joint Is Jumping," *Smithsonian*, Vol. 29, No. 12, March 1999, cover.

"Students Set Pace In Dance Invention: Their Novelties Are Closely Watched, Ballroom Teachers Are Told at Meeting Here," *New York Times*, July 12, 1932, p. 19.

"Swing Carnival Held To Benefit Charity: Goodman and Basie Bands Lure 6,000 to Garden," *New York Times*, Jun 13, 1938, p. 15.

"Swing Bands Put 23,400 in Frenzy; Jitterbugs Cavort at Randalls Island as 25 Orchestras Blare in Carnival," *New York Times*, May 30, 1938, p. 13.

"Swing: The Hottest and Best Kind of Jazz Reaches Its Golden Age," *Life*, Vol. 5, No. 6, August 8, 1938, Vol. 5, No. 6, pp. 50–60.

Vollmer, Albert A. DDS, "From the Bandstand: The Harlem Blues & Jazz Band," *Footnotes*, Vol. 1, No. 3, July–September 1986, p. 2.

Wadleigh, Frances E. "Pattin' Juba," *The Speaker's Garland Literary Bouquet*, Vol. VIII, xxx, 1900, p. 85.

Watkins, Mel, *American Experience*, "Stephen Foster," People & Events: Daniel Decatur Emmett, 1815–1904, pbs.org, http://www.pbs.org/wgbh/amex/foster/sfeature/sf_minstrelsy_3.html (accessed October 12, 2008).

Watson, Sonny, "BOP !" *Sonny Watson's StreetSwing.com*, http://www.streetswing.com/histmain/z3bop1.htm (accessed November 12, 2009).

Wilson, John, "Lecture on Dance Steals Jazz Fete," *New York Times*, July 6, 1958, p. 50.

Wilson, John S, "Bird Wrong Bop Must Get a Beat," *DownBeat*, October 7, 1949, np.

Winkle, Gabrielle, "Guest Stars at The Cat Club," *Footnotes*, Vol. 1, No. 3, July–September 1986, p. 3.

Winsten, Archer, "Wake of the News," *New York Post*, May 7, 1936, p. 21.

"Yehoodi.com: The website for the hardcore hep-cat swinger!", http://www.yehoodi.com/dashboard/.

"Yellow Charleston Pays Death Penalty; Julius W. Miller Dies at Sing Sing for Slaying Barron Wilkins, Negro Cabaret Owner," *New York Times*, September 18, 1925, p. 14, http://select.nytimes.com/gst/abstract.html?res=F60B10FE39 551B7A93 CAA81782D85F418285F9&scp=1&sq=9%2F18%2F1925+barron+wilkins&st=p (accessed February 23, 2009).

## Videos/DVDs

*42nd Street*. Directed by Lloyd Bacon, choreographed by Busby Berkeley, MGM Studios, 1933.

*America Dances! 1897–1948: A Collector's Edition of Social Dance in Film*. Produced by Dancetime Publications Kentfield, CA, http://www.DancetimePublications.

*The Call of the Jitterbug*. Jasper Sorensen, Vibeke Winding, and Tana Ross, Green Room Productions, 1988.

*Eye on Dance: Third World Dance: Tracing Roots*, Series #29. Program Director/Producer Celia Ipiotis, produced by Jeff Bush.

*Eye on LA*. KABC7–television interview with Jack Bridges, 1984. Rough-cut footage from PBDA video archives.

*Frankie Manning Never Stop Swinging.* Julie Cohen, Swing Bud Productions, 2009.

*Jazz A Film by Ken Burns:* Episode 4, "The True Welcome." PBS DVD Gold. Produced by Ken Burns and Lynn Novick. Directed by Ken Burns.

*Jazz A Film by Ken Burns*: Episode 5, "Swing: Pure Pleasure." PBS DVD Gold. Produced by Ken Burns and Lynn Novick. Directed by Ken Burns.

*Legends of Swing Jean Veloz and Ray Phelps.* An On Tap! Rusty E. Frank Presentation, 2009.

*The Mask.* Directed by Chuck Russell, New Line Studios, 1997.

Pasadena Ballroom Dance Association, private video archives, 1986, 1988, 1991, 1993, 1995, and 2005.

*Saturday Night Fever.* Directed by John Badham, Paramount Pictures, 1977.

*Shag, the Movie.* Directed by Zelda Barron, MGM, 1989.

*Swing Camp Catalina* video and DVD archives. Pasadena Ballroom Dance Association, 1994–2004.

*Swing Kids.* Directed by Thomas Carter, Hollywood Pictures, 1992.

## YouTube Videos

*After Seben* 1929 Shorty George Snowden, Paramount, May 7, 1929 (http://www.youtube.com/watch?v=22igp-ihYN4).

Al Minns and Leon James, DuPont Show of the Week "DuPont Show of the Month" NBC-TV, 1961 (http://www.youtube.com/watch?v=KJsBa2u9aMQ).

*American Graffiti* Trailer (http://www.youtube.com/watch?v=W6Jo1gH89VM).

Arthur Murray teaching/demo, collegiate shag, 1937 (http://www.youtube.com/watch?v=6SGvd5tseZY).

Balboa–Swing Dancing in the short *Maharaja*, 1943 (http://www.youtube.com/watch?v=ehVZktW0BK4).

Bobby McGee's Dance Party, 1982 (http://www.youtube.com/watch?v=SAz9HxrWL-k).

*Calypso Heat Wave* trailer, 1957 (http://www.youtube.com/watch?v=kZc1uaMoMKw).

Gap Commercial, "Khaki Swing" (http://www.youtube.com/watch?v=knW1hGwmEXQ).

*Happy Days* Dance Contest Part 3 (http://www.youtube.com/watch?v=mlVZjTfosWs).

In the Swing, Mary Ann Nuñez and Lance Shermoen, the Lindy Hoppers (http://www.youtube.com/watch?v=AlhkyS-Nn44).

Skippy Blair appearing with Larry Kern in *Queen of the Stardust Ballroom* (http://www.youtube.com/watch?v=_Fw0iTwVJnY).

## Personal Interviews

Randy Albers, March 13, 2010 (telephone).

Hilary Alexander, July 23, 2010 (e-mail).

Steve Bailey, May 28, 2010 and June 11, 2010 (telephone and in person).

Margaret Batiuchok, June 11, 2009, March 30, 2010 (e-mail).

Lance Benishek, July 26, 2010 (telephone).

Jonathan Bixby, February 28, 2010 (telephone).

Skippy Blair, Ph.D., February 26, 2010 (telephone).

Jack Carey, November 8, 2010 (telephone).

Paul Chipello November 12, 2008, February 21, 2009 and March 12, 2009 (in person, e-mail, and telephone).

Mary Collins, July 21, 2009, July 25, 2009 and August 8, 2009 (telephone).

Ruth Ettin, February 21, 2009 (telephone).

Rusty Frank, 2009 (telephone).

Stan Freese, March 20, 2010 (telephone).

Cliff Gewecke, March 29, 2010 (telephone).

Ralph Giordano, May 12, 2009 (e-mail).

Gene Hashiguchi, April 19, 2010 (e-mail).

Annie Hirsch, July 24, 2010 (telephone).

Alycia Keys, July 24, 2009 (in person and telephone).

Mark Knowles, February 13, 2009 (e-mail).

Paolo Lanna, November 29, 2009 (e-mail).

Ben Mankofsky, September 24, 2009 (telephone).

Frankie Manning, August 2008–April 2009 (in person and telephone).

Norma Miller, November 2008 (telephone) and May 31, 2009 (in person).

Cynthia Millman, July 10, 2010 (telephone) and July 17, 2010 (email).

Terry Monaghan, March 27, 2010 and March 28 (e-mail and telephone).

Margaret Newman, October, 2, 1998 (telephone).

Mary Ann Nuñez, March 4, 2010 (e-mail).

Jeannine Pedersen, February 26, 2010 (telephone).

Tony Perez, February 4, 2009 (in person).

Ruth Pershing, November 23, 2008 (e-mail).

Ray Phelps, October 28, 2009 (telephone).

Judy Pritchett, November 2008–May 2010 (in person and telephone).

Chuck and Sally Saggau, July 25, 2009, July 31, 2009 (telephone).

Larry Schulz, March 20, 2010 (telephone).

Erin Stevens (Key), January 2009–July 2010 (in person).

Jim Stevens, January 5, 2009, September 25, 2009 (in person).

Sugar Sullivan, December 14, 2009 (telephone).

Sylvia Sykes, March 2, 2010 (telephone).

Irene Thomas, August 6, 2009 (telephone).

Jean Phelps Veloz, July 2009 and June 2010 (in person and telephone).

Sonny Watson, October 26, 2009 (telephone).

Betty Wood, June 1999 (in person).

Freda Angela Wyckoff, November 4, 2009 (telephone).

Chazz Young, January 29, 2010 (telephone).

# Index

## About the Authors

**Tamara (Tami) Stevens**, an avid Swing dancer and Swing preservationist, has co-owned and operated the Pasadena Ballroom Dance Association in Pasadena, CA, since 1983, where she continues to teach all styles of American Social dance. She holds a bachelor's degree in philosophy from Cal State University Los Angeles, where she minored in English. She has traveled extensively as a Swing dance performer and instructor, has written and co-produced a series of instructional dance DVDs, and is often invited to speak on the subject of American Social dance. Along with her sister Erin, she has produced countless Swing dance events in the Los Angeles area, including Swing Camp Catalina, which brought thousands of Swing dancers together from around the world to Catalina Island, CA, from 1994 to 2004.

**Erin Stevens**, co-owner of the Pasadena Ballroom Dance Association (PBDA), is world-renowned for her teaching skills and her contribution to the "rebirth" of the Lindy Hop style of Swing in the 1990s. As a Swing dance historian and preservationist, she is credited with bringing legendary Swing dancer Frankie Manning out of retirement, getting him to teach Swing, and reigniting his dancing career, thus helping to launch the second era of swing. Erin graduated with a degree in dance teaching and choreography from the University of Irvine, CA. Along with her sister Tami, she continues to produce numerous Swing events in the Los Angeles area. From her performance at the White House to her international teaching engagements, Erin is one of the leading figures on the global Swing dance scene.